Political Process

Economy, Polity, and Society

***Series Editors*:** Virgil Henry Storr and Jayme Lemke, Mercatus Center

The foundations of political economy—from Adam Smith to the Austrian school of economics, to contemporary research in public choice and institutional analysis—are sturdy and well established, but far from calcified. On the contrary, the boundaries of the research built on this foundation are ever expanding. One approach to political economy that has gained considerable traction in recent years combines the insights and methods of three distinct but related subfields within economics and political science: the Austrian, Virginia and Bloomington schools of political economy. The vision of this book series is to capitalize on the intellectual gains from the interactions between these approaches in order to both feed the growing interest in this approach and advance social scientists' understanding of economy, polity, and society.

This series seeks to publish works that combine the Austrian school's insights on knowledge, the Virginia school's insights into incentives in non-market contexts, and the Bloomington school's multiple methods, real-world approach to institutional design as a powerful tool for understanding social behaviour in a diversity of contexts.

Titles in the series

Institutions and Incentives in Public Policy: An Analytical Assessment of Non-Market Decision-Making, edited by Rosolino Candela, Rosemarie Fike, and Roberta Herzberg

Market Process and Market Order: From Human Action, But Not of Human Design, edited by Rosolino A. Candela, Kristen R. Collins, and Christopher J. Coyne

Toward a Hayekian Theory of Social Change, edited by Peter J. Boettke, Erwin Dekker, and Chad Van Schoelandt

Knowledge and Entrepreneurship in Public Policy, edited by Christopher J. Coyne, Abigail R. Hall, and Eileen Norcross

Nudging Public Policy: Examining the Benefits and Limitations of Paternalistic Public Policies, edited by Rosemarie Fike, Stefanie Haeffele, and Arielle John

Economics and the Public Good: The End of Desire in Aristotle's Politics and Ethics, by John Antonio Pascarella

Culture, Sociality, and Morality: New Applications of Mainline Political Economy, edited by Paul Dragos Aligica, Ginny Seung Choi, and Virgil Henry Storr

Political Process

New Perspectives on the Virginia and Bloomington Schools

Edited by
Donald J. Boudreaux, Christopher J. Coyne,
and Brian Kogelmann

LEXINGTON BOOKS
Lanham • Boulder • New York • London

Published by Lexington Books
An imprint of The Rowman & Littlefield Publishing Group, Inc.
4501 Forbes Boulevard, Suite 200, Lanham, Maryland 20706
www.rowman.com

86-90 Paul Street, London EC2A 4NE

British Library Cataloguing in Publication Information Available

Library of Congress Cataloging-in-Publication Data Available

ISBN 978-1-66694-541-6 (cloth)
ISBN 978-1-66694-542-3 (ebook)

Contents

List of Figures

List of Tables

Introduction

Donald J. Boudreaux, Christopher J. Coyne, and Brian Kogelmann

The chapters in this interdisciplinary volume explore and engage the Virginia and Bloomington schools of political economy from a wide variety of contexts and several different disciplinary perspectives. The contributors come from philosophy, political science, economics, Germanic languages and literature, communication studies, among others. Consequently, the range of topics covered is extraordinarily wide, including public administration, historical Japanese constitutional settlements, technocracy, Abigail Adams and the American founding, and much more. The hope is that these contributions demonstrate the continued relevance of the Virginia and Bloomington schools of political economy and what they can teach us about collective choice processes.

AN OVERVIEW OF THE VIRGINIA AND BLOOMINGTON SCHOOLS

The Virginia school of political economy was founded by James M. Buchanan and Gordon Tullock (1999) with the publication of their coauthored book *The Calculus of Consent: The Logical Foundations of Constitutional Democracy*. It is called "the Virginia school" because its founders developed the main ideas while holding professorships at three different Virginia universities: the University of Virginia, Virginia Polytechnic Institute and State University, and George Mason University. Buchanan would go on to win the Sveriges Riksbank Prize in Economic Sciences in Memory of Alfred Nobel in 1986.

The Bloomington school of political economy was founded by Elinor and Vincent Ostrom. Elinor would go on to win that same prize in 2009. It is called "the Bloomington school" because its founders developed the main ideas while holding professorships at Indiana University, located in Bloomington, Indiana. Though there are important differences between the two, both schools of political economy place special emphasis on the *process* of governance. By "process" we refer to how people actually come together to make collective decisions, and how they revise those decisions through time.

Many associate the Virginia school of political economy with the idea of "politics without romance" (Buchanan 1999b). When economists analyze markets, they typically assume that actors in the marketplace are self-interested: firms want to maximize profits and consumers want to get the best products for the lowest prices. The Virginia school asks us to apply the same behavioral assumptions in our analysis of politics. Just as firms and consumers act in self-interested ways, so too do politicians, bureaucrats, and voters. As such, the Virginia school advises we "compare social institutions as they might be expected actually to operate rather than to compare romantic models of how such institutions might be hoped to operate" (Buchanan 1999b, 47). This emphasis on self-interested political actors is not original to the Virginia school; it is a continuation of the classical liberal tradition (Kogelmann 2023). David Hume, for instance, told us that when "contriving any system of government, and fixing the several checks and controuls of the constitution, every man ought to be supposed a knave, and to have no other end, in all his actions, than private interest" (Hume 1987, 42).

Another key tenet of the Virginia school is its emphasis on methodological individualism (Buchanan 1999b, 48–50). When talking about politics, it is easy to anthropomorphize large institutions and organizations. We say that Congress passed a certain bill, that Russia invaded Ukraine, or that the Supreme Court declared a law unconstitutional. The Virginia school reminds us that only individuals act, not institutions or organizations. Congress did not pass a bill; rather, a majority of individual members in both the House of Representatives and the Senate voted for it. Russia did not invade Ukraine; specific political leaders in Russia who exercised control over the military made that decision. The focus, then, is on individual choice in different institutional arrangements, which yield different knowledge and incentives.

More foundational than the Virginia school's emphasis on politics without romance or methodological individualism is its emphasis on politics as exchange (Buchanan 1999e, 1999b, 50–51). Even though politics is unlike markets in that it is fundamentally coercive, there is still "the potentiality of exchange in those social-political institutions that we normally consider to embody primarily coercive or quasi-coercive elements" (Buchanan 1999e, 40). Just as producers and consumers exchange goods and services in the marketplace to better themselves, so do political actors. A politician supplies desired policies in exchange for votes; a legislator votes for a bill she doesn't support in exchange for a colleague supporting her favored bill; a lobbyist exchanges campaign contributions for a politician's support on a desired area of policy, and so on.

These three ingredients—politics without romance, methodological individualism, and politics as exchange—offer significant insights into collective choice processes. Consider just one example: interest group politics. If voters are self-interested, then they will be reluctant to join interest groups. This is because they receive the benefits of an interest group's efforts even if they don't contribute to it (Olson 1971).

For instance, if the Sierra Club secures legislation protecting the environment, then you receive that benefit whether you contribute to the organization or not. Recognizing this, interest groups can engage in exchange with potential members. By providing exclusive benefits to members—for instance, personal firearms insurance for NRA members or discounts at Cabela's for corn farmers—interest groups incentivize individuals to join and support them when they otherwise would not (Olson 1971, 133). This explains why some interest groups are viable and others are not.

Also original to the Virginia school is the idea of government failure; it teaches us all the ways that politics can go wrong (Buchanan 1999a). Yet the Virginia school not only offers diagnoses but also remedies. Key here is a distinction between two levels of politics: the constitutional level and the postconstitutional or the ordinary level (Buchanan 2000, 41). The ordinary level of politics is what we typically think of when we think of politics: it consists of candidates running for office, voters voting for them, politicians passing public policy, and so on. The constitutional level of politics concerns the rules of the game that ordinary politics proceeds within. Given that politics without romance is a key assumption of the Virginia school, scholars in this tradition tell us to focus our energy on changing the rules of the game, not the players. If ordinary politics is not proceeding in a desirable way, then change the rules within which ordinary politics operate. There is no use searching for ethical political leaders.

This leads us to the final key aspect of the Virginia school: constitutional political economy, or the study of different constitutional designs and their downstream effects on ordinary politics (Buchanan 1999d). Constitutional political economy can be approached from a normative perspective, where scholars propose different constitutional rules that restrain self-interested political actors to produce better outcomes (Kogelmann 2018, 2022). Proposals range from generality amendments (Buchanan and Congleton 2003) to limiting the scope of government decision-making (Buchanan 1999c, 108), to redistributing the gains from rent-seeking (Buchanan 1999c, 111), and much more. Constitutional political economy can also be approached in a positive manner, where scholars examine how and why constitutional rules take the shape they do. Politics as exchange is a key part of this analysis: the kinds of constitutions we end up with are the result of exchanges between the various parties at the founding moment (Buchanan 2000, ch. 2).

There is much overlap between the Virginia and Bloomington schools. Elinor and Vincent Ostrom both emphasize the important influence *The Calculus of Consent* had on their thinking (Ostrom and Ostrom 2004). The Bloomington school embraces methodological individualism (Ostrom 2014, 257–258). It also emphasizes the importance of constitutional rules for understanding how collective choice processes work in practice as well as how to design better processes going forward (Ostrom and Ostrom 2014, 29–30). There are, however, some differences.

The Bloomington school embraces a richer behavioral model than the Virginia school, where individuals are motivated not just purely by self-interest but also by other factors such as reciprocity and relations of trust (Ostrom 1998). Moreover, the Bloomington school places less emphasis on the role of exchange in collective choice processes, and more emphasis on *self-governance*, or the ways in which ordinary individuals create and enforce governance institutions to overcome collective action problems. As Vincent describes it: "Democratic ways of life turn on self-organizing and self-governing capabilities rather than presuming that something called 'the Government' governs" (Ostrom 1997, 4).

The Bloomington school is a rich and multifaceted research tradition; as such, we can only cover some aspects of it (Aligica and Boettke 2009; Tarko 2016). One key insight of the Bloomington school is a more nuanced understanding of the complex nature of collective goods. Before the Ostroms, economists bifurcated goods into two types: private goods (rivalrous and excludable) and public goods (nonrivalrous and nonexcludable). The Ostroms rejected this dichotomy (Ostrom and Ostrom 1999). Some goods are nonrivalrous (like public goods) in that one person's consumption does not preclude the consumption of another, but excludable (like private goods) in that it is easy to prevent others from consuming them. The Ostroms call these *toll goods* or *club goods*, and they include things like theatres and swimming pools. Some goods are rivalrous (like private goods) in that one person's consumption prevents others from consuming, but it is very hard to exclude people from consuming them (like public goods). These are called *common pool resources* (CPRs), and include things like water basins, fisheries, and timber forests.

CPRs play a central role in Elinor's (1990) *Governing the Commons*, perhaps her most important work. CPRs are ripe for abuse: because it is difficult to exclude people from consuming them, they will be overconsumed; because they are rivalrous, and the resource will be exhausted. This is the *tragedy of the commons*. Before Elinor, solving the tragedy of the commons involved either privatizing CPRs or having the state step in to regulate them. However, through careful empirical observation Elinor found that successfully managed CPRs often involved neither approach. Successfully managed CPRs were governed by a complex mix of institutions that did not fall neatly into either camp. She writes: "Many successful CPR situations are rich mixtures of 'private-like' and 'public-like' institutions defying classification in a sterile dichotomy" (Ostrom 1990, 14). One of Elinor's most important contributions was codifying the principles that characterize successfully managed CPRs.

This rejection of old dichotomies goes beyond collective goods and CPR management. In her Nobel Prize address, Elinor begins by noting that "the market was seen as the optimal institution for the production and exchange of private goods. For nonprivate goods, on the other hand, one needed 'the' government to impose rules and taxes to force self-interested individuals to contribute necessary resources and refrain from self-seeking activities" (Ostrom 2010, 642). But even so, "undertaking empirical studies of how citizens, local public entrepreneurs, and public officials engage in diverse ways of providing, producing, and managing public service industries and common property regimes at multiple scales has generated substantial knowledge that is not explained by the two models of optimal organizational forms" (Ostrom 2010, 643). This rejection of the state-market dichotomy would lead the Ostroms to the idea of *polycentricity*.

Polycentricity was initially explored in a paper on metropolitan governance by Vincent Ostrom, Charles Tiebout, and Robert Warren (1961). The authors begin by noting that metropolitan governance usually consists of "overlapping jurisdictions" of authority, "duplication of functions" concerning the provision of public goods and services, and "many centers of decision making that are formally independent of each other" (Ostrom et al. 1961, 831). This is opposed to monocentric or "gargantuan" approaches to governance, where authority, decision-making, and the provision of public goods and services are limited to one centralized governance unit.

Monocentric governance structures are akin to one of the "optimal" organizational forms that Elinor decries—*the* state. Polycentric forms of governance are clearly distinct from this paradigm, and yet, polycentric systems are not markets, making them distinct from the other paradigm. We thus have a distinct form of governance that defies neat classification. Exploring the idea of polycentric governance would be a key contribution of Vincent (Ostrom 1999).

AN OVERVIEW OF THE VOLUME

This volume is broken into two parts. Chapters in the first part focus on theoretical foundations and assumptions of the Virginia and Bloomington schools of political economy. In the first chapter, "Politics Without Romance, Without Romance: the Meta-Problem for Virginia Political Economy," Jason Lee Byas points out a tension at the heart of the Virginia school of political economy. The Virginia school focuses on government failures that result from self-interested politicians. It also proposes constitutional rules to avoid these failures. Why, asks Byas, would self-interested politicians bind themselves with constitutional rules? Byas' paper looks at the Virginia school's theory of constitutional process and argues that it offers no plausible answer to this question; as such, a new theory of the constitutional process is needed, which Byas develops.

In chapter 2, Jordan J. Hunter offers an Austrian perspective on co-production and knowledge in public administration. In the traditional model of government supply of goods and services to citizens, government agencies are the producers while citizens are the consumers. Other than casting ballots during regular elections, citizens play no role in producing the outputs supplied to them by the state. The problem here is obvious. Because the production of most government-supplied outputs is funded with taxes, and because these outputs are not supplied in actual markets guided by competitively set prices, administrators confront serious challenges knowing just what to produce and how best to produce it. Even administrators with the best of intentions will often fail even to come close to "optimizing" the supply of outputs. Hunter, inspired by the work of Elinor and Vincent Ostrom, explores "co-production" as means of reducing this problem's magnitude.

Hunter argues that co-production, if carried out wisely, not only improves the quality of public services, but it also reinforces democratic values "by increasing citizen engagement and empowerment." With co-production, the "expert," while valued for his or her specialized knowledge, plays no role as unilateral director of citizens' affairs. After elaborating on co-production's potential, Hunter identifies the challenges of implementing it. These are real. Yet as the experience with the COVID pandemic made clear, citizens are well-advised to consider co-production as a source of potential protection from overbearing bureaucracies.

Next, Mariam Sedighi, in chapter 3, describes how differences in foundational assumptions about human rationality affect social science research, exploring the development of the "cybernetics" view of human behavior and society in the post-World War II period, tying the work of Hayek and the Ostrom's into these developments. In their work, Elinor and Vincent Ostrom, like Hayek, began with the realization that the human mind as we observe it to operate in society is largely a product of human interaction. And much of the human action that is classified by social scientists as "rational" obtains this property only because the actors share knowledge with each other, as well as receive, and respond to, feedback from others. Social scientists who begin with the assumption that human rationality is a fixed and abstract feature of the human mind interpret observed reality quite differently from scientists who, like the Ostroms, have at the core of their analyses the recognition that human rationality is contingent upon the interactions that humans have with each other, lending to their learning-process oriented approach to human social behavior, which Sedighi argues is consistent with developments in cybernetics thinking. Therefore, because social scientists are themselves human, Sedighi concludes that "the academic practices of knowledge production and transmission are bounded by the contingencies of epistemic modes of thinking."

It is now well-known that politicians face strong incentives to increase spending without raising taxes. Succumbing to this incentive yields strings of annual budget deficits, the accumulation of which threatens any government's fiscal stability. Risks of default on debt payments and of inflationary monetization of debt rise the longer politicians operate with this bias toward deficit financing. Few policy changes are more important, therefore, than those that correct, or at least diminish, this bias. Unfortunately, reducing this bias in ways that don't hamstring governments' ability to respond to significant challenges—such as wars, pandemics, and economic downturns—is devilishly difficult. In chapter 4, Andrew Berryhill forthrightly acknowledges this difficulty and compares different proposed means of instilling fiscal discipline. No such means exists that is guaranteed to work and is without downsides. Yet as explained by Berryhill, reform at the constitutional level of budgeting procedures—reform guided by the insights of James Buchanan and other public-choice scholars—likely is the option with most promise.

Both the Virginia and Bloomington schools were deeply concerned with bureaucracy and public administration. In chapter 5, Eryn Rozonoyer looks at technocracy—the idea that expert bureaucrats should rule—through the lens of Plato, arguing that Plato's concept of the "philosopher king" should not be considered a prototypical technocrat, and that, if considered alongside his understanding of epistemic humility, it offers insight into the *limits* of technocracy instead. Though technocracy has seen recent resurgent interest, Rozonoyer argues that Plato teaches us that the domain of politics possesses a unique *techne*, requiring types and degrees of knowledge that are extremely difficult, if not impossible to obtain, which makes it unlike other domains of expertise; the implication is that technocratic forms of bureaucratic governance are fatally flawed. Rozonoyer further argues that the flaws of technocracy can be avoided with polycentricity.

In chapter 6, "James M. Buchanan and the Unromantic Rhetoric of Public Choice," Alexander W. Morales looks at how economic expertise is consolidated and perpetuated by examining the rhetoric of Buchanan's public-facing work. Morales argues that Buchanan rhetorically frames public choice economists as having three specific qualities: good sense (*phronesis*), good will (*eunoia*), and good moral character (*arete*). He further argues that Buchanan was able to challenge orthodox approaches to political economy by framing public choice as a morally superior perspective that, when fully embraced, constrains the scope and autocratic tendencies of mainstream economists.

The second part of the volume includes chapters which apply key insights from the Virginia and Bloomington schools of political economy to analyze specific case studies. In chapter 7, Todd Maslyk examines the creation of Japan's Meiji Constitution in the late 1800s. His analysis explores the emergence of the constitution within the context of preexisting political arrangements and cultural beliefs. In doing so, his analysis emphasizes the importance of "institutional stickiness," which recognizes that in order for formal institutions to be sustained they must align, at least to a degree, with underlying belief systems. In addition to illuminating the specific process through which the Meiji Constitution emerged, Maslyk's chapter offers general insights into how we can think about constitutional and institutional emergence and change through time.

Next, in chapter 8, Sargis Karavardanyan explores the relationship between regime corruption and protest activities, with a focus on democratic societies. He empirically analyzes regime corruption scores on protest patterns in select democratic countries, finding a positive correlation between regime corruption and protest levels. Sargis also studies the connection between protest movements and perceived regime legitimacy. He finds that high levels of protest in some democracies may be orchestrated to signal regime stability to external observers, such as economic investors. At the same time, persistent protest movements often raise red flags about possible sociopolitical and human rights concerns within a country. This research sheds light on the role of corruption in shaping civil actions, and hence political processes, in democratic societies. In doing so, Sargis highlights how corruption can be insidious in democracies, undermining the collective decision-making processes of society and destabilizing core democratic tenets.

In chapter 9, Paa-Kwesi Heto engages the scholarship on commerce's impact on peace and conflict. He synthesizes the existing academic literature on these issues and highlights some of the overlooked aspects of commerce's impact on peace and conflict. A key contribution of his chapter is to frame international commerce as a signaling device that helps to overcome the political knowledge problem in two ways. First, Heto argues that trade reveals a ruling regime's orientation toward the international system—for example, the regime's view toward trade and the global economy and its security preferences. Second, he argues that international trade provides feedback to the political elite regarding the effects of their policies. In making these arguments, this chapter sheds light on the interconnection between the political process and the market process.

Close observation of real-world governments often reveals apparent mysteries. One of these is explored in chapter 10 by Curtis Bram. Put as a question, the mystery is this: Why do many authoritarian governments establish political parties? Viewed superficially, no authoritarian government should need any such appurtenance. Bram, however, reasons that political parties aligned with authoritarian rulers improve these rulers' ability to secure their hold on power by retaining the support of political elites. Specifically, when the number of elites whose support is required is large—when the number of coalitions that a ruler must satisfy is more than few—a political party affiliated with the authoritarian ruler can reduce the ruler's transaction costs of communicating with the elites and of securing their continued support. To test his hypothesis, Bram compares the Kim regime in postwar North Korea to the Rhee regime in South Korea. This comparison lends credence to Bram's intriguing hypothesis.

In the final chapter of the volume, Kirstin Anderson Birkhaug applies the theory of public entrepreneurship—a key part of the Bloomington school—to the American Revolutionary period through the lens of Abigail Adams's correspondences. During the war, there were major breakdowns of governance and disruptions in the provision of goods. By carefully examining Adams's correspondence, Birkhaug demonstrates how women throughout rural Massachusetts were able to coordinate their efforts and overcome these collective action problems during this tense period. The chapter deploys a historical case study to elucidate the connection between informal entrepreneurship in the wake of disaster and the political economy of the United States, as well as the historical role of women in the formation of American entrepreneurship, politics, and economics.

REFERENCES

Aligica, Paul Dragos and Peter J. Boettke. 2009. *Challenging Institutional Analysis and Development: The Bloomington School*. New York: Routledge.

Buchanan, James M. 1965. "An Economic Theory of Clubs." *Economica* 32 (125): 1–14.

———. 1999a. "Politics, Policy, and the Pigovian Margins." In *The Collected Works of James M. Buchanan, Vol. 1: The Logical Foundations of Constitutional Democracy*, 60–74. Indianapolis, IN: Liberty Fund.

———. 1999b. "Politics without Romance: A Sketch of Positive Public Choice Theory and Its Normative Implications." In *The Collected Works of James M. Buchanan, Vol. 1: The Logical Foundations of Constitutional Democracy*, 45–59. Indianapolis, IN: Liberty Fund.

———. 1999c. "Rent Seeking and Profit Seeking." In *The Collected Works of James M. Buchanan, Vol 1: The Logical Foundations of Constitutional Democracy*, 103–115. Indianapolis, IN: Liberty Fund.

———. 1999d. "The Domain of Constitutional Economics." In *The Collected Works of James M. Buchanan, Vol. 1: The Logical Foundations of Constitutional Democracy,* 377–395. Indianapolis, IN: Liberty Fund.

———. 1999e. "What Should Economists Do?" In *The Collected Works of James M. Buchanan, Vol. 1: The Logical Foundations of Constitutional Democracy*, 28–44. Indianapolis, IN: Liberty Fund.

———. 2000. *The Limits of Liberty: Between Anarchy and Leviathan*. Indianapolis, IN: Liberty Fund.

Buchanan, James M. and Roger D. Congleton. 2003. *Politics by Principle, Not by Interest*. Indianapolis, IN: Liberty Fund.

Buchanan, James M. and Gordon Tullock. 1999. *The Calculus of Consent: The Logical Foundations of Constitutional Democracy*. Indianapolis, IN: Liberty Fund.

Hume, David. 1987. *Essays: Moral, Political, and Literary*, edited by Eugene F. Miller. Indianapolis, IN: Liberty Fund.

Kogelmann, Brian. 2018. "Rawls, Buchanan, and the Search for a Better Social Contract." In *Exploring the Political Economy & Social Philosophy of James M. Buchanan*, edited by Paul Aligica, Christopher J. Coyne, and Stefanie Haeffele, 17–38. Lanham, MD: Rowman & Littlefield.

———. 2022. "Public Choice and Political Equality." In *Wealth and Power: Philosophical Perspectives*, edited by Michael Bennett, Huub Brouwer, and Rutger Claassen, 67–84. London: Routledge.

———. 2023. "In Defense of Knavish Constitutions." *Public Choice* 196: 141–156.

Olson, Mancur. 1971. *The Logic of Collective Action*. Cambridge: Harvard University Press.

Ostrom, Elinor. 1990. *Governing the Commons: The Evolution of Institutions for Collective Action*. Cambridge: Cambridge University Press.

———. 1998. "A Behavioral Approach to the Rational Choice Theory of Collective Action." *American Political Science Review* 92: 1–22.

———. 2010. "Beyond Markets and States: Polycentric Governance of Complex Economic Systems." *American Economic Review* 100: 641–672.

Ostrom, Elinor and Vincent Ostrom. 2004. "The Quest for Meaning in Public Choice." *American Journal of Economics and Sociology* 63: 105–147.

Ostrom, Vincent. 1997. *The Meaning of Democracies and the Vulnerability of Democracies: A Response to Tocqueville's Challenge*. Ann Arbor, MI: University of Michigan Press.

———. 1999. "Polycentricity (Part 1)." In *Polycentricity and Local Public Economies*, edited by Michael D. McGinnis, 52–74. Ann Arbor, MI: University of Michigan Press.

———. 2014. "Epistemic Choice and Public Choice." In *Choice, Rules and Collective Action: The Ostroms on the Study of Institutions and Governance*, edited by Filippo Sabetti and Paul Dragos Aligica, 243–270. Colchester, U.K.: ECPR Press.

Ostrom, Vincent and Elinor Ostrom. 1999. "Public Goods and Public Choices." In *Polycentricity and Local Public Economies*, edited by Michael D. McGinnis, 75–103. Ann Arbor, MI: University of Michigan Press.

———. 2014. "Public Choice: A Different Approach to the Study of Public Administration." In *Choice, Rules and Collective Action: The Ostroms on the Study of Institutions and Governance*, edited by Filippo Sabetti and Paul Dragos Aligica, 23–43. Colchester, UK: ECPR Press.

Ostrom, Vincent, Charles M. Tiebout, and Robert Warren. 1961. "The Organization of Government in Metropolitan Areas: A Theoretical Inquiry." *American Political Science Review* 55: 831–842.

Tarko, Vlad. 2016. *Elinor Ostrom: An Intellectual Biography*. Lanham, MD: Rowan & Littlefield International, Ltd.

Part I

THEORETICAL FOUNDATIONS

Chapter 1

Politics Without Romance, Without Romance

The Meta-Problem for Virginia Political Economy

Jason Lee Byas

PUBLIC CHOICE PESSIMISM?

Virginia Political Economy is a research tradition that can be characterized as the conjunction of two further research programs: public choice and constitutional political economy.[1] Public choice studies the workings of state institutions through the lens of the incentives faced by individuals within those institutions, on the assumption of behavioral symmetry with the way those same individuals make choices within markets (Buchanan 2003). Constitutional political economy is the study of how different possible institutional arrangements and rules might adjust the options available to those individuals, such that they are likely to make different choices, leading to different outcomes (Buchanan 1990). In addition to these positive research programs, scholars in the Virginia Political Economy tradition are likely to normatively subscribe to a distinctive kind of classical liberalism, committed to making good on the ideal of political equality through tools like a *norm of generality* that attempts to limit the possibility of discrimination and domination of some individuals by others through the state (Buchanan and Congleton 1998).[2]

It is easy to see how these pieces are meant to form a cohesive framework. Thinking through the incentives faced by political actors will very quickly lead to the thought that any serious improvement at the level of policy will require serious improvement at the level of the rules for selecting those policies. In turn, this will lead to a special concern for ensuring that those institutions are sufficiently restrained to prevent their use for the abuse or exploitation of anyone subjected to them. There is a logical fit between these components of the Virginian approach.

Yet there is also a serious tension between them. According to the Virginia Political Economist, qua public choice theorist, we should not pretend that human agents will be any less narrowly self-interested when they make choices as voters, politicians, or bureaucrats than they are when they are buyers or sellers. It is therefore naïve to expect such agents to follow the path of public interest, even when it diverges from that of their own private interest, simply because they are acting in one of these public roles. This is the basic case for saying we should instead look to change the rules behind those choices so that we can redirect that second path toward the first. However, the path to that point of convergence is even murkier: if incentives to abuse and exploit put policy-level progress out of reach, surely those same incentives will put constitution-level progress even further out of reach.

In this chapter, I explore and assess this challenge, which I call *the Meta-Problem of Virginia Political Economy*: to the extent that the Virginians' public choice analysis is correct, enacting their constitutional recommendations will be to that same extent infeasible, and so the political prospects of their normative values will dim in proportion to the truth of their positive claims. If this Meta-Problem cannot be solved, then the result is *public choice pessimism*: the conclusion that the pathologies of power Virginians highlight are institutionally inescapable, and so their liberal political vision will be impossible without a miracle (Munger and Villarreal-Diaz 2019).[3]

I argue that there is a credible solution to the Meta-Problem, and so public choice pessimism may be avoided, but not before showing just how grave the situation really is. In the following section, I start by outlining the basic problem and the kind of cycle that it predicts: a series of increasingly inefficient forms of intervention and exploitation, which then collapse from inefficiency, fostering modest liberalization, leading to growth, and then back to increasingly inefficient forms of intervention and exploitation. At times, constitutional political economists have argued that uncertainty about long-term interests inherent to constitutional deliberation can relax ordinary public choice problems, and that this suggests a way to break the cycle, but I argue that any such effect is not of a kind that could get us out of the Meta-Problem. There, I also consider the possibility of interest alignment, in which elites themselves might be incentivized to make meaningful reforms. While those fortuitous circumstances are not impossible, I give some reasons to think they are highly unlikely.

I then consider some possible fixes, first quick and then slow, for getting out of that cycle. The third section looks at the quick fix of abandoning the commitment to democracy for one of dictatorship or rigging the game for a particular coalition of well-aligned interests. I argue that Buchanan and other Virginia Political Economists have been right to reject these options. In short, even if we put aside normative worries with these quick fixes, they underestimate the nature of the problem and threaten to make it worse.

These problems point us to slower fixes to which I turn in the next section. These are much more abstract appeals to a change in ideas or the cultivation of a liberal spirit. While there is something right with these answers, they cannot be enough on their own. Just as ideas and spirit are not enough for stable, substantial policy improvement without constitutional constraints in place, they alone cannot be enough to put those constraints in place. There is also a further problem, especially relevant in a discussion of political economy: ideas and visions do not exist in institutional vacuums. An implication of this is that classical liberalism is simply less likely to flourish in the institutional environment it is meant to correct, and if some version of it does emerge triumphant, it is most likely to be one warped beyond recognition.

Having considered those quicker and slower fixes, I then observe that all of them hold fixed assumptions about the points at which political agency exists. When we open our conception of political agency beyond direct engagement with the state, or getting things ready for some future direct engagement, we start to see light at the end of this tunnel. In particular, there exist roundabout fixes, such as direct rule evasion and building countervailing institutions in civil society, which might serve to check the state.

One of the biggest problems for these solutions is that as long as institutionalized means of rent-seeking persist, there will be a temptation for successful nonstate institutions to retool their efforts toward rent-seeking. I then argue that this suggests a new direction for constitutional political economy: discovering ways that these nonstate institutions might be constructed to bind themselves against future rent-seeking. Alongside this constitutional political economy writ small also comes the Meta-Problem writ small. The difference is that once shrunk to this size, it is adequately addressed by something like our slower fixes.

As I stress in the conclusion, our best hope for a solution to the Meta-Problem for Virginia Political Economy is through an expansion of that same constitutional attitude that Virginia Political Economy traditionally prescribes. Rather than just taking institutions as they are and doing what we can, we should be prepared to change them. So too must we be prepared to think seriously about which institutions might be worth focusing on, even before we get the *most obvious* ones to change.

VIRGINIA POLITICAL ECONOMY AND ITS META-PROBLEM

Before discussing why the two components of Virginia Political Economy are in tension, it is worth first examining why they come together.

Public choice begins with two premises, which are fairly obvious once clearly stated. First, political processes and institutions do not exist on their own and so do not move on their own: they are made up of people, occupying various offices and functions, and so state action is always the action of many different individuals, each with agency, and each with their own set of incentives. Second, these individuals are the same individuals during state choice situations that they are during market choice situations. It is naïve, then, to assume they will be wholly public-spirited in state choice situations, given that they are not so spirited in the market. The tools used to analyze commercial exchange can also be used to analyze political exchange, and the difference between those analyses is the difference between the structure of each exchange.

The public choice paradigm is sometimes described as a view of politics *without romance* because it quickly points to deep, structural pathologies in modern political institutions (Buchanan 2003). For instance, the fact that the state provides a powerful means for coercing others means that it provides attractive avenues for profit: those who can more easily influence state actors can obtain wealth by simply extracting it from others. When the costs of securing this extraction are lower than the costs of producing some good or service that could be exchanged on the market for the same profit, these incentives will lead those in such a position to retool their efforts away from production and toward predation. This process is called *rent-seeking*.

The economic problem with rent-seeking, independent of any ethical objections, is that the resources expended in rent-seeking do not produce new wealth; they just move it from one hand to another. Thus, the total amount of wealth in society goes down, as social costs are borne without social benefits (Tullock 1967). Because the wealth of individual rent-seekers increases, and their incentives are for their individual wealth rather than overall social wealth, the process continues as long as opportunities for rent-seeking persist.

This same individualist analysis also explains why those opportunities will persist. Counterintuitively, state institutions will generally select policies that extract wealth from larger groups in the service of smaller groups (Olson 1965). The first reason for this is that each individual in the larger group bears a relatively minor cost, whereas each individual in the smaller group receives a significant benefit. Second, it is much harder for the larger group to secure cooperation and coordinate their interests.

For example, suppose that $50,000 total is taken from a hundred thousand people and given to one person. Here, the single person has a strong incentive to ensure that the transfer happens, as she will gain $50,000, but each individual in the larger group has only the trivial incentive of not losing fifty cents. Even though they don't want to lose the fifty cents, it's not worth the costs of making themselves aware of the problem, figuring out how to stop it, and getting others to coordinate. This is especially true given that if there were any such effort underway, it would be individually rational to free-ride, worsening the prospects for that defensive effort. Therefore, as long as the total cost of ensuring that the transfer happens is less than $50,000 to the beneficiary, it is more likely to happen than not, and total social wealth declines by however much that cost ended up being.

This basic logic of concentrated benefits trumping dispersed costs leads to phenomena like regulatory capture, in which industry leaders are incentivized to seek regulation of their industry in order to raise costs for competitors (Stigler 1971). Economically destructive limits to competition are also likely to persist well after they stop providing benefits to the initial rent-seeker because relaxing those limits will still create costs (Tullock 1975). Given the minimal likelihood of any one vote affecting the outcome of an election, voters are both rationally ignorant (Downs 1957) and rationally irrational (Caplan 2007): the costs of obtaining sufficient information on how to best vote far exceed the benefits, and so they are instead most likely to unreflectively vote in ways that fit with social allegiances (Brennan and Lomasky 1993). Politicians, who want to secure their position, are steered toward policies that flatter the unreflective prejudices of these ignorant and irrational voters while also satisfying the preferences of rent-seeking interest groups and donors. These systemic, structural problems cut deep, and the picture they paint of democratic government is bleak.

At least that much is true when assuming the rules governing the policy process stay fixed. The same rules create the same incentives, which will inevitably lead to the same outcomes. This is why the study of public choice motivates constitutional political economy, which is the study of different sets of rules for governing political decision-making. If we want significant, productive political change beyond the occasional miracle, we will need better rules for political deliberation and exchange.

In *The Calculus of Consent*, Buchanan and Tullock distinguish between the preconstitutional moment, at which point we choose which rules will govern our future collective choices, and the postconstitutional moment, at which point we make further choices from within the rules selected in the preconstitutional moment. From behind a veil of uncertainty about our postconstitutional positions, we can come to some degree of unanimity in choosing rules that will minimize the power of others to impose costs upon us once those rules are in place. Toward that end, we will want state action to be difficult to pursue in proportion to its potential for harm so that it cannot be used as an engine of discrimination or domination.

We need not construe Buchanan and Tullock's preconstitutional moment as a real, historical moment, and can instead interpret it as a device for discovering which rules are normatively best.[4] Nonetheless, it is worth noting that in the real world, we are very deep into the postconstitutional moment already, with rules not selected from behind a veil of uncertainty or through anything approximating unanimity. On the one hand, the observed consequences of this status quo have been exactly what Virginia Political Economy would predict. On the other hand, this now raises the Meta-Problem: how can we get to the "there" of the better rules outlined in constitutional political economy from the "here" of political pathologies predicted by public choice?

Channeling Knut Wicksell, Buchanan was fond of reminding economists that they were not proffering advice for a benevolent despot and so political realities had to play a part in thinking about the feasibility of their preferred policies (1987, 143). One way to emphasize the importance of the Meta-Problem is to add further that political economists are also not proffering advice to a benevolent despot who plans to abdicate power, and so the feasibility of any constitutional recommendations must also consider the political realities of our existing constitutional situation. From that position, it is hard to see how changing our constitutional rules from inside could be a serious suggestion, given that the same problems that hinder productive policy change will hinder productive constitutional change.

Worse still, the very fact that the effects of productive constitutional change would reach much further than productive change on any single policy is also a reason to think it will be even more difficult than productive change on any single policy.

For example, consider Buchanan's own suggestions when asked for amendments to the U.S. Constitution (2005a). One was for a balanced budget amendment, where estimated spending could exceed estimated tax revenues only when approved by three-fourths of the House and of the Senate. A second was for a ban on any discriminatory state action of any kind, eliminating targeted subsidies, tax credits, and nonuniversal transfers, except when these promote a general interest beyond their direct targets. Third, most dramatically, he proposed to guarantee natural liberty by prohibiting all government interference in voluntary exchange, both foreign and domestic.

Imagine how difficult it would be to actually get these amendments passed. I don't just mean the hurdles of the ratification process itself; I mean the special difficulties for Buchanan's particular proposals. Part of why he proposed them, of course, is that they would significantly curb the use of the state to seek and secure rents. For that same reason, every private entity whose current business model depends on existing or future rents, along with every special interest whose policy preferences conflict with a generality norm, would have reason to ferociously resist the Buchanan amendments.

To name just a few of these, the incentivized opposition would include all businesses that receive tax credits or subsidies, all regulatory agencies and the industry leaders that capture them, and any beneficiary of a tariff or otherwise discriminatory tax. These interests will have every reason to favor those legislators who oppose the amendments and to crush those who support them, which creates a heavy constraint on any legislator who wants to keep their job. The fact that the voting public as a whole would benefit from the Buchanan amendments doesn't help much, because those benefits are too widely dispersed, and so voters will have all the same reasons that they usually do to be rationally ignorant.

By contrast, we have reason to think that constitutional change which worsens public choice problems will be easier, even if still very difficult. As with any policy, the concentrated benefits to those who stand to gain from the change push the scale in its favor, with little resistance from those who bear the dispersed costs.

Such considerations tell strongly against one solution that Buchanan and his coauthors often suggested, which is that the perspective one must adopt in considering constitutional changes looks so far into the future that it is hard to tell where their interests really lie (Buchanan and Tullock 1962, 74; Brennan and Buchanan 1985, 137–140). This actually occurring veil of uncertainty would naturally incline us in a public-interested direction, seeing as we could know little about our position or the positions of those whom we care about. Unfortunately, this magic of the constitutional moment doesn't seem to do the trick: observably, real-world constitutions are made with enough certainty about future interests that those interests still tend to shape the final result.[5]

This should be unsurprising, given the points just raised. To those points, we can add two further ones: first, the blade of uncertainty cuts both ways. Those who already stand in a privileged position given existing arrangements will be averse to constitutional revision precisely because it might swing against them. If you don't know which persons will be favored once you walk into the political-economic dark of the postconstitutional moment, but you *do* know that you're doing pretty well back here in the status quo, this will give you reason to dig in your heels and block attempts at constitutional revision. After all—and this is the second point—if the generalized social benefit combined with uncertainty were enough to overcome ordinary public choice concerns, it seems like we would see a lot more productive constitutional change than we do. Instead, constitutional changes that do occur tend to follow typical public choice patterns, and a plausible explanation is that there is a reasonably clear rent-seeking element that helps to get over the elite anxiety inherent to constitutional change. In other words, insofar as the veil of uncertainty is a feature of real-world constitutional deliberation, it can actually make things worse.

The conclusion here is one of *public choice pessimism.* By this, I mean the thought that given the incentive dynamics of collective decision-making in large-scale cases like modern democracies, we have reason to expect these economic pathologies to get worse and worse, and that to whatever extent some reform would be meaningfully productive, it will be *to that same extent* politically infeasible. If public choice pessimism is true, then the project of Virginia Political Economy eats itself: exploring the problems with existing political arrangements and what would be needed to fix those problems will reveal that the exploration gave no practical guidance. As Buchanan wrote with Geoffrey Brennan, a pessimist conclusion would mean that their work "would have to have been driven by purely aesthetic purpose" (1985, 134). We could know exactly why the world is crumbling around us, but we could not do anything to stop it.

One response here might be to hold out for a *miracle*, wherein the narrow and concentrated interests of the powerful align with productive constitutional change.

Such a response can't be rejected out of hand, because in this context, miracles have happened. In Douglass North, John Joseph Wallis, and Barry Weingast's *Violence and Social Orders*, they argue that miracles of interest alignment explain the transition from closed access orders to open access ones.[6] In short, closed access orders are those where activity in civil society and the economy presumptively requires the permission of existing elites, and open access orders are those where such activity presumptively requires no permission. On their account, it is when those same elites stand to benefit from shifting to an open-access order that the move is made. This explains both how the change could ever happen and why it is so historically rare.

Perhaps something similar could lead a modern, democratic open-access order to further improve its structure when the interests of elites converge with the recommendations of constitutional political economy. In such a case, familiar public choice problems would actually be a godsend, as the power of concentrated interests would itself spell the end of that same power.[7]

Unfortunately, such miracles are unlikely. It is hard enough to fall into the miracles that allow for an open-access order to emerge. It is even harder for them to appear once an open-access order is in place, at least when we have in mind those miracles that are so substantial that they set the stage for constitutional-level change.

In the closed-access order, those with such power are actors whom some other elites have accepted into their fold. Under such an arrangement, what is in the interest of some elites will likely be in the interest of elites more generally, and so when miracles emerge, they will meet less resistance.

By its very nature, there are many more players with credible power in an open-access order, and many more competing interests. While it may be in the narrow self-interest of one rent-seeking or rent-dependent party to get out of the game and adjust the constitution, this suggests nothing about whether it will be in the narrow self-interest of others with meaningful power. This one party may push for productive change given how their interests align, but they will be pushing back against the much greater tide of parties whose interests are not so-aligned.[8]

If an efficacious miracle of the kind we need is to happen in an open-access order, it will have to be one that aligns the concentrated interests of elites in general, rather than just some small subset of them. An event that might have this effect is a *crisis* caused by ill-designed institutions, which those institutions are not currently equipped to handle. With serious elite interests in jeopardy, serious reform might be possible.

Unfortunately, this is also unlikely to work. As distortions in the economy accumulate, it becomes increasingly crisis-prone (Olson 1982), but there is more than one way to respond to a crisis. One option is to remove those policies that created the crisis and use constitutional reform to guard against anything similar happening in the future. Another is to respond by some other, distorting state action that pushes in the opposite direction (Higgs 1987).

For many reasons, the second option will generally win out: this countervailing state action will typically benefit a specific group, and so that group will have a concentrated interest in pushing that particular state action. At a psychological level, positive state action looks like "doing something," and liberalization can look like abandoning the problem. Moreover, since other interests depend on existing arrangements, targeted interventions will be preferred to liberalization or constitutional reforms that may threaten to upset those arrangements.

Sometimes, crises will be so deep that the harder option of liberalization is taken. Yet easing up just enough to resolve the current crisis will not require full liberalization, nor will it require constitutionally binding measures against future mistakes. Without the more dramatic response, the liberalization that does occur will generate more wealth, which will also generate more opportunities for rent-seeking and will start the cycle again.

The pessimist conclusion, then, inverts Ludwig von Mises's conclusion that mixed economies of markets with regular intervention are an impossibility. He argued that starting down the road of interventionism means that each intervention will require a countervailing one to deal with its ill effects and that these would slowly accumulate to the point where the state is functionally managing the economy (1940). If public choice pessimism is true, then perhaps interventionism is the only option: laissez-faire sows the seeds of its own demise by creating the wealth necessary for further rent-seeking, and for reasons Mises himself outlined, outright socialism must eventually collapse into something less totalizing in its control (1920).

If this cycle is to be avoided, we need more than a miracle. There needs to be some point of political agency from which we can adjust the game despite the built-in difficulties in doing so.

QUICK FIXES

When thinking through the logic pointing toward the pessimist conclusion, it becomes salient that what got us there was the logic of democracy. To some, this might suggest the quick fix of abandoning the Virginian normative commitments against discrimination or domination, in favor of dictatorship or rigging electoral rules to favor some preferred coalitional interests. Both options have been vigorously rejected by Buchanan and others affiliated with Virginia Political Economy (Farrant and Tarko 2019; Boettke and Thompson 2022), but some who are otherwise sympathetic to their views might think this is a problem. It is worth briefly working through why these quick fixes will not work even if we ignore their more directly normative problems.

The first and most minor problem with these options is still quite severe: the very problem they are trying to solve just replicates. Even if these changes were desirable, they would still be significant changes. While occasional gerrymandering might not be so hard, more substantial changes to electoral rules and installing a new, autocratic government certainly would be. The quick fix, then, would generally not be very quick.

A second problem is that the cost of failure for any serious attempt would be very, very high. Most obviously, attempting to install a dictator would likely involve violent, destabilizing conflict. Even trying to shift electoral rules toward terms favorable to a preferred coalition is likely to intensify existing political tribalism. Neither environment is hospitable to freedom. Moreover, if such attempts are clearly associated with classical liberalism, others will associate classical liberals with an attempt to tyrannize them, which further worsens further still the long-term prospects for liberty.

A third problem is that these are still particular interests, and actively empowering particular interests means becoming dependent on those interests' arbitrary whims. Suppose that a given dictator is committed to classical liberalism in everything except the fact of his dictatorship. There is no guarantee that he will remain committed as time goes on, and the policy pendulum will immediately swing with him. He could, formally speaking, impose constitutional restraints on himself, but if he is powerful enough to unilaterally impose them, then that fact will itself undermine their credibility.

Similarly, the people in a winning coalition of interests are still people, and as cultural winds shift, so too will their political allegiances. Even if, however unlikely, a particular set of interests is near-perfectly amenable to classical liberalism today, those same groups may be near-perfectly hostile to it tomorrow. Observe, for instance, that Alaska and Hawaii were admitted to the United States near the same time, so that the Republican Hawaii would offset the Democratic Alaska. Since then, the two have switched. Similarly, the now near-uniformly Republican Oklahoma was admitted as only one state, instead of two, out of fear over admitting two Democratic states.[9] Political demography is always much more fleeting and fickle than it seems in the moment.

Fourth, and perhaps most concerning, the dynamics of maintaining autocratic rule or a permanent winning coalition incline against liberalism. To maintain power, it is not enough that a dictator does not hold elections. He will generally also need to limit freedom of speech and association, while also holding off violent challengers to his power through increasingly unscrupulous means. Similar concerns are at play when trying to maintain a permanent winning coalition (Boettke and Thompson 2022).

The general problem with these quick fixes is that, in trying to be quick, they ignore the nature of the problem they are meant to solve. What makes bad policy so seemingly inescapable is that the rules of the game so dependably tilt in perverse directions because coercive power is insufficiently restrained. Making the use of coercive power even less restrained for particular players, then, will lead to even worse versions of this same problem.[10]

SLOW FIXES

If we take interests as given, then barring a miracle, public choice considerations will prevent any long-lasting, productive constitutional changes, and this will be especially so the more significant those changes are. The magic of the constitutional moment and its veil of uncertainty is not forthcoming and may even be part of what holds us back. Seemingly straightforward shortcuts around the democratic process are illusory and come with many problems of their own. From within the game in which we are already engaged, it seems that the pessimistic conclusion follows.

Buchanan's own suggestion was to reject the assumption that we must take interests as given. Writing with Geoffrey Brennan, he conceded that if we assume a narrow, *homo economicus* model of actors' motivations, then the political process ensures a pessimistic conclusion. However, they continued, real-world agents are more complicated than that. Public choice corrected the naïve view that self-interested agents magically devote themselves wholly to the public interest when they enter politics, but it would be an overcorrection to say that they never had or acted on any idea of the public interest at all (1985, 146–147). The task before political philosophers and social scientists, then, is to shape our understanding of what that public interest is, and to emphasize the importance of constitutional thinking, shifting our attention toward the rules of the game rather than any moment of play (1985, 149–150).

Writing on his own, Buchanan continued this theme, arguing that it is not just ideas, narrowly construed, that matter for this task. There is also an important role in constructing a coherent, inspiring narrative for how those ideas fit together, which he called discovering a movement's "soul" (2000). With a properly animating soul, a movement can hope to have the power necessary to make big, constitutional changes, rather than just tinkering around the edges of particular policies.

Efforts appealing to ideas and spirit are quite slow, but they do hold some promise. While there is something surprising about public choice theorists stressing the importance of ideas about the public interest and a romantic vision, there is surely something right about it.

For instance, it is not even *internally coherent* to think outcomes mechanically proceed from interests without any mediation from ideas. After all, for people to act on their interests, they must have ideas about what those interests are. Our preferences depend on our self-conception, what we think will satisfy those preferences depends on our model of how the world works, and what we will do when pursuing them will depend on what political options we think are available to us (Rodrik 2014, 190–195). As Dani Rodrik writes, a consequence of this is that "ideas can . . . relax political constraints," widening the scope of the possible (2014, 205, emphasis removed). With that in mind, we may have hope in the role of social and intellectual entrepreneurs, who discover opportunities for improvement and bring this knowledge to the public (Leighton and Lopez 2012; Boettke and Coyne 2009; Hayek 1949).

I am very sympathetic to this suggestion, and as I will argue later, I think it must be a part of the right solution to the Meta-Problem. Yet it cannot go all the way on its own.

In Wayne Leighton and Edward Lopez's *Madmen, Intellectuals and Academic Scribblers*, they outline three examples of successful intellectual entrepreneurship in twentieth-century America that are likely to be viewed as positive by Virginia Political Economists (2012, Ch. 6). These are the FCC auctioning off licenses for parts of the radio spectrum, airline deregulation, and welfare reform. All three of these are impressive achievements that should not be downplayed.

However, notice that these are also all instances of particular policy changes within existing constitutional arrangements, rather than fundamental changes to the constitution that produced these policies. I do not mean that they were not literal amendments to the U.S. Constitution; I mean that they were significant changes in play, but not in the rules of the game. The FCC now distributes spectrum licenses by auction, but the FCC still controls the airwaves. Airlines have been greatly deregulated, but this was not because of any general restrictions raised against regulation. Welfare programs have changed, but this was not because of restrictions placed upon the state's power to redistribute. These changes were policy choices within rules that grant legislators and regulators broad discretion, not fundamental institutional changes that bind legislators and regulators by removing their discretionary power.

Placed in this context, it is also worth noting that these were not the only changes to economic policy in that same time frame. Both the redistributive and regulatory states have greatly grown, even if there are occasional wins—even major wins—on particular policies. That is why public choice calls our attention to the rules of the game, rather than moments of play, and so it is worth considering putting classical liberal ideas about the rules of the game into focus, and seeing how they might fare under existing rules.

Ideas themselves, like any other product, will flourish or languish in different institutional contexts (Tarko 2015, 18–21). Unfortunately, institutional environments marked by the pathologies Virginians describe are also institutional environments especially inhospitable to the kind of classical liberalism Virginians prescribe. Buchanan's slow fixes of ideas and spirit are not enough to get wide-reaching, constitutional change off the ground on their own.

A first reason for this is the effect existing institutions have on ideology. Ideology, in this sense, is "a somewhat coherent, rather comprehensive belief system about social relations, . . . [which] structures a person's perceptions and predetermines his or her understandings of events in the social world" (Higgs 2008, 548). A plausible feature of many accounts of ideology is that ideologies come tethered to particular social institutions and practices, and that regular participation within those institutions and practices will reinforce the hold of an ideology (Haslanger 2017).

If this is so, then our familiarity with the existing game, and regular deliberation within its rules, will be a powerful block against any attempt to change them. An industry caked in layers of regulation and subsidy will be difficult to imagine in any other way. The very idea that *all* such regulations and subsidies might be barred across the board will sound insane. We are used to our purchases being guided by what drugs the Food and Drug Administration (FDA) approves, and so we come to equate safety with FDA approval. *No FDA approval*, then, is taken to mean *no safety*, and the proposal to eliminate the regulatory state will be rejected out of hand. Even if the tide turns against the FDA in particular, familiarity with regulation itself will block applying the lesson more generally.

This is also a way in which fighting public choice pathologies becomes harder the worse they get. As Robert Higgs documents, state expansion follows crises, as the destabilizing of expectations allows for a change in ideology that permits greater state power. When the crisis ends, state power retracts, but not to precrisis levels, and this is due to the ideological shift (Higgs 1987). Applying this to the earlier exposition of the cycle predicted by the pessimist conclusion suggests pushing back at the level of ideas will be enormously difficult, as it is at the level of ideas that the problem reinforces itself.

That is a way that the existing institutional setting hinders slow fixes that rely on developing the constitutional mind. Slow fixes that rely on developing a constitutional spirit face related problems. For example, a world familiar with countless varieties of state action, through which different ideas and commitments are expressed, will find liberal restraint uninspiring. In such a context, saying that the state should greatly reduce its role seems to mean greatly reducing the extent to which we care about the social world. It is this kind of concern, for example, that led Robert Nozick to significantly moderate his libertarianism, writing that "[t]he libertarian view looked solely at the purpose of government, not at its *meaning*; hence, it took an unduly narrowly view of purpose, too" (1989, 288, emphasis in original).

In a world where meaning is so commonly taken to come from state action, the gospel of state restraint will find few natural converts. In those same conditions, many converts that are made will be contrarians or people who simply care less, and both groups are unlikely to stay very committed to any cause for very long. As long as the state has not lost all credibility, then increases in its scope will mean decreases in how many people might be committed to constraining it. If the state has lost credibility, this also might not be enough, since the revolt triggered could be a populist one of replacing players, rather than a liberal one of changing the rules.[11]

A further worry, for both ideas and spirit, is that when classical liberal ideas seem to triumph under existing institutions, they are prone to being warped by those institutions. If the classical liberal message of freedom is to be electorally successful, it must come attached to candidates who can actually win. Given that candidates who can actually win will need to placate both rent-seeking concentrated interests and an electorate marked by rational ignorance and rational irrationality, that abstract liberal message is likely to find itself attached to concrete policies of a much less liberal sort. When those ill-fitting concrete policies fail, this in turn motivates a rejection of the abstract message used to rationalize them.[12]

Of course, there are clear cases where the thrust of ideas alone led to productive constitutional changes from within the ordinary operation of a democratic system. Two that jump to mind are the British abolition of slavery and the American expansion of suffrage to women.[13] Yet it is worth taking a second to see why these are exceptions that prove the rule's punishing applicability in other cases.

In both cases, there is an extremely straightforward moral concern, and that moral concern requires very little, if any understanding of political economy to see: some people are being treated as less than people, and some people are being subjected to laws yet are explicitly barred from any decision about who crafts those laws. As both cases show, the slow fixes of ideas and spirit are still very slow and still require a heroic effort to do their work. So too must that slow tide come up against the dam of ideology, with familiarity being conflated with necessity. However, when the moral concern and its application to the question are so straightforward, at least that tide's waters need not peter out when the ordinary person lacks understanding of political-economic minutiae, nor will those waters get rerouted through the tunnels of state action that have come to stand in for that concern. It is quite hard to fake commitment to liberal ideals about moral equality while slavery persists and very easy to notice the discrepancy; it is not so hard to warp moral worries about the power of economic elites into support for webs of regulation that entrench that same power.[14]

RETHINKING POLITICAL PROCESS AND POLITICAL ORDER

Public choice pessimism feels inescapable. From inside the machine that public choice describes, it looks impossible to rewire it into something better. The answer, then, may be to look outside the machine.

If we take "the political process" to mean *the process of direct engagement with the state*, and limit our understanding of political order to *those rules by which state action is chosen and executed*, then the pessimistic conclusion cannot be avoided. However, Billy Christmas and I have elsewhere criticized the conflation of politics with engaging the state, even when the political aims in question are how to check state power (Byas and Christmas 2020).

There, we contrast two approaches, which we call "The Policy Framework" and "Methodological Anarchism." The former takes questions about justice or politics to necessarily be questions about the state, its actions, and its constitution. The latter instead takes questions about justice or politics to be questions about the norms, practices, and institutions that govern a given society—a scope that includes but is not limited to the state (2020, 53–54).[15]

What is important for our purposes here is that once our conception of political processes and political order is expanded in this way, so too is our understanding of where political agency lies.

Within the Policy Framework, our options appear to be what Christmas and I call *reform* or *revolution* (2022, 62). "Reform," in this context, refers to attempts to get an existing state to change its own policies or constitution, in some way mediated through the state's own channels. "Revolution" is the attempt to simply overthrow one state and replace its constitution with another. Both of these are state-mediated forms of political action, because whatever change they seek to effect in society must pass through some change that they seek to effect in the state.

We contrast this with a form of political agency we call *direct action*. Direct action is "direct" because it is unmediated, seeking to change the governance of society in its norms, practices, and institutions whether the state complies or not.

If direct action can serve to place constraints upon the state from outside of the state, then this will avoid the Meta-Problem. The process of political action in question here is not operating from within the game of the state, and so is not governed by the rules that govern policy choices within that game. Accordingly, any attempted imposition of constraints in this way will not face the particular problems outlined by public choice. Because we are not using the machine to repair the machine, we are not subject to its mechanics.

For this solution to work, of course, it will have to be the case that meaningful constraints can be imposed upon the state from outside. Otherwise, this will not bring us any further with respect to the Meta-Problem.

A fully adequate defense of direct action as a strategy is beyond the space I have remaining here, and so I will not attempt to give one. Instead, I will provide some reasons to think direct action might possibly be a means of providing meaningful constraints on the state.

Consider two categories of direct action: creating and securing *avenues of evasion* and *alternative institutions*. These categories are not meant to be exhaustive of the forms direct action might take, nor is there a hard separation between them. In broad strokes, avenues of evasion are the ways that those subjected to state coercion might be able to bypass that coercion more safely, and alternative institutions are organizations or practices within markets and civil society that provide goods and services currently provided by the state.

For example, the Underground Railroad was an avenue of evasion, whereas fraternal societies were alternative institutions (Beito 2000). Parts of the Bitcoin community aspire for it to be both, as a form of money outside the state, which then helps to enable prohibited transactions (Nakamoto 2008; Bailey, Rettler, and Warmke 2021). Cryptocurrencies like Bitcoin then enabled the Silk Road, by which I mean the now-defunct marketplace for drugs on the deep web, not the historic trade route, which also sought to provide both. Most obviously, it was a means of evading drug policy, but it also provided some protection against violence and fraud in a domain where the state would not: purchasing drugs (Aldridge and Décary-Hétu 2016; Barratt, Ferris, and Winstock 2016). Lest these examples suggest too extreme a picture of direct action, they can also be perfectly ordinary: privately administered, extensive welfare services such as those offered by the Church of Jesus Christ of Latter-Day Saints are an especially successful instance of an alternative institution (Goodman and Herzberg 2019).

How can these sorts of things serve as checks upon the state? In short, by changing what the state can realistically do, through raising the costs of successfully executing state actions and lowering public acceptance of state policy.

For a potentially controversial but illustrative example with respect to avenues of evasion, consider copyright. Some economists reject the practice as a clear instance of rent-seeking in its provision of a monopoly (Boldrin and Levine 2010). Despite this, both legislation and court decisions have lengthened the duration and widened the scope of copyright over time. Nevertheless, the political reality is that copyright's effect on consumer activity has become weaker with time, as file-sharing has become commonplace. So too does that same avenue of evasion weaken public acceptance of copyright.

With respect to alternative institutions, the case for state action will be less plausible the more the relevant goal is adequately achieved privately.

For instance, there is widespread agreement that mass incarceration is one of the worst pathologies of American political institutions. Unfortunately, there is also a plausible case that mass incarceration is a product of inflexible punitiveness toward *violent* crime, and that politically popular reforms like legalizing marijuana or eliminating private prisons are unlikely to make much of a dent (Pfaff 2017). It could be taken as a fixed political point that mass incarceration will stay with us since voters are unlikely to soften their approach to violent crime, and politicians will follow their lead.

An alternative approach is taken by Danielle Sered's Common Justice, an organization that specializes in responding to serious, violent cases of interpersonal harm through restorative justice. As explained in her *Until We Reckon: Violence, Mass Incarceration and the Road to Repair*, her motivation is explicitly political. According to Sered, reversing mass incarceration will require providing a credible response to the problem of violent crime that is compatible with scaling back those responses that have produced mass incarceration. Because this experimentation is not forthcoming from the state itself, it must be built outside of the state in order to produce any results. As examples like this indicate, the building of alternative institutions can break the ideological hold of the status quo by giving people not just an intellectual understanding of alternatives, but an experiential one.

When avenues of evasion and alternative institutions are sufficiently successful, the state must eventually own up to the constraints placed upon it and accommodate them. Many instances of deregulation have followed sufficiently widespread evasion of the prior regulation, making the explicit deregulation little more than a formal recognition of what was already happening (Leitzel 2003, 41). In a common law system, the precedent of custom can come to change official law even when that custom emerged illegally (Leitzel 2003, 43).[16]

CONSTITUTIONAL POLITICAL ECONOMY FROM BELOW AND THE META-PROBLEM WRIT SMALL

While there are many worries about the politics of direct action, I will consider only the most relevant to our present discussion: when alternative institutions develop alongside an ill-structured state, with its standing opportunity for rent-seeking, there will necessarily be a temptation for those alternative institutions to pursue those rents.

To the extent that these alternative institutions become successful, there will to that same extent be a stronger temptation, because their success will often entail a greater capacity for winning and wielding political power. When a group has come to coordinate well for productive ends, this will also enable them to better secure rents. For instance, Emily Chamlee-Wright and Virgil Storr demonstrate how, in the post-Katrina environment, groups retooled their social capital from providing mutual assistance to securing favorable distribution of resources in state rebuilding efforts (2011).

This is a very serious problem, and I do not myself have a clear answer. However, I can nonetheless point in the direction of one. Institutions, including those within civil society, deliberate according to rules, and the structure of their rules for decision-making will determine the projects they pursue. In other words, they have constitutions, and those constitutions are themselves open for amendment. An important task for political economy, then, can be discovering how institutions designed for projects like mutual assistance might successfully bind themselves to prevent acting on the temptation of future rent-seeking.[17]

At the beginning of Book IV of *The Wealth of Nations*, Smith describes political economy as "a branch of the science of a statesman or legislator." In Buchanan's own description, it is the study of exchange relationships and their institutional context (1964). While Buchanan took himself to be channeling Smith, his description is actually much broader, and it is amenable to the point I am making here. State institutions are not the only institutions we find ourselves in, and they are not the only ones where exchanges might be made to adjust their structure. The practical importance of an economics that sees less like a state and more like a citizen (Boettke 2019), then, can be to discover those exchanges. This is a constitutional political economy from below, which does not assume that outcomes proceed mechanically from the rules of those institutions that stand on high.[18]

Yet suggesting this direction for answers also invites another problem. This is that if we mean to solve the public choice problems for organizations in civil society with the tools of constitutional political economy, those public choice problems will themselves make the implementation of any recommendation more difficult. In other words, we return to the Meta-Problem of Virginia Political Economy, writ small.

The answer here is straightforward: once the Meta-Problem has been shrunk to the scale of civil society and market institutions, it can be adequately addressed by something like Buchanan's slow fixes. In general, it is much easier to maintain a shared intellectual understanding and animating spirit within a particular institution of civil society than it is to do so across society at large, especially when that society is marked by the kind of pluralism and diversity that liberalism creates. Because particular institutions pursue specific aims, they carry a much greater sense of shared commitment. It is easier for most everyone in a fraternal society to get roughly on the same page about its long-term plans than for everyone in a nation to do so.[19]

Moreover, consider again the reasons the slow fixes were insufficient for the original Meta-Problem. The first was that familiarity with existing institutions will make alternatives unthinkable, the second was that familiarity with shared commitments being expressed through state action will make classical liberalism uninspiring, and the third was that the variety of classical liberalism likely to find electoral success will be one warped by the requirements of that success.

On *all three counts*, the slow fixes stand a much better chance against the Meta-Problem writ small than they did against the original Meta-Problem. By the very fact that the institution in question pursues its task outside the state, its members will have intimate familiarity with the alternative it presents. They are actively doing something through their shared project, and so they cannot be said to be doing nothing. When considering the success of any attempt to bind against future rent-seeking, the dynamics to be considered are not the dynamics of state institutions, but the internal dynamics of this alternative institution itself.

Insofar as they have secured a means of coordination to rationally pursue their shared aim, they will be able to coordinate to prevent falling into temptation once the long-term costs and benefits are made abundantly clear. At least, this is true if they are fellow-spirited with respect to the institution in question. Plausibly, because there are not already ripe opportunities for rent-seeking through that institution, present participation is a much better indicator of this fellow-spiritedness than participation in government and can be taken as an indicator of broader public-spiritedness.

CONCLUSION: CONSTITUTIONAL OPTIMISM

It is a distressing feature of our institutions that their deep-seated ills make those same ills seem inescapable. We can imagine ways we might reconstitute those institutions and break free from their problems, but there needs to be something within our institutions that we can grab onto in order to make that change. If we are going to get there, there must be a path from where we already are.

The miracle where elite interests align with productive constitutional reform is possible, but we should not hold out for it, especially when elite interests themselves can diverge: even when some elites might have something to gain from reform, it is likely that their efforts will be crushed by those with something to lose.

The quick fixes of dictatorship and permanent winning coalitions are normatively unacceptable, but this should not distract us from the fact that they would not even work. The entire problem is that some persons are empowered to pursue their interest at public expense, and so making it even easier for particular parties to do so takes us in the wrong direction.

The slow fixes of spreading ideas and a unifying vision for these ideas are at least the right place to look for a solution. Yet we still need to look a little further, because those efforts, too, are made harder by the very problem they seek to solve. The familiar feels necessary. Rejecting the way things are done can look like refusing to do anything. When ideas that push against the grain triumph, they often come out warped and torn by that grain's resistance.

All this, however, is not a reason to fall back on pure pessimism. Rather, it is a reason to back up and look for a path without these same persistent problems. Once we take stock of where we are, we find an attractive path in bypassing existing institutions instead of trying to push through them.

This isn't to give up on the constitutional attitude, but to expand it. Not only should we think about how the fundamental institutions of our society might be different, but we should also think about which institutions are truly fundamental. If the state is not so supreme in its power that its rules are the only rules of the social game we play, we can constrain it by adjusting those other rules in the social world.

Once this possibility is raised, pessimism turns to optimism. We have tried only the most obvious portion of options available to us; entrepreneurial opportunities still lie all around us, untapped. Among these are ways that social insurance might be provided truly socially (Beito 2000), that we might respond to wrongdoing without being chained to current criminal policies (Sered 2019), or even that defense against nations might be secured without the problems familiar to national defense (Coyne and Goodman 2020). We need not wait on leviathan to profit from them.

NOTES

1. Thanks to Alex Wade Craig, Nathan Goodman, M. Scott King, other contributors to this volume, and its editors, especially Brian Kogelmann, for their very helpful feedback at multiple stages of this chapter.

2. See also Kogelmann (2023) for more on Virginia Political Economy as an approach to the normative ideal of political equality.

3. While I do not refer directly to Munger and Villarreal-Diaz's paper in this chapter beyond this one citation, it will be apparent to readers familiar with their essay that my points here are very much in line with the problems they raise.

4. However, at many points in the *Calculus of Consent* and other works by Buchanan, it does appear that the veil of uncertainty is proposed as a persistent feature of real-world constitutional deliberation. On this ambiguity, see Kogelmann (2018, 28–30). Here, I collapse the ambiguity in favor of the thought experiment interpretation to make a specific point about the situation we are in now, regardless of what might have made for good constitutional deliberation. Later in this same section, though, I also suggest that if we do take the interpretation in which the veil of uncertainty is a feature of real-world constitutional deliberation, it is not very plausible, or at least not to an extent that would help us with the Meta-Problem.

5. For an extensive empirical treatment of uncertainty about future interests in constitutional deliberation, which unfortunately consistently comes down against Buchanan's predictions, see the essays collected in Imbeau and Jacob (2015). For an influential, albeit controversial, discussion of how economic interests shaped the U.S. Constitution, see Beard (1913). Sometimes, perceived future interests make themselves quite plain in the text of written constitutions, as with the partial inclusion of slaves as persons in the U.S. Constitution, which served no purpose beyond protecting the power of the slaveholding aristocracy. On this general line of argument about uncertainty in constitutional deliberation from Buchanan, see Kogelmann (2018, 28–30). See also Brennan and Buchanan (1985, 134–150), which repeats the argument before conceding some of its limits, turning then to slow fixes of the sort discussed in this chapter.

6. North, Wallis, and Weingast (2013) use the term "natural states" for closed-access orders. Here, I use "closed access orders" to make the contrast clearer.

7. Potentially relevant to note is that North, Wallis, and Weingast take their framework to cut against Virginia Political Economy's picture of the state in modern liberal democracies (2013, 140–142). Nonetheless, it is easy to imagine how the ideas might be combined in the way suggested here.

8. Two possible questions here: First, why assume there will be a "much greater tide of parties whose interests are not so aligned?" In short, because existing institutional arrangements have made rent-seeking a dependable business model. Foreclosing future rents will often dramatically disrupt long-term plans. Given the transitional gains trap, even those without future plans for rent-seeking, and who do not benefit from their existing rent dependency, will have reason to oppose uprooting their existing dependency. Second, does the claim that this much larger tide will be successful rely on reversing the logic of concentrated benefits and dispersed costs, since here the much larger group wins out? Fully responding to this worry would take things a bit far from my main point but see Holcombe (2018) for more on how the transaction costs of political exchange are lower for elites in ways that make coordination more feasible.

9. This should not be taken to imply one party or the other was more amenable to classical liberalism than the other, either now or when any of these states were admitted. The point here is just that even the most seemingly solid political alignments are more contingent than this quick fix would require. Additionally, some readers may be inclined to respond to these examples by saying, "but the parties switched sides." This is not accurate, at least not in the full-scale, musical chairs way this phrase suggests. There have been significant political realignments, but it is not as if Woodrow Wilson and FDR would have fit naturally in the Republican Party post-realignment, nor that Warren Harding and Calvin Coolidge would have fit naturally in the Democratic Party post-realignment. Rather, segments of those parties' respective coalitions regrouped. With that regrouping often came shifts within those subsets' own politics to better fit their new coalition. This reemphasizes my point that a demographic group's present political tilt is never written in stone.

10. For related criticisms of the appeal many development economists see in "benevolent autocrats," see Easterly (2014).

11. Buchanan's own most pessimistic moment also seems to be a reflection of how existing institutions provide an inhospitable intellectual environment for market liberalism. His concern, somewhat different from mine, was that after abdicating so much responsibility to the state, people will increasingly yearn for it to take on a parental role (2005b).

12. As Don Lavoie wrote during the middle of the Reagan administration, which heavily utilized classical liberal rhetoric:

> By its largely rhetorical devotion to the free market and its actual policies of constructing a permanent war economy, conservatism helps to perpetuate the myth that it is the policies of free markets rather than those of planning that have been obstructing peace, and that it is an existing market economy rather than an established system of noncomprehensive planning which is responsible for our current economic distress. (1985, 231)

13. Those constitutional amendments that brought the abolition of slavery, equal protection of the law, and expansion of suffrage to Black men in the United States resulted from the extraordinary circumstances of postbellum reconstruction and so did not emerge from within the ordinary operation of democracy.

14. On points related to these, see Huemer (2016; 2018). The second paper specifically raises the possibility that legitimate moral concerns are re-routed through public choice mechanics into policies that do not fit them (2018, 322–323).

15. This is closely related and amenable to, yet distinct from, "analytical anarchism," a social scientific framework which "neither takes rules as given nor assumes that monopoly enforcement of such rules occurs" and places a special focus on the study of endogenous rule formation (Boettke and Candela 2020, 222). As Christmas and I would have it, methodological anarchism is a philosophical complement to the scientific framework of analytical anarchism.

16. See also Thierer (2020) generally, who argues for evasive entrepreneurship as a means of political action.

17. In suggesting that actors concerned with the state's power should build up institutions within civil society to check that power, there is some similarity in my thought to that of Acemoglu and Robinson (2019). Yet part of their idea is that government must also grow to check civil society. I am significantly more skeptical of this part of their approach, and indeed, part of the idea I am defending is for alternative institutions to build power that can *frustrate* state growth and perhaps eventually *overtake* the state in spheres it has so far secured for itself, with those stable alternative institutions providing a check against the state returning to those spheres. Another difference is that where they see civil society's mobilization as an alternative to relying upon checks and balances, I take stable alternative institutions and avenues of invasion as *a form of* constitutional checks. If one agrees with the general thrust of my points here but is much less skeptical of state growth and much more skeptical of effective institutions of self-governance, then their conclusions will end up looking a fair bit like Acemoglu & Robinson's, but through a Buchanan-esque lens.

18. For a recent example of work that might be described as constitutional political economy from below, see Novak (2021), which explores how social movements function and different methods for achieving their goals. See also Leeson (2011), which discusses the constitutional political economy of clubs and argues that maintaining constitutional commitment is much easier in clubs than in governments.

19. Of course, this also means that organizations built for predatory purposes, such as the mafia, will also have an easier time sticking to their original, predatory purpose. However, the constitutional question I'm concerned with here is preventing an organization built for productive purposes from sliding into predatory purposes, and, in particular, purposes shaped by predatory profit opportunities made available through the state.

REFERENCES

Acemoglu, Daron, and James A. Robinson. 2019. *The Narrow Corridor: States, Societies, and the Fate of Liberty*. New York: Penguin.

Beard, Charles A. 1913. *An Economic Interpretation of the Constitution of the United States*. New York: Macmillan.

Beito, David. 2000. *From Mutual Aid to the Welfare State: Fraternal Societies and Social Services, 1890–1967*. Chappell Hill, NC: University of North Carolina Press.

Boettke, Peter J. 2019. "The Role of the Economist in a Free Society: The Art of Political Economy." *Econlib*. https://www.econlib.org/library/Columns/y2019/BoettkeeconomistsroleIII.html.

Boettke, Peter J., and Rosolino A. Candela. 2020. "The Positive Political Economy of Analytical Anarchism." In *The Routledge Handbook of Anarchy and Anarchist Thought*, edited by Gary Chartier and Chad Van Schoelandt, 222–34. New York: Routledge.

Boettke, Peter J., and Christopher J. Coyne. 2009. "An Entrepreneurial Theory of Social and Cultural Change." In *Markets and Civil Society*, edited by Víctor Pérez-Díaz, 77–103. New York: Berghahn Books.

Boettke, Peter J., and Henry A. Thompson. 2022. "Identity and Off-Diagonals: How Permanent Winning Coalitions Destroy Democratic Governance." *Public Choice* 191 (3–4): 483–99.

Boldrin, Michele, and David K. Levine. 2010. *Against Intellectual Monopoly*. Cambridge: Cambridge University Press.

Brennan, Geoffrey, and James M. Buchanan. 1985. *The Reason of Rules: Constitutional Political Economy*. Cambridge; New York: Cambridge University Press.

Brennan, Geoffrey, and Loren Lomasky. 1993. *Democracy and Decision: The Pure Theory of Electoral Preference*. Cambridge: Cambridge University Press.

Buchanan, James M. 1964. "What Should Economists Do?" *Southern Economic Journal* 30 (3): 213–22.

———. 1987. "The Constitution of Economic Policy." *The American Economic Review* 77 (3): 243–50.

———. 1990. "The Domain of Constitutional Economics." *Constitutional Political Economy* 1 (1): 1–18.

———. 2000. "The Soul of Classical Liberalism." *The Independent Review* 5 (1): 111–19.

———. 2003. "Public Choice: Politics Without Romance." *Policy* 19 (3): 13–18.

———. 2005a. "Three Amendments: Responsibility, Generality, and Natural Liberty." *Cato Unbound*. https://www.cato-unbound.org/2005/12/04/james-m-buchanan/three-amendments-responsibility-generality-natural-liberty.

———. 2005b. "Afraid to Be Free: Dependency as Desideratum." *Public Choice* 124 (1–2): 19–31.

Buchanan, James M., and Roger D. Congleton. 1998. *Politics by Principle, Not Interest: Towards Nondiscriminatory Democracy*. Cambridge: Cambridge University Press.

Buchanan, James M., and Gordon Tullock. 2008 [1962]. *The Calculus of Consent: Logical Foundations of Constitutional Democracy*. Ann Arbor, MI: University of Michigan Press.

Byas, Jason Lee, and Billy Christmas. 2022. "Methodological Anarchism." In *The Routledge Handbook of Anarchy and Anarchist Thought*, edited by Gary Chartier and Chad Van Schoelandt, 53–75. New York: Routledge.

Caplan, Bryan. 2008. *The Myth of the Rational Voter: Why Democracies Choose Bad Policies*. Princeton, NJ: Princeton University Press.

Chamlee-Wright, Emily, and Virgil Henry Storr. 2011. "Social Capital, Lobbying and Community-Based Interest Groups." *Public Choice* 149 (1–2): 167–85.

Coyne, Christopher J., and Nathan Goodman. 2020. "Polycentric Defense." *The Independent Review* 25 (2): 279–92.

Downs, Anthony. 1957. *An Economic Theory of Democracy*. Nachdr. Boston: Addison Wesley.

Easterly, William. 2014. *The Tyranny of Experts: Economists, Dictators and the Forgotten Rights of the Poor*. New York: Basic Books.

Farrant, Andrew, and Vlad Tarko. 2019. "James M. Buchanan's 1981 Visit to Chile: Knightian Democrat or Defender of the 'Devil's Fix'?" *The Review of Austrian Economics* 32 (1): 1–20.

Goodman, Nathan P., and Roberta Q. Herzberg. 2020. "Gifts as Governance: Church Welfare and the Samaritan's Dilemma." *Journal of Institutional Economics* 16 (5): 703–14.

Haslanger, Sally. 2017. "Racism, Ideology, and Social Movements." *Res Philosophica* 94 (1): 1–22.

Hayek, F. A. 1949. "The Intellectuals and Socialism." *The University of Chicago Law Review* 16 (3): 417–33.

Higgs, Robert. 1987. *Crisis and Leviathan: Critical Episodes in the Growth of American Government*. New York: Oxford University Press.

———. 2008. "The Complex Course of Ideological Change." *The American Journal of Economics and Sociology* 67 (4): 547–66.

Holcombe, Randall G. 2018. *Political Capitalism: How Economic and Political Power Is Made and Maintained*. New York: Cambridge University Press.

Huemer, Michael 2016. "A Liberal Realist Answer to Debunking Skeptics: The Empirical Case for Realism." *Philosophical Studies* 173 (7): 1982–2010.

———. 2018. "Debunking Leftward Progress." *Ratio* 32 (4): 312–24.

Imbeau, Louis M., and Steve Jacob. 2015. *Behind a Veil of Ignorance?: Uncertainty and Power in Constitutional Design*. New York: Springer.

Kogelmann, Brian 2018. "Rawls, Buchanan, and the Search for a Better Social Contract." In *Exploring the Political Economy and Social Philosophy of James M. Buchanan*, edited by Paul Aligica, Christopher J. Coyne, and Stefanie Haeffele, 17–38. Lanham, MD: Rowman and Littlefield.

———. 2023. "Public Choice and Political Equality." In *Wealth and Power: Philosophical Perspectives*, edited by Michael Bennett, Huub Brouwer, and Rutger Claassen, 67–84. London: Routledge.

Lavoie, Don. 1985. *National Economic Planning: What Is Left?* Cambridge, MA: Ballinger Pub. Co.

Leeson, Peter T. 2011. "Government, Clubs and Constitutions." *Journal of Economic Behavior and Organization* 80 (2): 301–8.

Leighton, Wayne A., and Edward J. López. 2013. *Madmen, Intellectuals, and Academic Scribblers: The Economic Engine of Political Change*. Stanford, CA: Stanford University Press.

Leitzel, Jim. 2003. *The Political Economy of Rule Evasion and Policy Reform*. New York: Routledge.

Mises, Ludwig von. 2011 [1940]. *Interventionism: An Economic Analysis*. Edited by Bettina Bien Greaves. Indianapolis, IN: Liberty Fund.

Munger, Michael C., and Mario Villarreal-Diaz. 2019. "The Road to Crony Capitalism." *The Independent Review* 23 (3): 331–44.

North, Douglass Cecil, John Joseph Wallis, and Barry R. Weingast. 2013. *Violence and Social Orders: A Conceptual Framework for Interpreting Recorded Human History*. First paperback edition. Cambridge: Cambridge University Press.

Novak, Mikayla. 2021. *Freedom in Contention: Social Movements and Liberal Political Economy*. Lanham, MD: Lexington Books.

Nozick, Robert. 1989. *The Examined Life: Philosophical Meditations*. New York: Simon and Schuster.

Olson, Mancur. 1971 [1965]. *The Logic of Collective Action: Public Goods and the Theory of Groups*. Harvard Economic Studies 124. Cambridge MA; London: Harvard University Press.

———. 1982. *The Rise and Decline of Nations: Economic Growth, Stagflation, and Social Rigidities*. New Haven, CT: Yale University Press.

Pfaff, John F. 2017. *Locked in: The True Causes of Mass Incarceration--and How to Achieve Real Reform*. New York: Basic Books.

Rodrik, Dani. 2014. "When Ideas Trump Interests: Preferences, Worldviews, and Policy Innovations." *Journal of Economic Perspectives* 28 (1): 189–208.

Sered, Danielle. 2019. *Until We Reckon: Violence, Mass Incarceration, and a Road to Repair*. New York: The New Press.

Smith, Adam. 1981 [1776]. *An Inquiry into the Nature and Causes of the Wealth of Nations*. Edited by R. H. Campbell, Andrew S. Skinner, and W. B. Todd. Indianapolis, IN: Liberty Classics.

Stigler, George J. 1971. "The Theory of Economic Regulation." *The Bell Journal of Economics and Management Science* 2 (1): 3–21.

Tarko, Vlad. 2015. "The Role of Ideas in Political Economy." *The Review of Austrian Economics* 28 (1): 17–39.

Thierer, Adam. 2020. *Evasive Entrepreneurs and the Future of Governance: How Innovation Improves Economies and Governments*. Washington, DC: Cato Institute.

Tullock, Gordon. 1967. "The Welfare Costs of Tariffs, Monopolies, and Theft." *Economic Inquiry* 5 (3): 224–32.

———. 1975. "The Transitional Gains Trap." *The Bell Journal of Economics* 6 (2): 671–78.

Chapter 2

Co-production and the Use of Knowledge in Public Administration

Jordan J. Hunter

One of Elinor and Vincent Ostrom's major insights into effective public service delivery was that it is the nature of some services to require inputs from both the regular producer and the user of that service. Otherwise, "the service may deteriorate into an indifferent product with insignificant value" (Ostrom and Ostrom 1999, 93). This alternative logic of service provision stands in contrast to the typical consumer models in mainstream economics, where there exists a clear divide between regular producers and consumers (Aligica, Boettke, and Tarko 2019; Ostrom 1996). The concept of co-production entails crossing this traditional producer-consumer divide as an alternative mode of service production and delivery. Sorrentino, Sicilia, and Howlett (2018) further explain the significance of co-production when they state, "The reason why co-production has been proposed as an alternative solution to this traditional model is the belief that, unlike the production of goods, the production and delivery of services is difficult without the active participation of the recipients" (ibid. 279).

The question I wish to address in this chapter is simple: why is the production and delivery of services difficult without the participation of the recipients? First, however, it will be helpful to further define co-production. For a good or service to be co-produced means that nontrivial resources from service users are used as inputs in conjunction with the resources provided by the organization involved in the production of that good or service. It is a relationship between a paid employee or an organization and (groups of) individual citizens that requires a direct and active contribution from these citizens to the work of the organization (Brandsen and Honingh 2016). When organizations and individuals co-produce, they ideally make use of each other's resources to achieve better outcomes than they otherwise could (Loeffler and Bovaird 2020). In the context of public administration specifically, co-production refers to the involvement of citizens in the production of public services.

Whereas traditional frameworks of government services position citizens as consumers of a service that is produced entirely by another entity, the theory of co-production encourages one to view citizens as consumer-producers that share inputs in the production function (Parks et al. 1981). For example, citizens may "consume" the service of community safety provided by police officers; they may also help produce community safety by notifying the police of criminal behavior. Thus, co-production describes a more participatory model of governance that seeks to move decision-making to the "street levels" of the administration for both clients and workers of the organization (Pestoff 2018).

The idea of co-production inherently encourages one to view citizens as (potential) agents of change, in contrast to the depiction of impotent citizens that Elinor Ostrom criticized (Ostrom 1996, 1998). This Ostromian view of citizens capable of self-government can be mapped to Vincent Ostrom's (2008) juxtaposition of democratic administration and bureaucratic administration. Bureaucratic administration emphasizes a sharp line between politics and administration, somewhat analogous to Elinor Ostrom's (1996) "great divide" between rule-makers and rule-followers.

Democratic administration and co-production notably see citizens in a different role compared to New Public Management and traditional public administration, both of which tended to ignore the active role of citizens and focus on service providers. Both approaches were still centered on bureaucracy. Bovaird (2007) summarizes co-production's uniqueness among these other modes of governance:

> Whereas traditional public administration saw public servants acting in the public interest and New Public Management suggested ways in which service providers could be made more responsive to the needs of users and communities, the co-production approach assumes that service users and their communities can—and often should—be part of service planning and delivery. This is a revolutionary concept in public service. It has major implications for democratic practices beyond representative government because it locates users and communities more centrally in the decision-making process. (846)

Co-production was one of the pioneering concepts that gained traction in the Indiana Workshop in Political Theory and Policy Analysis in the 1970s. The Ostroms and their colleagues' research highlighted that part of what determined the effectiveness of a service was collaboration between those who used a service and those who supplied it (Aligica, Boettke, and Tarko 2019). Although there was an initial flurry of work on the topic, co-production receded from scholarly attention in the 1990s and mid-2000s. Brudney (2021) attributes this decline in academic work on co-production to several factors, perhaps most importantly being the diversion of scholarly interest to so-called "New Public Management." In contrast to the co-production view, which cast service users as partners with government professionals, New Public Management emphasized viewing the public as customers (Hood 1991).

In recent years, the concept of co-production has enjoyed a revival of interest (Alford 2014; Nabatchi, Sancino, and Sicilia 2017; Verschuere, Brandsen, and Pestoff 2012). This renewed attention to co-production has developed alongside what public administration scholars call "new public governance" (Bingham, Nabatchi, and O'Leary 2005; Hartley 2005) or the "participatory state" (Bovaird et al. 2014), wherein collaborative arrangements, networks, participatory governance, and multiactor relationships (Emerson, Nabatchi, and Balogh 2012) are emphasized in contrast to more bureaucratic or managerial modes of administration. Amid this revival, co-production has even been recognized globally as a major tool for policy reform by governments and NGOs (OECD 2011).

Co-production is thought to yield many desirable results (Loeffler and Bovaird 2018). At least two broad categories can be used to describe aspirations regarding co-production. One of these is to increase performance and service quality (Andrews and Brewer 2013; Bovaird 2007; Needham 2008; Voorberg, Bekkers, and Tummers 2015). For example, Zambrano-Gutierrez, Rutherford, and Nicholson-Crotty (2017) find empirical evidence of co-production in public education increasing standardized test scores and even moderating the negative performance effects of school violence. Another aspiration of co-production is its potential to uphold democratic values by increasing citizen engagement and empowerment (Levine and Fisher 1984; Pestoff 2018; Needham 2008; Sancino 2016), improving government accountability (Tuurnas, Stenvall, and Rannisto 2016), and developing trust in government institutions (Fledderus 2018).

The renewed interest and contributions to the co-production literature are welcome. They have tuned in to provide insightful evidence for co-production's promises and limitations and have also provided helpful theoretical adjustments that allow for a more nuanced understanding of co-production in the twenty-first century. Indeed, research has tended to focus on the outcomes of co-production as well as the question of who participates (Alonso et al. 2019; Jakobsen and Andersen 2013; Voorberg, Bekkers, and Tummers 2015). In other words, modern co-production research has focused on the *who* and *what* of co-production (Nabatchi, Sancino, and Sicilia 2017). While this "zoomed-in" approach is both helpful and necessary to advance understanding, it is important to take a large step back and address the *how* of co-production beyond its consideration as a matter of policy and implementation.

Co-production boasts impressive claims. How is it that the involvement of citizens in what is today often considered the domain of bureaucratic agents should yield improvements in not just public services but also in the democratic quality of political organizations and processes?

In this chapter, I argue that co-production has the potential to achieve these goals because it ideally ameliorates the enduring tension between bureaucracy and democracy—especially their modes of administration—and that it does so by attempting to reconcile types of epistemic properties biased by each. On the one hand, bureaucratic administration is biased in favor of expert and scientific types of knowledge. On the other hand, democratic administration is biased in favor of informal and contextual types of knowledge.

Little attention has been given to co-production's epistemic processes that make it a significant departure from other approaches to the administrative state. Moreover, co-production is often not considered in the political economy context that its progenitors operated in (Jackson 2021), where epistemic features, feedback mechanisms, and learning are key aspects of political and market processes. While the Ostroms' work on complex systems and the evolution of institutions has been recognized as sharing much in common with Friedrich Hayek (Aligica, Boettke, and Tarko 2019; Earl and Potts 2011; Lewis 2017), the strains of Hayekian thought that undergird co-production have gone underappreciated.

What results from reconnecting Hayek to the co-production project is a reconceptualization of co-production as a *division of knowledge labor* between experts and citizens that highlights the importance of epistemic processes for public administration. This potentially not only improves understanding of the underlying mechanisms for successful co-production but also provides clues about under what types of conditions co-production may be more or less feasible as an operating framework for public services. Highlighting the epistemic processes in service administration that makes co-production fruitful matters for public administration since public organizations are left to operate without the disciplining parameters of property, prices, and profit and loss (Boettke 2018). The realization that co-production has some of the same mechanical characteristics as market processes implies the potential for co-production to help fill in (some of) the gaps left by the absence of market prices.

Understanding co-production from this perspective has the potential to improve knowledge on three fronts. First, considering co-production in light of some of Friedrich Hayek's work may help explicate its underlying mechanisms. Second, considering the epistemic features of public production highlights the value of citizen involvement in public service delivery and the limits of traditional, bureaucratic modes of administration. Finally, this work may provide a first stage for future research to be better prepared to consider what kinds of services may be better suited to intensive co-production.

In the following sections, I first lay out the landscape of public administration and the tension between bureaucratic administration and democratic administration. Next, I explore Hayek's knowledge problem, alongside similar work by other scholars, and how the epistemic features of public administration are significant for good government. Finally, I discuss co-production as a means of epistemic reconciliation.

PUBLIC ADMINISTRATION AND CO-PRODUCTION

The academic study of public administration highlights an enduring tension between democracy and bureaucracy (Cook 2020; Durant 2010; Redford 1969; Ostrom 2008; Waldo 1948). Unelected government employees often hold substantial authority and discretion over administrative law and the implementation of policy. In theory, elected representatives are held accountable to citizens via the voting system, where citizens can censure or approve their elected delegates. However, the selection, ongoing employment, and discretion of personnel in an administrative state are not subject to popular vote. This insulation of government bureaucracy from the public—whether seen as a feature or a bug—has raised many questions, including concerns regarding accountability (Dubnick and Yang 2015; McCubbins, Noll, and Weingast 1987), the efficacy of democracy in the administrative state (Ariely 2013; Redford 1969; Waldo 1948), and the interface between citizens and government employees (Moynihan, Herd, and Harvey 2015; Nabatchi, Goerdel, and Peffer 2011; Vigoda 2002).

Elinor Ostrom was critical of how this tension between democracy and bureaucracy has been treated by other scholarly fields. She noted that "As long as public officials and citizens . . . continue to see a great divide between them . . . potential synergies will remain mere potentialities." This "great divide" took different forms across disciplines. In public administration, few textbooks "discuss the skills needed to work effectively in problem-solving activities with citizens." In economics, "problems of market failure assert that 'the' government must provide in those cases where the market fails." Political science often ignored *how* services were administered and instead tended to "focus on the formal aspects of national governments" while the "role of citizens is depicted as casting ballots and watching the action" (Ostrom 1996, 1083). These critiques demonstrate various assumptions, explicit and implicit, about both administration and the role of citizens.

Much of Elinor and Vincent Ostrom's work can be seen as a rebuttal to overly rigid prescriptions of governance. They saw utility in multi-organizational arrangements in the provision of public services (Ostrom and Ostrom 1971). Vincent Ostrom's public administration classic, *The Intellectual Crisis in American Public Administration,* describes traditional public administration—or bureaucratic administration—as centered around theories of the unity of command, hierarchy, and rules, and consolidation and homogeneity. Fragmented jurisdiction and duplication of services were considered inefficient. Jean Hartley (2005) describes this approach to governance in her review of public administration paradigms:

> The public administration approach, evident particularly in the post-war period and up to the early 1980s, is largely based on a legislative, bureaucratic and rule-based approach to public service provision. The population is assumed to be fairly homogeneous, and the definition of needs and problems is undertaken by professionals, who provide standardized services for the population. Power and authority lies with government, and the provision of welfare and regulatory services is assumed to emanate from the state, through elected representatives. (29)

Bureaucratic administration held very little room, if any, for citizens, and government services were produced largely by government organizations for passive clients, whose inputs were relegated to supplementary or marginal at best and insignificant at worst (Brudney 2021). By contrast, Vincent Ostrom tried to propound a new theory of democratic administration. This democratic theory of administration sought to be compatible with a democratic constitution and sought to solve the problem of political inequality. A theory of democratic administration, according to Vincent Ostrom, includes principles of egalitarianism, dispersed decision-making capabilities, overlap between politics and administration, and variety in organizational and contractual arrangements (Ostrom 2008).

While Vincent Ostrom was incisive about the limitations of bureaucratic administration, he was not against bureaucratic administration anywhere and everywhere. He notes that

> A theory of democratic administration does not preclude a theory of bureaucratic administration. But acceptance of a theory of democratic administration does imply a rejection of the assertion that a theory of bureaucratic administration is the only theory of good administration for all governments alike. (Ostrom 2008, 99)

Vincent Ostrom was also concerned about the fit between modes of administration and the broader constitutional system upon which government administration is based. Thus, Vincent Ostrom did not preclude bureaucratic forms of administration but rather advocated that their scope be circumscribed based on context. Bureaucratic administration thus may be appropriate for some circumstances, some of the time (Aligica and Tarko 2013).

It is no coincidence that the concepts of polycentricity and co-production both emerged from the Indiana Workshop. Co-production, as a theory pertaining to the administration of public services, can be considered a special case of polycentric order. A service that is co-produced implies shared or overlapping jurisdiction over the administration of a public service, at least at the street level where users of the service get a say in how those services are produced and consumed. A parallel trend can be seen in the development of the street-level bureaucracy concept (Lipsky 1983) which, interestingly, emerged around the same time as these Ostromian concepts. It seems that multiple scholars at the time were noticing that the schematic of a bureaucracy that robotically followed codified procedures did not match reality. Lipsky highlighted the overlooked fact that front-line government staff, who directly interact with citizens, had substantial influence over public policy in the sense that they exercise considerable discretion over the execution of policy (Lispky 1983). What seems to have emerged from these concurrent developments was a greater focus on policy at the ground level, and thus a greater focus on the citizens themselves.

The acceptance of bureaucratic administration as a permissible mode of administration highlights that democratic administration allows for a variety of institutional arrangements that meet the needs of the situation. A closely related concept that emerges from the work of both Vincent and Elinor Ostrom is that of polycentricity, which connotes multiple centers of decision-making with nested and overlapping systems, whereas bureaucratic administration prefers a single decision-maker whenever possible (V. Ostrom, Tiebout, and Warren 1961). The value of polycentricity can be seen when considering Robert Dahl's dilemma regarding democracy. The ideal of democracy is to expand the opportunities for individuals to live under laws of their own choosing as much as possible; however, living among equal others often necessitates submitting to collective decisions that can impinge upon otherwise personal choices. "The problem, then, is to discover a way by which the members of an association may make decisions binding on all and still govern themselves" (Robert Dahl 2008, 89). Polycentricity may thus be a "structural" solution to this dilemma (Aligica, Boettke, and Tarko, 2019) since polycentric orders have the potential to consider the variety of heterogeneous values, preferences, and circumstances of individuals (Aligica and Tarko 2013), whereas traditional, bureaucratic administration carries the assumption of governing a "fairly homogenous" population (Hartley 2005, 29).

THE KNOWLEDGE PROBLEM IN PUBLIC ADMINISTRATION

Uncertainty, and the diversity of circumstances and preferences, provide a challenge to the administrative state. This is why, according to Scott (1998), administrations try to simplify, codify, and otherwise make legible complex phenomena and orders. However, as Scott warns in *Seeing Like a State*, these processes of simplification run the risk of ignoring otherwise important knowledge that is lost in this process of weeding out complexity. Furthermore, if combined with high modernist views of progress, an authoritarian power, and an impotent civil society, such administrative activity can lead to tyrannical and lethal outcomes.

This threat of bureaucratizing all aspects of life through an administrative state was anathema to Hayek, who was an ardent critic of public administration and the aspirations of centralized economic planning. Central planners presumed that free markets were chaotic and irrational and that a top-down, "rational" approach could be used to plan economies with the advancement of social-scientific means (Lavoie 1985). Hayek was critical of the notion that the tools of science could be applied to social phenomena in the same manner as the natural sciences and with similar success. He rejected the idea that the problem of organizing society is one of calculation. He further dismissed the belief that the main impediment to centralized economic planning was to simply acquire the requisite statistical information and that *if* all the relevant information were possessed, one could calculate the best use and allocation of goods and services in an economy (Hayek 1945).

Hayek's dissent from the mainstream of economic planning optimism was largely based on ontological and epistemic grounds. Hayek argued that the problem of a rational economic order was not simply a lack of enough scientific facts, methods, and logic. Instead, "the 'data' . . . are never for the whole society 'given' to a single mind which could work out the implications, and can never be so given" (Hayek 1945, 93). The utilization of societal resources is not a math problem per se, but a knowledge problem, and the system that can make better use of existing knowledge will be the more efficient one.

Moreover, and essential to Hayek's argument, is his demarcation of scientific knowledge as something categorically different from what Hayek (1945) calls "the knowledge of the particular circumstances of time and place" (95). According to Hayek, this knowledge of time and place is distinct from scientific knowledge to the extent that scientific knowledge is knowledge of general rules. Instead, this particular kind of knowledge possessed by individuals is unorganized, dispersed, and uniquely available to those who use it in their own decisions. Here, Hayek emphasizes the experiential element in how individuals obtain knowledge relevant to their circumstances:

> We need to remember only how much we have to learn in any occupation after we have completed our theoretical training, how big a part of our working life we spend learning particular jobs, and how valuable an asset in all walks of life is knowledge of people, of local conditions, and of special circumstances. (95)

Importantly, the planner and the expert are limited in their roles even if they possess the relevant scientific knowledge because this localized, subjective knowledge "by its nature cannot enter into statistics and therefore cannot be conveyed to any central authority in statistical form" (98). Hayek argued that the free market was a rational order, but that this rationality was emergent and decentralized. What made it rational was that individuals could have reliable information about the decisions they make through the emergence of the price system, which provided signals about relative value and coordinated individual action. No economic expert was required to control prices and outputs across the whole economy.

This dispersion of knowledge is what makes markets so effective at increasing wealth relative to nonmarket settings. Through the price system, signals of this dispersed knowledge act as a mechanism for communicating information to others in a manner such that no single mind needs to know the details of the whole picture in order to act. No central planner is required to make decisions about resource allocation in a dynamic society in which the "facts" of the situation are rapidly in flux. Market prices play the important institutional role of communicating knowledge to producers and consumers about the value of a commodity or service. Markets distribute these decentralized signals without requiring a centralized authority adjudicating prices and outputs. Thus, a great advantage of markets over centralized economic planning is an emergent and decentralized knowledge "management" system. In complex phenomena such as a social order, no single individual can "acquire the full knowledge which would make mastery of the events possible" (Hayek [1975] 2014, 371).

Scott, as mentioned earlier, is also skeptical of the high-modernist "imperialism" that elevates scientific knowledge to a synoptic, all-seeing level and largely dismisses practical knowledge and informal processes as relics of the ignorant. Like Hayek, he rejects the notion that only one kind of knowledge, a super rational, scientific knowledge of general rules, is meaningful in social and political order. He borrows the Greek concept of *mētis* to describe forms of knowledge found in local experience and practicality. *Mētis* describes not just traditional wisdom or practical skills, Scott says, but also conveys a wide breadth of practical skills and acquired intelligence that, importantly, is obtained and applied in a dynamic human and natural setting. Significant for the current discussion is that *mētis* resists the codification and simplification that is amenable to bureaucratic administration (Scott 1998, 314).

While Hayek's arguments are made specifically against centralized economic planning, the issues he identifies constitute general problems associated with social order. In this vein, Hayek and Scott, although they have other disagreements, find a significant common concern for the potential "imperialism" of what Scott calls high-modernist rationality and what Hayek calls scientism. Notably, neither is against science qua science or the validity of universal truths discovered via the scientific method. They are not relativists, at least in my reading. Instead, these scholars seem concerned that the impressive and relatively novel power of modern science and technology appears to afford a certain hubris and synoptic delusion in those inclined toward using such tools.

Taking Hayek and Scott's insights about knowledge and its use in society together, the knowledge problem clearly exists as an obstacle to political organizations and processes. The danger is that decision-making within organizations occurs with only a portion of the relevant knowledge or information pertaining to a situation, resulting in inefficient or ineffective outcomes at best, and tyrannical lethality at worst. Essentially, a scientistic imperialism potentially leaves unused abundant resources of knowledge and information relevant to any given decision.

In the political sphere, actors must make use of the available store of human knowledge to make decisions about scarce resources. All decisions have trade-offs. This brings us to the knowledge problem in public administration. If markets provide the decentralized means of transmitting and coordinating relevant information, how will public organizations operate without the local knowledge or *mētis* that Hayek and Scott were convinced were essential to a free and flourishing society? Within public administration, neither property rights nor the disciplining feedback mechanisms of profit and loss exist in the same authentic way that they do in market systems. Boettke (2018, 948) frames the problem frankly by asking: "how is government going to accomplish the task of economic management? What alternative mechanisms in public administration will serve the role that property, prices, and profit and loss serve within the market setting?"

To put the knowledge problem in public administration another way, government experts and professionals face the problem of operating with only a restricted set of relevant knowledge to meet the preferences and needs of citizens. Even if bureaucrats operate from altruistic and public-oriented motivations, the knowledge problem persists. Although bureaucrats may be equipped with technical tools and may be given instructions from unelected managers and vague political goals from politicians, they face the issue of coordinating many dispersed bits of knowledge into a coherent plan. Public administration scholars have admitted that "street-level bureaucrats have to respond to citizens with only a limited amount of information or time to make a decision" and that the rules they are supposed to abide by often do not "correspond to the specific situation of the citizen" (Tummers and Bekkers 2014, 528). While experts may have access to rational-scientific forms of knowledge, they lack informal knowledge about specific circumstances and, especially, specific individuals. The limitations of a scientific-dominant approach to administration are mentioned by Brandsen (2021, 536): "At the level of management and strategy, it can be hard to see the relevance of individual views and experiences, but few would deny that people are experts on their own . . . lives."

While I do not believe it is the case that public servants are incapable of good judgment and sympathy, as a rule, it seems reasonable to think that the more insulated any professional is from the person they intend to serve, the greater a challenge it is to serve that person. Both traditional public administration, with its focus on top-down rule-making and administrative processes, and New Public Management, with its focus on top-down performance management, maintain this simplification of citizens as passive service users or consumers. When organizational incentives are geared toward rule-following and processes, the significance of context tends to take a backseat in the decision-making of public employees. Loeffler and Bovaird (2021, 46), referencing Jon Pierre (2013), highlight the tension between context-specific knowledge and scientific knowledge in public policy and administration:

> such situations, where context is so important, may mean that generalization, and therefore "cumulative science," is very difficult. However, the corollary may be that some aspects of public policy and management will remain relatively impervious to 'science' in the narrow sense, and be better dealt with by craft or art—and this should not be regarded as a defeat for "knowledge" but rather a recognition of the need to contextualise what kinds of knowledge are relevant in tackling different classes of problem.

Aligica, Boettke, and Tarko (2019) suggest that an appropriate analysis of governance involves examining the "epistemic properties" of different institutions. Revisiting the bureaucracy-democracy tension using Hayek's insights on the knowledge problem that decision-makers face, Table 2.1 juxtaposes bureaucratic administration and democratic administration and compares how these different modes of administration implicitly conceptualize and use knowledge. This table highlights several assumptions these two modes of administration make regarding properties of knowledge, helping to explain why there exists tension between democracy and bureaucracy. Table 2.1 is helpful to see the ways in which bureaucratic and democratic administration are configured to be at odds with each other in terms of their epistemic properties. Contrasting these properties of knowledge between

Table 2.1 Knowledge in Bureaucratic Administration and Democratic Administration

Bureaucratic Administration	Democratic Administration
Knowledge is . . .	*Knowledge is . . .*
Centralized	Dispersed
"Scientific"	"Circumstantial" (i.e., nonscientific)
Used by experts	Used by anyone
Static	Dynamic

Source: Created by author.

bureaucratic and democratic administration is helpful for highlighting their differences, but it should be remembered that these are not necessarily mutually exclusive modes of administration. Hayek and Scott, as mentioned earlier, similarly do not outright dismiss scientific knowledge, planning, and expertise.

These epistemic properties of public institutions undergird some of the fundamental tensions of public administration. Further, this juxtaposition is not to imply that one mode of administration or one type of knowledge is strictly dominant over the other. Recall Vincent Ostrom's insight that bureaucratic administration precludes democratic administration, but not the other way around. That bureaucratic administration and scientific knowledge should be outright rejected has not been the purpose of this chapter. Rather, it has been to emphasize that strictly dominant bureaucratic administration is epistemically deficient.

Hayek argues for the existence and relevance of local forms of knowledge and states that "scientific knowledge is not the sum of all knowledge" (1945, 95). While his overall argument is aimed against total scientific imperialism, his wording here leaves open the possibility that scientific knowledge may still play a role in decision-making in society. An analogue vis-à-vis political organization can be found in Vincent Ostrom's admission that bureaucratic administration is not precluded in a theory of democratic administration. For both scholars, the thrust of their efforts was to redirect attention from scientism (for Hayek) and scientific management (for Ostrom) toward a more balanced approach that considers more seriously the limitations of rationality. However, if individuals are to regularly engage in trade and cooperation, they must share some common sensibilities about the world, and as such, a rejection of scientific knowledge and objectivity that wanders too near to radical subjectivism will undermine their ability to communicate and cooperate. Instead, this tempered approach is similar in some regards to Herbert Simon's concept of bounded rationality, which escapes the false dichotomy of rational versus irrational agents. Some balance of these two seemingly competing kinds of knowledge is required in the administration of public governance. Indeed, these distinct types of knowledge are potentially complementary.

Democratic administration allows for greater use of the dispersed, local knowledge that Hayek and Scott are concerned about. Vincent Ostrom notes that perfection in hierarchy under a single source of political authority reduces the capability of government to respond to diverse preferences among citizens and to cope with dynamic environmental conditions (Ostrom 2008). Democratic administration, by contrast, provides for many, potentially overlapping points of authority. Scott's insight is that centralization in administration not only reduces its capacity but also increases the incentive to oversimplify and make illegible complex phenomena. Such complexity can include preferences about education and labor conditions, natural resource management, and poverty.

Thus, it is prudent to imagine ways of reconciling the epistemic tensions that modern liberal democracy faces. How can democratic administration, if it is to coexist to some extent with bureaucratic administration, earnestly undertake Hayek's challenge to make the greatest use of knowledge in society, in all its types? Can public institutions make use of contextual, local knowledge while not dismissing the value of science and expertise?

CO-PRODUCTION AS DIVISION OF KNOWLEDGE LABOR

Many of the frustrations in society—especially political frustrations—can be framed as a tension between experts and laypersons. This framing seems especially salient at a time when populism and antipathy toward established institutions seem to be increasing. Obviously, the existence of experts implies some demand by laypersons for those who have obtained highly specialized knowledge of some matter; yet any honest expert will admit with chagrin to times of not seeing the obvious when laypersons were able to see it easily. As Wagner (2016, 39) puts it, "Everyone, private citizens and political figures alike, acts on partial and incomplete information, for there is no other option in the presence of the scale and complexity of contemporary societies." But when it comes to decision-making in the public realm about regulations, resource allocation, and the provision of public services, experts are given a high degree of status deference and sometimes behave as though they are sitting in a panoptic position. Public employees, such as police officers, teachers, traffic engineers, or public health officials, are recognized as trained experts in their respective fields, and they hold substantial discretion over the implementation of policy and the delivery of public services. Because they hold such discretion and political power, many lives are vulnerable to their actions.

This matter of the role of experts returns us to co-production, which was identified by Elinor and Vincent Ostrom as a fundamental matter for many kinds of activities. Interestingly, the way that Vincent and Elinor Ostrom ([1977] 1999) originally frame co-production was as a problem, not a solution: "Another *problem* [emphasis mine] in proportioning supply to patterns of use arises when users of services also function as essential coproducers" (93). The problem they identify is that without meaningful involvement and effort from service users, some services are rendered ineffective. Implied here is that expert knowledge in the bureaucracy is an insufficient condition for effective service delivery. It may be necessary or complementary, but nevertheless insufficient in many cases. Yet the traditional mode of analysis in public administration conforms more closely to a top-down approach that gives preference to experts as the best judges of value in public administration settings. The result is that citizens are typically forgotten in the design and analysis of public services and thus cast as passive recipients, realizing one of Tocqueville's fears about democracy in America.

If all administrative activities are seen as a regular production problem that neatly divides consumers and producers, government professionals are bound to rely excessively on scientific or expert kinds of knowledge and stumble upon public administration's knowledge problem. Again, we see the temptation for administrations to simplify complexity for the sake of legibility, reduction of uncertainty, and efficiency. However, by doing so, they systematically draw from a smaller reservoir of usable knowledge. But when services are analyzed through a co-production lens, it can be seen how institutions may access a greater store of available knowledge to be used in the production of services and the design of general rules. When institutions are designed and managed to draw from both general, scientific knowledge and local, informal knowledge, from professionals and from laypersons, a greater store of knowledge is available to be used in the epistemic problem that public institutions face.

Co-production, beyond being a policy prescription or even a deference to citizen inputs, can be framed as a mediator of the tension between professionals and laypersons, between bureaucracy and democracy. Co-production helps to ameliorate this tension by directly infusing bureaucracy with more democracy by involving citizen inputs in service delivery. It does so by providing an avenue for contextual knowledge to play a role in service delivery. In this light, co-production can also be seen as a Smithian *division of knowledge labor*. This division of knowledge labor entails two general roles: (1) professionals who provide general, formal knowledge via scientific methods, and professional experience and (2) laypersons who provide local, informal knowledge via personal experience. Given Hayek's and Scott's arguments about the use of knowledge in society, it is argued that neither type of knowledge ought to hold special privileges in all cases. Each type of knowledge has its comparative advantage in the governance of society. Instead of viewing bureaucrats as public masters, bureaucrats can be recast as public servants and political equals who fulfill a more generalized epistemic role of providing general knowledge and general solutions. Instead of viewing citizens as passive consumers, citizens can likewise be recast as public partners who fulfill a more specialized epistemic role of providing localized knowledge and specific solutions.

Consider the example of co-producing education – an archetypal example of co-production. Elinor and Vincent Ostrom recognized that educators cannot achieve their goals without active input from students and their parents. A teacher is trained in general principles of pedagogy and provides this professional portion of the knowledge required to produce education, but a teacher is trained to teach students generally, not any one student in particular. Each student has specific needs. Brandsen (2021) also appeals to the relevance of different types of knowledge when he discusses education as an example of co-production that illustrates the utility in the division of knowledge labor:

> A teacher has better knowledge of didactics, but the parent has the better knowledge of the child. Combining the two types of knowledge makes obvious sense. Co-production therefore makes it easier to integrate experiential knowledge, because in individual cases these are inherently relevant and because it does not demand specialist scientific knowledge. (536)

Even if a randomized control trial produces a statistically significant effect for some pedagogy on some outcome, this value only represents a statistical average. Essentially, this value is what works for the abstract "average" student, not necessarily for any particular student. Students and/or parents may then complement the general principles with specific knowledge about circumstances. These may be the deportment of the student, her home life, her interests, or any other information that is relevant to the goal of education. The important aspect of any co-production case is that the user of the service "possesses unique information of which beneficial use might be made, but of which use can be made only if the decisions depending on it are left to him *or are made with his active co-operation*" (Hayek 1945, 95, emphasis mine).

The importance of co-production does not dismiss the role that experts or bureaucratic administration might play. Ronald Coase (1937), in his work on the nature of the firm, noted that there may be costs to using the market's price system. Thus, it may be less costly to carry out some transactions within the direction of administration. In a similar vein, some transactions for citizens may be less costly within an administrative environment. The bureaucracy, in some cases, may be a way to reduce uncertainty and access scientific and expert knowledge. Thus, co-production should not be thought of as a method to supplant bureaucratic administration, but rather to enhance it with more relevant knowledge.

An important question that remains in co-production literature is: under what circumstances is co-production more likely to be effective? The potential for co-production to improve service quality and democratic values is not without limits. Scholars are quick to qualify that co-production is not a panacea for every public or private problem (Bovaird 2007). Optimists and skeptics alike have raised their concerns. Co-production might exacerbate existing inequities because more resources are required by individuals (Jakobsen and Andersen 2013). Some citizens may simply not be interested in co-production or may need to be trained or have resource constraints lifted to participate more. On the organizational side, public employees might be hesitant to work with citizens, as coordination costs will now play a significant role (Yang and Callahan 2005). Professionals and laypeople will need to adopt effective ways of communicating in the work of co-governing.

Finally, not every service is likely to be improved by increased citizen participation. While there is not sufficient room in this chapter to cover the research on this topic, the concepts about types of knowledge discussed in this chapter provide a starting point. The following features are likely to be significant factors in predicting the efficacy of co-production. Services in contexts that are novel, dynamic, and complex may be more likely to benefit from co-production; contexts that are rote and static may be less appropriate for extensive co-production.

Some fields/topics are more scientific by nature and thus require more scientific knowledge input from experts. Nevertheless, science as an institution does not operate in an apolitical vacuum. For example, the U.S. Geological Survey has recently given attention to "adopting a coproduction approach to conducting science," stating that "coproduced knowledge and tools are more likely to be seen as credible, relevant, and timely" (Selby et al. 2024; Wall, Meadow, and Horganic 2017). Another example of co-production in a more science-oriented context is in meteorology and weather safety. Some individuals volunteer as "storm spotters" for the National Weather Service, collecting "ground truth" weather data that complements the remote sensing efforts by scientists. More research is needed to get a clearer picture of what co-production might mean in more scientific and technological fields.

If co-production as a division of knowledge labor increases the total knowledge from which the design and delivery of public services can draw, perhaps co-production can also be conceptualized as a means to channel the information that prices would normally provide in market settings. This potential of co-production returns us to Boettke's question: "What alternative mechanisms in public administration will serve the role that property, prices, and profit and loss serve within the market setting?"

It is difficult to see how price-like information would be utilized in co-production since it is still a nonmarket setting. Then again, nonmarket signals have been demonstrated to work in postcrisis situations, as discussed by Storr, Haeffele-Balch, and Grube (2015) in their work on social entrepreneurs in times of crisis. These authors suggest that social status can work as a substitute for the price mechanism in times of postcrisis rebuilding when social order has been disrupted. Although they are careful to qualify that prices communicate information at a much greater and more efficient scale, they nevertheless provide case studies of individuals coordinating their means and knowledge and acting to rebuild community outside both the force of government and the incentives of prices. It may be that co-production is unable to signal information at the level of market prices at scale, but this only emphasizes the importance of local governance.

SUMMARY

Scott ends his book, *Seeing Like a State,* with a call for more *mētis*-friendly institutions. This chapter has sought to describe co-production as at least one way to make such institutions. Indeed, co-production is part of many aspects of public administration in practice, as I have already mentioned. What seems to be lacking is more recognition of it from the upper echelons of academia and government. I have also tried to contrast the epistemic features of bureaucratic and democratic administration with an eye toward the role that co-production plays. Vincent Ostrom was concerned about the problem of political inequality and saw unitary, hierarchical command in politics as a threat to political equality. Here, I have tried to argue that co-production may help ameliorate political inequality within bureaucracies by placing decision-making more centrally with citizens. More specifically, I have tried to argue that co-production's value is found largely in its epistemic features. These epistemic features of polycentric governance and co-production go together. Just as polycentric governance has multiple centers of decision-making, co-production also disperses decision-making between bureaucrats and service users.

Public administration has largely been keen to presume bureaucratic expertise to be sufficient to provide value and satisfy citizens' preferences, yet much of the work that public organizations seek to do regards services: public safety, education, elderly care, public health, job training, and more. These kinds of services often face the co-production problem: their effective production requires inputs from the consumer. Even if a service does not strictly require consumer input, it is often the case that the involvement of service users provides unique value on multiple fronts. In many ways, the co-production problem is a special case of the knowledge problem described by Hayek and Scott. While the role of types of knowledge in co-production has been mentioned briefly in other literature, it has received scant attention. Moreover, other literature on co-production has not explicitly connected Hayek's and Scott's arguments about distinct types of knowledge. Thus, the co-production literature has been unable to sufficiently communicate why citizen involvement within a system of democratic administration has the potential to provide more value to society relative to more bureaucratic modes of public administration. While Hayek's influence is recognized in Elinor Ostrom's work on common-pool resources (Earl and Potts 2011), this connection is rarely seen in her work on co-production.

The concept and practice of co-production in political organization seek to make complimentary use of the resources of government professionals and citizens to produce greater value than either could on their own (Pestoff 2018). The reason that co-production can do so is best articulated by appealing to Hayek's and Scott's arguments about the use of knowledge in society: not all knowledge of worth is of the scientific kind. For matters of service design and delivery, decentralized, informal knowledge is especially pertinent to producing value for individuals, given their heterogeneous preferences and specialized circumstances. Without co-production, administration takes on a provider-centric model that ignores the role citizens play and relies too heavily on experts to do the work of governing. Even if the government does not directly provide professionalized services itself, it may "provision expertise" in other sectors of society via contractual relationships and seek to establish overarching parameters that foster co-production. Empowering individuals to have greater personal control and responsibility in public services can enable them to better fulfill their own values and reduce uncertainty in the administration of services (Pestoff 2018).

Conceptualizing co-production as a division of knowledge labor helps to strengthen understanding of a subject that has often evaded careful definition and contiguous theoretical advancement. Future work can also dive further into the epistemic features of different stages of the co-production cycle: co-commissioning, co-designing, and co-evaluating (Nabatchi et al. 2017). Ideally, a greater appreciation for the importance of the epistemic properties of institutions involved in public governance can promote better public administration and a stronger citizenry.

REFERENCES

Alford, John. 2014. "The Multiple Facets of Co-Production: Building on the Work of Elinor Ostrom." *Public Management Review* 16 (3): 299–316.

Aligica, Paul Dragos, Peter J. Boettke, and Vlad Tarko. 2019. *Public Governance and the Classical-Liberal Perspective: Political Economy Foundations*. Oxford: Oxford University Press.

Aligica, Paul Dragos, and Vlad Tarko. 2013. "Co-Production, Polycentricity, and Value Heterogeneity: The Ostroms' Public Choice Institutionalism Revisited." *American Political Science Review* 107 (4): 726–41.

Alonso, José M., Rhys Andrews, Judith Clifton, and Daniel Diaz-Fuentes. 2019. "Factors Influencing Citizens' Co-Production of Environmental Outcomes: A Multi-Level Analysis." *Public Management Review* 21 (11): 1620–45.

Andrews, Rhys, and Gene A. Brewer. 2013. "Social Capital, Management Capacity and Public Service Performance." *Public Management Review* 15 (1): 19–42.

Ariely, Gal. 2013. "Public Administration and Citizen Satisfaction with Democracy: Cross-National Evidence." *International Review of Administrative Sciences* 79 (4): 747–66.

Bingham, Lisa Blomgren, Tina Nabatchi, and Rosemary O'Leary. 2005. "The New Governance: Practices and Processes for Stakeholder and Citizen Participation in the Work of Government." *Public Administration Review* 65 (5): 547–58.

Boettke, Peter. 2018. "Economics and Public Administration." *Southern Economic Journal* 84 (4): 938–59.

Bovaird, Tony. 2007. "Beyond Engagement and Participation: User and Community Coproduction of Public Services." *Public Administration Review* 67 (5): 846–60.

Bovaird, Tony, Elke Loeffler, Gregg G. Van Ryzin, and Salvador Parrado. 2014. "User and Community Coproduction of Public Services: What Influences Citizens to Coproduce?" In *Public Administration and the Modern State*, edited by Eberhard Bohne, John D. Graham, Jos C. N. Raadschelders, and Jesse Paul Lehrke, 109–24. London: Palgrave Macmillan UK.

Brandsen, Taco. 2021. "Vulnerable Citizens: Will Co-Production Make a Difference?" In *The Palgrave Handbook of Co-Production of Public Services and Outcomes*, edited by Elke Loeffler and Tony Bovaird, 527–39. Cham, Switzerland: Springer International Publishing.

Brandsen, Taco, and Marlies Honingh. 2016. "Distinguishing Different Types of Coproduction: A Conceptual Analysis Based on the Classical Definitions." *Public Administration Review* 76 (3): 427–35.

Brudney, Jeffrey L. 2021. "Co-Production in Political Science and Public Administration." In *The Palgrave Handbook of Co-Production of Public Services and Outcomes*, edited by Elke Loeffler and Tony Bovaird, 61–77. Cham, Switzerland: Springer International Publishing.

Coase, R. H. 1937. "The Nature of the Firm." *Economica* 4 (16): 386–405.

Cook, Brian J. 2021. *The Fourth Branch: Reconstructing the Administrative State for the Commercial Republic*. Lawrence, KS: University Press of Kansas.

Dahl, Robert A. 2008. *Democracy and Its Critics*. New Haven, CT: Yale University Press.

Development, Organisation for Economic Co-operation and. 2011. *Together for Better Public Services: Partnering with Citizens and Civil Society*. Paris: OECD Publishing.

Dubnick, Melvin, and Kaifeng Yang. 2010. "The Pursuit of Accountability: Promise, Problems, and Prospects." SSRN Scholarly Paper. Rochester, NY.

Durant, Robert F. 2010. "A Heritage Made Our Own." In *The Oxford Handbook of American Bureaucracy*, edited by Robert F. Durant, 3–22. Oxford: Oxford University Press.

Earl, Peter E., and Jason Potts. 2011. "A Nobel Prize for Governance and Institutions: Oliver Williamson and Elinor Ostrom." *Review of Political Economy* 23 (1): 1–24.

Emerson, K., T. Nabatchi, and S. Balogh. 2012. "An Integrative Framework for Collaborative Governance." *Journal of Public Administration Research and Theory* 22 (1): 1–29.

Fledderus, Joost. 2018. "The Effects of Co-Production on Trust." In *Co-Production and Co-Creation*, 258–65. New York: Routledge.

Hartley, Jean. 2005. "Innovation in Governance and Public Services: Past and Present." *Public Money & Management* 25 (1): 27–34.

Hayek, F. A. 1945. "The Use of Knowledge in Society." *The American Economic Review* 35 (4): 519–30.

Hood, Christopher. 1991. "A Public Management for All Seasons?" *Public Administration* 69 (1): 3–19.

Jackson, Peter M. 2021. "The Political Economy Foundations of Co-Production." In *The Palgrave Handbook of Co-Production of Public Services and Outcomes*, 79–94. Cham, Switzerland: Palgrave Macmillan.

Jakobsen, Morten, and Simon Calmar Andersen. 2013. "Coproduction and Equity in Public Service Delivery." *Public Administration Review* 73 (5): 704–13.

Lavoie, Don. 1985. *National Economic Planning: What Is Left?* Washington, DC: Cato Institute.

Levine, Charles H., and Glenn Fisher. 1984. "Citizenship and Service Delivery: The Promise of Coproduction." *Public Administration Review* 44: 178–89.

Lewis, Paul. 2017. "The Ostroms and Hayek as Theorists of Complex Adaptive Systems: Commonality and Complementarity." In *The Austrian and Bloomington Schools of Political Economy*, 22: 35–66. Bingley: Emerald Publishing Limited.

Lipsky, Michael. 1983. *Street-Level Bureaucracy: The Dilemmas of the Individual in Public Service*. New York: Russell Sage Foundation.

Loeffler, Elke, and Tony Bovaird. 2018. "Assessing the Effect of Co-Production on Outcomes, Service Quality and Efficiency." In *Co-Production and Co-Creation*, 269–80. London: Routledge.

———. 2020. "Assessing the Impact of Co-Production on Pathways to Outcomes in Public Services: The Case of Policing and Criminal Justice." *International Public Management Journal* 23 (2): 205–23.

———. 2021. "User and Community Co-Production of Public Services and Outcomes—A Map of the Current State of Play." In *The Palgrave Handbook of Co-Production of Public Services and Outcomes*, edited by Elke Loeffler and Tony Bovaird, 3–30. Cham, Switzerland: Springer International Publishing.

McCubbins, Mathew D., Roger G. Noll, and Barry R. Weingast. 1987. "Administrative Procedures as Instruments of Political Control." *The Journal of Law, Economics, and Organization* 3 (2): 243–77.

Moynihan, Donald, Pamela Herd, and Hope Harvey. 2015. "Administrative Burden: Learning, Psychological, and Compliance Costs in Citizen-State Interactions." *Journal of Public Administration Research and Theory* 25 (1): 43–69.

Nabatchi, Tina, Holly T. Goerdel, and Shelly Peffer. 2011. "Public Administration in Dark Times: Some Questions for the Future of the Field." *Journal of Public Administration Research and Theory* 21 (suppl. 1): i29–43.

Nabatchi, Tina, Alessandro Sancino, and Mariafrancesca Sicilia. 2017. "Varieties of Participation in Public Services: The Who, When, and What of Coproduction." *Public Administration Review* 77 (5): 766–76.

Needham, Catherine. 2008. "Realising the Potential of Co-Production: Negotiating Improvements in Public Services." *Social Policy and Society* 7 (2): 221–31.

Organisation for Economic Co-operation and Development. 2011. *Together for Better Public Services: Partnering with Citizens and Civil Society*. Paris: OECD Publishing.

Ostrom, Elinor. 1996. "Crossing the Great Divide: Coproduction, Synergy, and Development." *World Development* 24 (6): 1073–87.

Ostrom, Vincent. 2008. *The Intellectual Crisis in American Public Administration*. Tuscaloosa, AL: University of Alabama Press.

Ostrom, Vincent, and Elinor Ostrom. 1971. "Public Choice: A Different Approach to the Study of Public Administration." *Public Administration Review* 31 (2): 203–16.

———. 1999. "Public Goods and Public Choices." In *Polycentricity and Local Public Economies,* edited by Michael D. McGinnis, 75–103. Ann Arbor, MI: University of Michigan Press.

Ostrom, Vincent, Charles M. Tiebout, and Robert Warren. 1961. "The Organization of Government in Metropolitan Areas: A Theoretical Inquiry." *American Political Science Review* 55 (4): 831–42.

Parks, Roger B., Paula C. Baker, Larry Kiser, Ronald Oakerson, Elinor Ostrom, Vincent Ostrom, Stephen L. Percy, Martha B. Vandivort, Gordon P. Whitaker, and Rick Wilson. 1981. "Consumers as Coproducers of Public Services: Some Economic and Institutional Considerations." *Policy Studies Journal* 9 (7): 1001–11.

Pestoff, Victor. 2018. *Co-Production and Public Service Management: Citizenship, Governance and Public Services Management*. London: Routledge.

Pierre, Jon. 2013. "Context, Theory and Rationality: An Uneasy Relationship." In *Context in Public Policy and Management: The Missing Link*, edited by Christopher Pollitt, 124–30. Cheltenham: Edward Elgar.

Redford, Emmette Shelburn. 1969. *Democracy in the Administrative State*. New York: Oxford University Press.

Sancino, Alessandro. 2016. "The Meta Co-Production of Community Outcomes: Towards a Citizens' Capabilities Approach." *Voluntas: International Journal of Voluntary and Nonprofit Organizations* 27: 409–24.

Scott, James C. 1998. *Seeing Like a State: How Certain Schemes to Improve the Human Condition Have Failed*. New Haven, CT: Yale University Press.

Sorrentino, Maddalena, Mariafrancesca Sicilia, and Michael Howlett. 2018. "Understanding Co-Production as a New Public Governance Tool." *Policy and Society* 37 (3): 277–93.

Storr, Virgil Henry, Stefanie Haeffele-Balch, and Laura E. Grube. 2015. *Community Revival in the Wake of Disaster: Lessons in Local Entrepreneurship*. New York: Palgrave Macmillan US.

Tummers, Lars, and Victor Bekkers. 2014. "Policy Implementation, Street-Level Bureaucracy, and the Importance of Discretion." *Public Management Review* 16 (4): 527–47.

Selby, Lea B., Sarah K. Carter, Travis S. Haby, David J. A. Wood, Aparna Bamzai-Dodson, Patrick J. Anderson, Jeffrey E. Herrick, Ella M. Samuel, and John C. Tull. 2024. "A Toolkit for Coproducing Actionable Science to Support Public Land Management." Denver, CO: U.S. Department of the Interior, Bureau of Land Management. https://www.blm.gov/noc/report/toolkit-coproducing-actionable-sci-encesupport-public-land-management

Verschuere, Bram, Taco Brandsen, and Victor Pestoff. 2012. "Co-Production: The State of the Art in Research and the Future Agenda." *VOLUNTAS: International Journal of Voluntary and Nonprofit Organizations* 23 (4): 1083–101.

Voorberg, W. H., V. J. J. M. Bekkers, and L. G. Tummers. 2015. "A Systematic Review of Co-Creation and Co-Production: Embarking on the Social Innovation Journey." *Public Management Review* 17 (9): 1333–57.

Wagner, Richard E. 2016. *Politics as a Peculiar Business: Insights from a Theory of Entangled Political Economy*. Cheltenham: Edward Elgar Publishing.

Waldo, Dwight. 1948. *The Administrative State: A Study of the Political Theory of American Public Administration*. New York: Transaction Publishers.

Wall, Tamara U., Alison M. Meadow, and Alexandra Horganic. 2017. "Developing Evaluation Indicators to Improve the Process of Coproducing Usable Climate Science." *Weather, Climate, and Society* 9 (1): 95–107.

Zambrano-Gutiérrez, Julio César, Amanda Rutherford, and Sean Nicholson-Crotty. 2017. "Types of Coproduction and Differential Effects on Organizational Performance: Evidence from the New York City School System." *Public Administration* 95 (3): 776–90.

Chapter 3

How Public Governance and Markets Became Learning Processes

Mariam Sedighi

This chapter explores the conceptualization(s) of human knowledge and rationality in classical liberal scholarship in the mid-twentieth century through a focus on the epistemic principles embedded in the formulations of public governance and markets as learning processes.[1] It draws upon and builds on interdisciplinary research in Science and Technology Studies (STS) and particularly genealogical studies that examine the emergence and movements of epistemic principles in (social) scientific theories, empirical studies, and expertise in the post-World War II era (Erickson et al. 2013; Gilman 2003, 2016; Heyck 2012, 2015; Popkewitz, Pettersson, and Hsiao 2021; Solovey and Cravens 2012). Through a focus on epistemic principles, the discussion situates mid-twentieth-century theorizations of polycentric political systems, price systems, and market processes within the confines of post-World War II scholarly knowledge and expertise. In so doing, the chapter emphasizes how what F. A. Hayek theorized as the "knowledge problem" is (re)articulated in knowledge-making processes in the social sciences, including in classical liberalism and Hayek's own scholarship. As with any knowledge-making process, expertise and scholarly practices are limited by the boundedness of human knowledge and reason. In this regard, the chapter contributes to the body of research in STS and classical liberalism concerned with how the widespread assumptions about the universality, independence, and objectivity of expertise can be an "escape from democracy" (Levy and Peart 2017).

The next section provides an epistemic framework through a review of recent genealogical studies that investigate epistemic principles embedded in American social science in the post-World War II era. It particularly attends to the way human knowledge, rationality, and agency were increasingly conceived as limited and bounded in post-war social science, and how the problems, solutions, and units of analysis across different disciplines constructed the human subject as *homo adaptivus*. It also discusses the entanglements of these modes of thinking about human knowledge and rationality with system theory's and cybernetics' concepts of system, process, information, communication, and feedback. It highlights how the re-articulations of these epistemes in different disciplines of (social) science entailed the construction and reconstruction of systems and processes as having the ability to generate kinds of knowledge and rationality that were beyond the ability of individuals.

The chapter then shows how the principles discussed in the epistemic framework were assembled with scholarship in the classical liberal tradition concerned with public administration, governance, and market processes. Specifically, it examines how the problem of human's limited knowledge and rationality in an emergent world was addressed in the theorizations of polycentricity by Vincent and Elinor Ostrom and market processes by Hayek. It explores how, in these theorizations, systems and processes were construed as able to generate knowledge that no individual could collect or calculate. Hence, rather than relying on the ability of self-interested, fully rational humans (*homo economicus* in neoclassical economics), the theorizations of the polycentric political system and price system embody the figure of *homo adaptivus*—that is, a subject of limited knowledge and rationality who constantly adapts their decisions and actions to the emerging contexts in which they are situated. The chapter concludes with remarks about the salience of attending to the limits of scholarly practices.

EPISTEMIC PRINCIPLES IN POST-WORLD WAR II SOCIAL SCIENCES

Finite Rationality and Infinite Adaptation

As historians of American post-World War II social science explain, in the aftermath of two catastrophic world wars and deep concerns about the possibility of a nuclear war, the idea of the human being as a fully rational subject whose decisions and choices were merely based on the principles of reason seemed implausible (Erickson et al. 2013; Heyck 2015; Solovey and Cravens 2012). In this context, a new epistemic mode of thinking about human reason and rationality emerged in social science. In this mode of thinking, human beings were no longer conceived through the model of *homo economicus*, that is, the rational subject who made decisions and acted based on reason, self-interest, and rational economic calculations. Instead, the human subject came to be perceived and studied in social science as having finite knowledge and bounded rationality. Human decisions and choices were thus seen to be always limited by the complexity and infinity of the world.

Since the model of human subjectivity as a rational *homo economicus* did not fit the ontology and epistemology of bounded rationality in a complex and emerging world, a new model of human agency gradually became intelligible (Grove 2018; Heyck 2015). This "new model," Heyck (2015) explains, "was not the perfectly rational, free to choose *homo economicus* of neoclassical dreams, nor was he the irrational, wholly malleable creature . . . that both Skinnerian and Freudian psychology imagined" (ibid, 82). Heyck (2015) calls this new model "*homo adaptivus*," that is, "the finite but inventive problem solver of bounded rationality" in an infinite world (ibid, 82). As a creature of limited knowledge and rationality in an uncertain and complex world, homo adaptivus was not expected to be able to control the environment or know or predict the future with certainty. Rather, homo adaptivus was a subject who expected uncertainties, engaged with complexities, and constantly adjusted their decisions and adapted to the emerging environments in which they were situated.

It should be noted that this view of humans as having a limited capacity to reason and as being fallible was not entirely new. Not only could it be found in David Hume's concerns about the limits of human reason but also in centuries-old narratives of the fall of man in Abrahamic religions. Yet, entailed in the re-articulation of this view of the human subject in post-World War II social science was an epistemic shift regarding the site of rationality and "truth," and a new mode of thinking about human agency. The new aspect of this mode of social scientific thinking about human reason, rationality, and subjectivity, Heyck (2015) argues, pertained to how it "saw our very limits as the keys to our power and the path to our progress, if never quite our perfection" (ibid, 83). Although humans were seen as creatures of limited capacities with only limited ability to reason and know, human minds were perceived as "marvelously effective adaptive tools, especially when they were brought together, organized, and used in combination" (ibid, 201). In other words, the limits of human minds to know the truth were tied to their capacity to adapt to the truth. Human minds, particularly when in combination, were able to adapt themselves to the complex and changing environment, to learn from/with others, to become part of a learning process, and eventually find the pathways to survival and progress. In this regard, the sites of truth and rationality were neither the individual (i.e., the *homo economicus*), nor an external entity (e.g., the divine). Rather, truth and rationality were seen to emanate from the very processes and systems in which the individual was a component.

Indeed, certain aspects of these new modes of conceiving human subjectivity, rationality, collective minds, and adaptability were in tension with the construct of *homo economicus* as a self-interested subject equipped with the tools of reason. This tension was reflected in social scientific studies, including the scholarship of Herbert Simon, a prominent social scientist in the postwar era.[2] Simon (1955) explicitly criticized the postulation of "an economic man" as one who embodied rationality and had "clear and voluminous" knowledge (if not complete knowledge) of the relevant aspects of his environment (ibid, 99). To him, the "severe demands" made upon the economic man to perform complex calculations and computations were practically impossible and thus unrealistic. Simon thus argued that "there is a complete lack of evidence that, in actual human choice situations of any complexity, these computations can be, or are in fact, performed" (ibid, 104).[3]

Heyck's (2015) quantitative and qualitative study of American flagship journals for anthropology, economics, political science, psychology, and sociology in the period between the 1920s and 1970s illustrates this epistemic change. Across different disciplines, the dominant conception of the human subject shifted from the rational "*homo economicus* of neoclassical dreams" to "the finite but inventive" *homo adaptivus* with "bounded rationality" (ibid, 82). As I discuss later in this chapter, classical liberal scholarship in the mid-twentieth century embodies these epistemic doubts about conceptualizing the individual as a rational subject able to know, reason, and plan within a complex and emergent world. Like many other arenas of theory and research, the classical liberal approach entails emphasis on adaptation and collective actions within market processes and systems. Given the salience of systems thinking in postwar scholarship broadly, and in classical liberal approaches specifically, the next section provides a review of its foundational elements.

Systems Thinking

Concurrent with the construction of homo adaptivus, another epistemic mode of thinking was fashioned in post-World War II social science, particularly between 1955 and 1975. As Heyck (2015) explores in detail in his book, *Age of System*, the mainstream concepts, methods, tools, practices, and institutional relations in different fields of social (and even natural) science were reconceptualized in terms of systems. He shows that many studies in this era reformulated their central objects as complex, relationally and hierarchically structured systems that were defined more by their structures and organizations than their components. Systems were conceived as more or less self-contained wholes that were larger than the sum of their constituting parts. In this regard, an important aspect of the epistemic shift in post-World War II social science was a shift from preoccupations with components toward the study of wholes (Halpern 2015). Hence, instead of focusing on features and characteristics of individual components, research increasingly examined whole structures, systems, processes, relations, and their transformations and outcomes across time.

Consequently, terms and concepts of systems thinking became increasingly popular in different disciplines and approaches, including, as this chapter shows, classical liberal scholarship. There were indeed disciplinary, institutional, and individual variations among the studies employing systems thinking. Yet, Heyck's (2015) research shows that systems thinking's core concepts and methods rose from only 7 percent of the sample in 1930 to over 60 percent in 1970. Among these terms and concepts are system, structure, organization, hierarchy, model, (system) behavior, function, process, mechanisms, relationships, communication, control, input and output, feedback, synthesis, and (dis)equilibrium. Moreover, it should be noted that thinking in terms of organizations and systems was not limited to the machine or the nonhuman; rather, all organisms and creatures were now conceived as systems or subsystems. For instance, in the scholarship of Herbert Simon, the human subject was conceived as "a complex, hierarchically structured adaptive system, a system that existed within systems and that was itself a system of systems" (Heyck 2015, 82). Rather than a self-interested individual, *homo adaptivus* was thus a system comprised of subsystems and situated within other systems. Furthermore, the notion of adaptation itself was re-articulated in terms of systems. Adaptation was now "understood as success in maintaining internal equilibrium, with equilibrium usually seen as a dynamic thing achieved through homeostatic mechanisms. Such mechanisms involved both interactions with the environment and internal adjustments to the stresses imposed by that environment" (Heyck 2015, 83).

As noted in the previous section, in the context of the post-World War II era, human reason was increasingly conceived as limited and bounded. However, with systems thinking, according to Heyck (2012, 2015), a new interest emerged to explore if and how it would be possible to employ science to create systems and models able to generate rational choices and decisions, despite human beings' limited knowledge and rationality. Consequently, alongside the "pessimism about the scope and quality of human reason," postwar social science generated "optimism about the power of social and technical mechanisms for producing rational choices" (Heyck 2015, 100). Rather than the individual human mind being the source of knowledge and rationality, the hope was to generate rational decisions, choices, or actions as the *outputs* of processes and systems. Hence, an assemblage was formed in which the notion of bounded rationality connected with technical knowledge about processes and systems. As Heyck (2015) argues, a subtle, yet significant, shift took place in the social sciences that made it possible to think about rational choices without having rational subjects: the main units of analysis shifted from the decision-maker to the decision, from the chooser to the choice, from the person to the process. As I will discuss later in this chapter, this epistemic mode of thinking can also be seen in social scientific scholarship concerned with market processes and polycentric political systems.

Heyck (2015) posits that microeconomics was among the disciplines intertwined with these epistemic principles in the age of system. He situates the influential power of Keynesian policies in the post-World War II political economy within the era's epistemic concerns with systems. Keynesian economics, Heyck (2015) argues, was based upon the "understanding of the economy as a complex organized system that tended to move toward an equilibrium state" while conceptualizing the state as "a kind of thermostat" that set "the level (of unemployment, say) at which equilibrium should be reached and that intervened, when necessary" (202). Despite the opposition that is often established between Hayekian or free market economics and Keynesian economics, the analysis section of this chapter will show that the epistemic principles of systems thinking constitute the former as well as the latter. For instance, system thinking's concepts of process, information, communication, and equilibrium are assembled with Hayek's theorization of the market and price system.

Another epistemic mode of thinking related to systems theory, which emerged in the context of military research during World War II and the Cold War, was related to research in cybernetics (Erickson et al. 2013; Halpern 2016; Hayles 1999; Kline 2015, 2020; Pickering 2010). Cybernetics was pioneered in the work of MIT-based mathematician, Norbert Wiener, on military research aiming to enhance the accuracy of anti-aircraft defense systems. The term "cybernetics" (a neo-Greek word meaning steersman) was coined by Wiener himself to refer to the studies of communication and control in the animal and the machine. Epistemically, and similar to systems theory, as histories of science have demonstrated, cybernetics is concerned with modeling, communication, flows of information, functions, and control. It is also informed by modes of thinking in terms of (interdependent) feedback loops, and inputs and outputs. Although these notions emerged in military and defense research, the epistemic principles underlying them soon migrated to other areas of research. For instance, in the famous Macy Conferences on Cybernetics (1946–1953),[4] Wiener's concept of "negative feedback," stemming from his research on the antiaircraft defense system, was among the main concepts that migrated to human sciences (Scott 2004).

In cybernetics, Halpern (2015) posits that the differences between micro-level and system-level actions and behaviors were a "fundamental epistemological quandary" (36). To navigate these differences and address the issues of communication and control, cyberneticians employed the concepts of "feedback" and "feedback loop." Indeed, these concepts were developed and employed in the nineteenth century in the context of attempts to increase the stability of mechanical systems (e.g., steam engines). Yet, it was only in the

1930s and 1940s that a feedback loop was explicitly theorized as the flow of information (Hayles 1999). In this regard, a cybernetic model/system was conceived to have three parts: (1) receptors able to absorb informational input from the environment; (2) a processing unit to record and process the input and produce instructions; (3) an output mechanism to impact the environment in the desired way. Cyberneticians posited that as new outputs led to new flows of input, and as information linked together all components of the system, feedback loops allowed a system to respond to changes in the perceived environment and adapt to it. Notions of communication and feedback in the flow of information made it possible for cybernetics to offer a "holistic understanding of a system in which the components enter into relations of causal circularity" (Bousquet 2009, 109). This cybernetic mode of thinking about holistic understanding and causal relations had important implications for other disciplines and areas of research, from sociology to political economy to education (Hayles 1999; Popkewitz, Pettersson, and Hsiao 2021).

It should be noted that for some post-World War II scientists, including neuropsychiatrist Warren McCulloch, the chair and the co-organizer of the Macy Conferences, cybernetics was a "universal" science that could unify different disciplines, from engineering to biology, psychology, and anthropology. This ability to connect different disciplines was linked to cybernetics' universal language (e.g., communication, information, feedback), its broad application (e.g., human behavior, political systems, firms, society, machines), as well as its modeling practices. Hence, cybernetic research enjoyed high status in the 1950s. However, several scholars have highlighted that the presumably "universal" meanings and applications of cybernetics varied from discipline to discipline and place to place and that its premises faced scholarly resistance early on (Geoghegan 2020; Kline 2020; Pickering 2010). These scholars push back against "the positivistic claims made by the Unity of Science movement in Europe" and the United States (Kline 2020, 13). Focusing on the disunity of cybernetics in the United States, Kline (2020) argues that attending to "the disunity of cybernetics, its multiple interpretations, modelling practices, subfields, and epistemologies" is significant to understanding "the history of the human sciences in the United States from about 1940 to 1980" (12). While acknowledging cybernetics' disunity, this chapter focuses on commonalities to draw attention to the epistemic resemblances and their articulation in the conceptualization of market and public governance as systems and learning processes.

Hence, in the post-World War II context, despite variations, some of the main constructs of the social sciences, including the notion of society itself, were rearticulated in terms of cybernetic epistemic principles, such as the facilitation of communication as the exchange of information through feedback and feedback loops. For instance, Wiener (1948) himself posited that the "social system is an organization like the individual, that is bound together by a system of communication, and that it has a dynamics in which circular processes of a feedback nature play an important role" (in Bousquet 2009, 116). Although cybernetics fell out of favor in the 1970s and "few scientists or academics would refer to themselves as cyberneticists today" (Bousquet 2009, 118), the epistemic principles and core concepts underlying cybernetics continue to get connected to the modes of thinking in different arenas of research, including (as the rest of this chapter will show) theories and debates about markets, entrepreneurship, and public governance. Among such cybernetic concepts and epistemic principles are the emphasis on information, feedback, communication, circularity, homeostasis, emergent futures, and so forth.

The rest of this chapter examines how the epistemic principles that became prevalent in the context of post-World War II social science are (re)articulated in classical liberal scholarship produced in the same era. The discussion examines the principles underlying conceptualizations of public administration and market processes. More specifically, it shows how notions and concepts related to systems theory, cybernetics, and the model of *homo adaptivus* are entangled with the theorizations of polycentric political systems by Ostroms and in the formulations of the knowledge problem and price system by Hayek.

EPISTEMIC PRINCIPLE IN MID-TWENTIETH-CENTURY CLASSICAL LIBERALISM

Polycentricism as a Continuous Process of Learning and Adaptation

The concept of polycentricity was first introduced in Michael Polanyi's (1951) *The Logic of Liberty.* Following an anti-positivist approach to the philosophy of science, Polanyi grounds his social analysis in an analogy of the scientific community as a successful polycentric system (Aligica and Tarko 2012). He notes how the decentralized and polycentric authority structure in a scientific community allows scientists to independently define problems and pursue scientific truths and discoveries. Although this authority structure does not impose specific research goals upon researchers, it guides the scientists to submit to certain "scientific standards." Consequently, despite the absence of an external, centralized authority, writes Polanyi (1951), all participants in a scientific community enjoy autonomy and freedom as they "jointly pursue a single systematic purpose"—that is seeking scientific truths (88).

Polanyi's argument about the relationship between polycentric wholes, individual freedom, adjustment, and development is not limited to social systems and scientific communities. He also sees polycentricism as the key to living organisms' growth and survival:

> The nature of scientific systems is more akin to the ordered arrangement of living cells which constitute a polycellular organism. The progress of science through the individual efforts of independent scientists is comparable in many ways to the growth of a higher organism from a single microscopic germ-cell. Throughout the process of embryonic development each cell pursues its own life, and yet each so adjusts its growth to that of its neighbours that a harmonious structure of the aggregate emerges. This is exactly how scientists co-operate: by continually adjusting their line of research to the results achieved up to date by their fellow scientists. (ibid, 88)

This analogy between a scientific community and a polycellular organism entails the ideas, concepts, and logic used in systems theory and cybernetics, as it employs notions of organism, system, structure, order, holism, arrangement, and process. It also highlights the salience of continuous adjustment, and thus communication and exchange of information, for the emergence and development of a whole organism or body of scientific knowledge. Hence, it is emphasized that a living cell has to adjust "its growth to that of its neighbors" and a scientist with "the results achieved up to date by their fellow scientists." The output of the process of adjustment is the emergence of what he calls "a harmonious structure of the aggregate" beyond the capacity of an individual cell. Similarly, "in adjusting himself to the others," Polanyi writes, "each scientist acts independently, yet by virtue of these several adjustments scientists keep extending together with a maximum efficiency the achievements of science as a whole" (ibid, 34–5). Hence, systems thinking concerns with the process, harmony, efficiency, and growth of a system "as a whole" are well reflected in Polanyi's conceptualization of polycentric systems—whether it is an individual living organism, a scientific community, or a social system.

Furthermore, Polanyi's scientist invokes the post-World War II figure of *homo adaptivus*, a subject whose rationality lies in continuous adaptation within a changing—yet bounded—environment. He emphasizes that a scientist has to continually adjust "their line of research to the results achieved up to date by their fellow scientists" for science to progress. In other words, the "progress of science" as a whole and the discovery of scientific truths are not achieved merely through the fixed calculations or plans of one single scientist working in isolation (i.e., *homo economicus*). Rather, progress is achieved through the continuous cooperation of *homo adaptivus* within a scientific system. "Research continues to advance on the lines of the universal system of science," (ibid, 84). The polycentric nature of this system, Polanyi emphasizes, allows science to advance even in the context of the Cold War, as "the

Russian pieces fit in with the British, the Swiss and the Japanese pieces, as well as with other pieces from all over the world" (ibid, 84). Hence, similar to other social scientific discourses in the age of system, truth, growth, progress, and even survival depend on the adaptive actions of *homo adaptivus*, rather than the self-interested actions of *homo economicus*.

According to Polanyi (1951), the "argument for freedom in science bears a close resemblance to the classical doctrine of economic individualism" (154). The polycentric structure of scientific communities "is very similar to Adam Smith's claim with regard to a team of businessmen" whose efforts "would be co-ordinated, as by an invisible hand, to the most economical utilization of the available resources for the purpose of satisfying different parts of the same system of demand," he adds (ibid, 154). He reiterates that

> The allocation of raw materials through the market to the plants constituting a productive system, and the suitable readjustment of this allocation in view of the changing supplies of raw materials and the varying demands of consumers . . . is clearly another instance of a large self-co-ordinating system in which each decision of one unit re-adjusts its relations to a great number of other units. (ibid, 118)

Polanyi thus posits that markets—due to their polycentricity—allow individual actors to freely act, adjust, and re-adjust their actions to those of others, thus achieving a level of coordination and growth as a whole that could not be attained through the monocentric structures of socialism. Like a living organism or a scientific community, growth and efficiency in the markets are conceived by Polanyi to be the outputs of a self-coordinating system functioning based on ongoing adjustment and adaptation. Hence, the figure of the *homo adaptivus* is present in the polycentric conception of the market.

The concept of polycentricism was later employed and further theorized in the field of governance studies, thanks to the scholarship of Vincent Ostrom, Elinor Ostrom, and the Bloomington School of Political Economy (Aligica and Boettke 2009). As a public administration paradigm, polycentricism was contrasted with the monocentric approach that dominated governance doctrines and political science in the twentieth century. As in Polanyi's (1951) scholarship, the notion of polycentricity in governance studies and in the scholarship of the Ostroms is entangled with the post-World War II mode of thinking in terms of systems theory, cybernetics, and the human subject as *homo adaptivus*.

The epistemic construction of societies, institutions, and relations as complex and beyond the capacity of the human being to know and design is reflected in the Ostroms' theorization of the polycentric political system. According to Ostrom (1972), in the monocentric vision, the "fragmentation of authority and overlapping jurisdiction" is presumed to generate "a state of affairs often described as 'chaotic'" (in McGinnis 1999, 53). This presumption of chaos thus makes it necessary for *one* center (e.g., the state) to obtain a monopoly over the legitimate exercise of power. The Ostroms, however, challenge this theoretical orientation, positing that monocentric approaches do not differentiate between chaos and complexity. They maintain that monocentricism overlooks the fact that the social context, institutional arrangements, and public governance entail complexities that cannot be captured in the standard public-private duality of monocentric visions (Aligica, Boettke, and Tarko 2019). As Aligica et al. (2019) explain, "the complex, contextual, and dynamic nature of the public-private interface" renders universal governance formulae, even those of a "minimal state," impossible (61).

In addition to their conception of the world as complex, the Ostroms re-cast what appears to be "chaos" in monocentric visions as an order and system—thus connecting with other post-World War II studies that emphasize the ability of systemic relations to generate an order greater than the sum of individual parts. "By conceptualizing . . . polycentric political systems," Ostrom (1972) explains, "we were suggesting that a *system of ordered relationships* [emphasis mine] underlies the fragmentation of authority and overlapping jurisdictions that had frequently been identified as 'chaotic' and as the principal source of institutional failure in the government of metropolitan areas" (Ostrom 1972 in McGinnis 1999, 53). Ostrom (1972) posits that a polycentric political system has "many centers of decision making that were formally independent of each other" in a "system" that is "viewed as a set of ordered relationships that persists through time" (ibid, 53). In this regard, the polycentric approach in governance studies resembles the postwar era's epistemic conceptualization of systems as larger than the sum of their components. Although it may appear as chaos, the relations within a polycentric political system are theorized by the Ostroms as having a logic and order beyond the ability of any entity or individual to independently produce.

Systems and cybernetic principles are also re-articulated in the emphasis placed on the functions and outputs of polycentric political systems. The concern in the Ostroms' theorization of polycentricism as a system is not the identification of relations or the multiplicity of centers per se. What matters is the *output* of such political systems—that is, their ability to prevent and/or correct the failures of monocentric approaches while also being more responsive to people's needs and freedoms. According to Elinor Ostrom (1998), "a system that has multiple centers of power at differing scales provides more opportunity for citizens and their officials to innovate and to intervene so as to correct maldistributions of authority and outcomes" (8). She thus insists that "polycentric systems are more likely than monocentric systems to provide incentives leading to self-organized, self-corrective institutional change" (ibid, 8). In this vision, when "multiple centers of power overlap in competition and cooperation as individuals act in specifically defined social and institutional settings," the outcome is the production of an "ecological rationality—with an emphasis on the dynamics that take place between ideas, rules, decisions, and learning" (Aligica et al. 2019, 70). In other words, polycentric political systems can generate an output and a kind of rationality larger than the sum of what is produced in different centers. In this regard, the Ostroms' conceptualization of polycentric political systems performs the post-World War II episteme of seeing truth and rationality as the outputs of systemic relationships.

The conceptualization of polycentric governance in the classical-liberal tradition as the process of learning and adaptation is indeed entangled with the conceptualizations of the market and the roles that market relations are seen to play in bringing order to the world. The next section explores Hayek's conception of the market as another ongoing process of learning and adaptation.

The Market as a Continuous Process of Learning and Adaptation

Like his contemporaneous scholars, Hayek's conception of the world in general, and economics in particular, is one replete with complexities. This conception is most vividly reflected in Hayek's 1974 Nobel Prize lecture, where he reiterates that economics is a science of essentially complex phenomena. In his remarks, he explicitly cautions against the rationalist pretense of being able to know the world through a presumed "power of prediction and control," stating that to "act on the belief that we possess the knowledge and the power which enable us to shape the processes of society entirely to our liking, knowledge which in fact we do *not* possess, is likely to make us do much harm" (Hayek 1974/1990, 33). In this regard, the notion of a complex world about which human beings have only limited knowledge is apparent in his thought. In the same lecture, he adds:

> [I]f man is not to do more harm than good in his efforts to improve the social order, he will have to learn that in this, as in all other fields where essential complexity of an organized kind prevails, he cannot acquire the full knowledge which would make mastery of the events possible. He will therefore have to use what knowledge he can achieve, not to shape the results as the craftsman shapes his. (Hayek 1974/1990, 33)

To Hayek (1988), rather than shaping the results, economics' task "is to demonstrate to men how little they really know about what they imagine they can design" (76). Hayek's model of the human subject is thus distant from the model of a fully rational subject.

In addition, the paradigmatic modes of thinking about the ability of systems to generate a kind of rationality that is unavailable to humans are overwhelmingly present in Hayek's scholarship and are well reflected in his discussions of the "knowledge problem" and the "fatal conceit" (1945, 1988). For instance, in "The Use of Knowledge in Society," Hayek (1945) draws theoretical attention to a major limitation in classical political economy: its "assumption that people's knowledge corresponds with the objective facts of the situation" and that perfect knowledge is the defining characteristic of a perfectly-competitive economic model (530).

The "knowledge problem," according to Hayek (1945), underscores the fact that the "economic problem of society" is not resource allocation, but "a problem of the utilization of knowledge not given to anyone in its totality" (519–520). In elaborating on the knowledge problem, Hayek draws attention to two important challenges that humans encounter in accessing and exchanging information and knowledge about complex phenomena. The first challenge is that knowledge is not yet in existence in the context of an emerging world. Crucial to this challenge is an understanding of knowledge as emergent and context-specific. Hayek (1945) explicitly asserts that knowledge depends on "the particular circumstances of time and place" and is always in the process of emerging within new constellations of circumstances (522). In other words, knowledge cannot be collected, but it emerges within the context.

The second challenge pertains to the fact that, even if existent, knowledge does not lend itself to human's consciousness and articulation (Hayek 1945, 1948; Kiesling 2015; Lavoie 1986). It thus pertains to Hayek's conceptualization of knowledge as at least partly unconscious and "tacit." He argues that the knowledge that humans can possess does not entirely lend itself to articulation and thus communication. As a result, to Hayek, much of the knowledge relevant to decision-making and planning in the market cannot be articulated and communicated and is thus beyond the ability of any entity to collect and use for planning (Hayek 1935, 1945). In this regard, and in line with the paradigmatic construction of the human subject as having bounded rationality and knowledge, the knowledge problem calls for seeing people as "imperfect creatures who interact with other imperfect creatures in an imperfect world" (Aligica et al. 2019, 73). It asks: how could these imperfect creatures possibly know, exchange, or collect something that is yet to emerge or something that cannot be communicated? Given the conviction that the knowledge available to any human (whether an ordinary citizen, an economist, or a political figure) is always partial and incomplete, it becomes impossible to communicate and incorporate relevant knowledge into centrally developed plans because the collection and use of nonexistent and noncommunicable knowledge is an impossible task for a central planner (such as the state). As Hayek (1945) maintains, knowledge "by its very nature cannot enter into statistics and therefore cannot be conveyed to any central authority in statistical form" (524). Stressing that the majority of the variables that "appear to be subsumed" under a centrally developed plan are "out of . . . any single agent's control," Hayek maintains that central planning, and the planners themselves, are irrational. Hence, the paradigmatic mode of thinking about the limits of human knowledge in a complex world is at the heart of Hayek's critiques of classical political economy and the rejection of central planning and state interventions in the economy.

Given the knowledge problem, Hayek argues that only economic actors who are part of market processes can communicate, exchange, acquire, and utilize relevant knowledge through their participation in emerging economic situations and in relationships with other economic actors. Through these market interactions, economic actors can gain partial access to tacit and emergent knowledge. Hence, the communication and exchange roles in the market account for the ever-changing state of the world (Kirzner 1997, 67). In this regard, the construct of the market is, in Mises' (1949) words, "not a place, a thing, or a collective entity"; instead, "a process, actuated by the interplay of the actions of the various individuals cooperating under the division of labor" and is thus "entirely a resultant of human actions" (258). Similarly, entrepreneurship is not the quality of a special kind of person, but the function. As Mises posits, "in any real and living economy every actor is always an entrepreneur" (ibid, 253). This conception of the market as a learning or entrepreneurial process is a fundamental diversion from the state of general market equilibrium in neoclassical microeconomics, which leaves no place for entrepreneurial activity (Kirzner 1997).

Hayek's proposition that the discovery and use of relevant knowledge can only take place through participation in the processes of interactions and adaptations to changing circumstances is regarded as one of his greatest contributions to political economy. This contribution and the formulation of the knowledge problem, as discussed above, are entangled with the critiques of rationalism and reflect paradigmatic concerns about the limits of human knowledge, rationality, and agency in a complex and emerging world. In Hayek's (1948) words, a human is a "very irrational and fallible being, whose individual errors are corrected only in the course of a social process, and which aims at making the best of the very imperfect material" (9). Not only does this statement show Hayek's rejection of the notion of homo economicus as a fully rational subject, but it also shows his emphasis on the way social processes enable the individual to correct errors, indicating a conception of humans as *homo adaptivus* and a belief in the ability of whole processes and systems to generate a rationality beyond the ability of one individual.

Hayek's scholarship connects with the era's social scientific epistemic principles beyond its rejection of the notion of *homo economicus* as a fully rational subject. If his works reflect the era's pessimism about human knowledge and rationality, they also embody the hope and optimism in the ability of systems and processes to produce rationality. For Hayek, the potential for producing rationality for irrational humans lies in market processes and price systems. As Aligica, Boettke, and Tarko (2019) note, "Hayek's key argument is that knowledge communicated and acted on in the *process of adaptation* [emphasis mine] to changing tastes, technologies, and resource availability is not the sort of knowledge that can be entered into statistics" (73). Instead, they maintain that "one must reconceive that

> economic problem of society is mainly one of rapid adaptation to changes in the particular circumstances of time and place' and see the price system as the solution that guides production plans and coordinates those plans with the consumption demands of buyers in the marketplace. (ibid, 73).

In "The Use of Knowledge in Society," Hayek (1945) describes the price system as a "marvel," which although "not the product of human design," is able to solve the problems that humans are not able to solve consciously (527). "Where the knowledge of the relevant facts is dispersed among many people," he writes, "prices can act to coordinate the separate actions of different people" (ibid, 526). He adds that the price system is

> a kind of machinery for registering change or a system of telecommunications which enables individual producers to watch merely the movement of a few pointers, as an engineer might watch the hands of a few dials, in order to adjust their activities to changes of which they may never know more than is reflected in the price movement. (527)

In the statement above, Hayek's analogies between producers and engineers and between prices and the hands of dials entail cybernetics' preoccupation with the salience of information and communication for both the machine and the human. Similarly, he maintains that "we must look at the price system as . . . a mechanism for communicating information" (ibid, 526). In this regard, he echoes the concerns of systems thinking and cybernetics with information and communication. To Hayek, prices operate as signals that articulate tacit knowledge, creating "a system of telecommunications" that transmits relevant information to individual buyers and sellers who, in the absence of these signals, would not be able to access and utilize that information. "The most significant fact about this system," Hayek notes, "is the economy of knowledge with which it operates, or how little the individual participants need to know in order to be able to take the right action" (ibid, 527). He thus puts emphasis on "the indispensability of the price system for any rational calculation in a complex society" (ibid, 528). In so doing, Hayek reflects the faith in the ability of the price system to produce a kind of rationality that individuals, due to their limited knowledge and rationality, cannot produce outside such a system.

As Heyck (2015) argues, the view of the economy as a complex system can be seen in Keynes' thought as well (202). However, whereas for Keynes it was possible for a central entity like the state to have access to relevant knowledge and thus act like a thermostat and move the economy toward equilibrium, for Hayek the state (as any other central entity or individual) cannot collect relevant knowledge and thus is incapable of producing rational decisions, interventions, and plans. It is thus "the assumption of more or less perfect knowledge on the part of almost everyone"—that is, their epistemic understanding of human rationality and knowledge—that is an important difference between Keynes and Hayek's economic models and systems (Hayek 1945, 527). In other words, the assemblage of the "knowledge problem" and systems thinking in Hayek's reasoning reconfigures the roles that the state and prices could possibly play regarding the generation of rational and just outcomes.

In his theorization of market processes, Hayek (1948) stresses that in order to ensure the communication of tacit and emerging knowledge through the price system, another process is also necessary: competition—a key concept that is also constituted by and constitutes the epistemic principles of systems thinking.[5] In this regard, as Boettke (2018) explains, although Hayek is often understood in mainstream economics to claim that the price system is a sufficient condition for attaining market equilibrium, he himself acknowledges that the price system (albeit necessary) is not a sufficient condition (ibid, 104–11). Instead, Hayek (1948) reiterates that

> Competition is essentially a process of the formation of opinion: by spreading information, it creates that unity and coherence of the economic system which we presuppose when we think of it as one market . . . It is thus a process which involves a continuous change in the data and whose significance must therefore be completely missed by any theory which treats these data as constant. (106)

As can be seen in this quote, akin to his conception of the price system and the market, Hayek's theorization of competition connects with the epistemic principles of systems thinking and cybernetics: he gives salience to flows of information, data, process, system, and emergence. Similar to the way systems thinking conceives of the whole as larger than the sum of its constituent parts, Hayek argues that the knowledge and rationality produced as the result of competition and market processes are larger than the sum of individual knowledge and rationality. In later elaborations, Hayek argued that competition, as the dynamic driving force for discovery in the market process, was in fact a "discovery process."

Cybernetic thinking is also articulated in the role of errors, mistakes, and failures in Hayek's conception of the market processes. He acknowledges the fact that the information signaled by prices is not always accurate—which is the case for "disequilibrium prices." Yet, it is maintained that even though the information conveyed by disequilibrium prices may not have the "accuracy" of what is transmitted by equilibrium prices, they still are able to communicate information about the initially uncoordinated decisions of market participants and thus signal valuable information that would not otherwise be known. As a result, market participants can learn from the "inaccuracy" of the information (and from their own disappointments), discover information and incentives that would otherwise remain hidden, revise their decisions, and better coordinate their decisions in the market and society, in ways that would go beyond the capacity of any central planning.

Hence, the conceptualization of market processes, market actors, and price systems in Hayek's scholarship is constituted by, and itself constitutes, the post-World War II epistemic modes of thinking about systems and feedback, and the concerns about the limits of human knowledge, rationality, and agency in a complex world. These principles, alongside the faith in the power of adjustments and adaptations, reconstituted the notions of "market" and "entrepreneurship" as processes that could generate outputs beyond the knowledge and capacity of individuals and central planners.

FINAL REMARKS

The discussion in this chapter shows how classical-liberal contributions concerned with governance and markets in the mid-twentieth century entail contingent—and yet taken-for-granted—modes of thinking about life and the human subject in the social sciences of this era. Neither universal nor objective, theories and research about the roles of the state and economic actors, political systems, and markets in this tradition are inscribed by the epistemic principles that contingently constructed the human as a subject of limited and bounded knowledge and rationality in a complex world. As in other disciplines in post-World War II social science, the human subject in the Ostroms' polycentric political system and in Hayek's price system is asked to participate in a process of learning, adjustment, and adaptation. Moreover, there is faith that systems, processes, feedback, and adaptation in markets and polycentric systems will generate an "organic rationality" through the ongoing flow of information that is beyond the ability of any individual or entity to independently produce. In this regard, the conceptualization of markets and public governance as ongoing processes of learning and adjustment embodies contingent principles that shape and limit human knowledge and rationality. The chapter thus shows how the academic practices of knowledge production and transmission are bounded by the contingencies of epistemic modes of thinking. In other words, rather than being objective, theory and research are inscribed by the historical and cultural contingencies of human knowledge and thought.

NOTES

1. Acknowledgments: I would like to thank the editors of this volume and the staff, facilitators, and fellows at the Mercatus Center's Adam Smith Fellowship colloquia series for their incredible support, insightful comments, and feedback. Special thanks to Jordan Lofthouse for his unwavering support and patience.

2. Whereas Simon's work does not fit disciplinary boundaries, his interest was in analyzing complex, hierarchical organizational structures in cognitive processes (in humans or machines), economic transactions, and bureaucratic organizations; thus, he drew on disciplines like cybernetics, physiology, and psychology.

3. Although not focusing on epistemic entanglements, Chandler (2013) demonstrates that Simon's arguments and scholarship about the limits of human knowledge and reason influenced F. A. Hayek and institutional economics.

4. The Macy Conferences on Cybernetics, sponsored by the Macy Foundation, took place between 1946 and 1953 in New York with the aim of promoting interdisciplinary thinking in the social, behavioral, and medical sciences to study the "governance" of human systems. These conferences brought together a number of prominent scientists in mathematics, psychology, engineering, anthropology, physics, ecology, psychiatry, neurophysiology, linguistics, and sociology. Anthropologists Gregory Bateson and Margaret Mead were among the participants of the Macy Conferences.

5. As Kirzner (1997) explains, the concept of competition for Hayek and other Austrians differs from the notion of the "perfectly competitive model" used in neoclassical theory.

REFERENCES

Aligica, Paul D., and Peter J. Boettke. 2009. *Challenging Institutional Analysis and Development: The Bloomington School.* London: Routledge.

Aligica, Paul D., and Vlad Tarko. 2012. "Polycentricity: From Polanyi to Ostrom, and Beyond." *Governance* 25 (2): 237–62.

Aligica, Paul Dragos, Peter J. Boettke, and Vlad Tarko. 2019. *Public Governance and the Classical-Liberal Perspective: Political Economy Foundations*. New York: Oxford University Press.

Boettke, Peter J. 2018. *F. A. Hayek: Economics, Political Economy, and Social Philosophy*. London: Palgrave Macmillan.

Bousquet, Antoine. 2009. *The Scientific Way of War*. New York: Columbia University Press.

Chandler, David. 2013. "Resilience and the Autotelic Subject: Toward a Critique of the Societalization of Security." *International Political Sociology* 7 (2): 210–26.

Erickson, Paul, Judy L. Klein, Lorraine Daston, Rebecca Lemov, Thomas Sturm, and Michael D. Gordin. 2013. *How Reason Almost Lost Its Mind: The Strange Career of Cold War Rationality*. Chicago and London: University of Chicago Press.

Geoghegan, Bernard Dionysius. 2020. "Textocracy, or, the Cybernetic Logic of French Theory." *History of the Human Sciences* 33 (1): 52–79.

Gilman, Nils. 2003. *Mandarins of the Future: Modernization Theory in Cold War America*. Baltimore and London: JHU Press.

———. 2016. "The Cold War as Intellectual Force Field." *Modern Intellectual History* 13 (2): 507–23.

Grove, Kevin. 2018. *Resilience*. New York: Routledge.

Halpern, Orit. 2015. *Beautiful Data: A History of Vision and Reason since 1945*. Durham, NC: Duke University Press.

———. 2016. "Circuits of Amnesia: Cybernetic Memory and Real-Time Analytics." *Cultural Studies? Critical Methodologies* 16 (5): 442–51.

Hayek, Friedrich A. 1945. "The Use of Knowledge in Society." *The American Economic Review* 35 (4): 519–30.

———. 1948. *Individualism and the Economic Order*. Regnery.

———. 1974. "The Pretense of Knowledge." *Mainline Economics: Six Nobel Lectures in the Tradition of Adam Smith*, edited by Peter J. Boettke, Stefanie Haeffele-Balch, and Virgil Henry Storr, 25–39. Arlington, VA: Mercatus Center at George Mason University.

———. 1988. *The Fatal Conceit: The Errors of Socialism*. London: Routledge.

Hayles, N. Katherine. 1999. *How We Became Posthuman: Virtual Bodies in Cybernetics, Literature, and Informatics*. Chicago: University of Chicago Press.

Heyck, Hunter. 2012. "Producing Reason." In *Cold War Social Science*, edited by Mark Solovey and Hamilton Cravens, 99–116. New York: Springer.

———. 2015. *Age of System: Understanding the Development of Modern Social Science*. Baltimore, MD: JHU Press.

Kiesling, Lynne. 2015. "The Knowledge Problem." In *The Oxford Handbook of Austrian Economics*, edited by Peter J. Boettke and Christopher J. Coyne, 45–64. New York: Oxford University Press.

Kirzner, Israel M. 1997. "Entrepreneurial Discovery and the Competitive Market Process: An Austrian Approach." *Journal of Economic Literature* 35 (1): 60–85.

Kline, Ronald. 2015. *The Cybernetics Moment: Or Why We Call Our Age the Information Age*. Baltimore, Maryland: JHU Press.

———. 2020. “How Disunity Matters to the History of Cybernetics in the Human Sciences in the United States, 1940–80.” *History of the Human Sciences* 33 (1): 12–35.

Lavoie, Don. 1986. “The Market as a Procedure for Discovery and Conveyance of Inarticulate Knowledge.” *Comparative Economic Studies* 28 (1): 1–19.

Levy, David, and Sandra Peart. 2017. *Escape from Democracy: The Role of Experts and the Public in Economic Policy*. Cambridge: Cambridge University Press.

Mises, Ludwig Von. 1949. *Human Action*. New Haven: Yale University Press.

Ostrom, Elinor. 1998. “The Comparative Study of Public Economies. Presented upon Acceptance of the Frank E. Seidman Distinguished Award in Political Economy.” Memphis, TN: PK Seidman Foundation.

Pickering, Andrew. 2010. *The Cybernetic Brain*. Chicago: University of Chicago Press.

Polanyi, Michael. 1951. *The Logic of Liberty: Reflections and Rejoinders*. Oxon: Routledge.

Popkewitz, Thomas S., Daniel Pettersson, and Kai-Jung Hsiao. 2021. “How Contemporary Educational Sciences Became Reasonable: The International Emergence of Educational Sciences in the Post–World War Two Years.” In *The International Emergence of Educational Sciences in the Post-World War Two Years: Quantification, Visualization, and Making Kinds of People*, edited by Thomas S. Popkewitz, Daniel Pettersson, and Kai-Jung Hsiao, 1–24. New York: Routledge.

Scott, Bernard. 2004. “Second-Order Cybernetics: An Historical Introduction.” *Kybernetes* 33 (9/10): 1365–1378.

Solovey, Mark, and Hamilton Cravens. 2012. *Cold War Social Science: Knowledge Production, Liberal Democracy, and Human Nature*. New York: Palgrave Macmillan.

Chapter 4

Rule-Based Fiscal Governance

Challenges, Alternatives, and a Path for Reform

Andrew Berryhill

As international government debt continues to rise, the weaknesses of modern fiscal governance have become increasingly salient. In 2022, twenty-three countries, including the United States, had public debts greater than 100 percent of their respective GDPs (IMF 2023). To reduce their debt burdens, many governments have implemented fiscal rules that ostensibly encourage fiscal responsibility. However, research suggests that these rules tend to be weakly designed and ultimately ineffective at improving fiscal outcomes. Heinemann et al. (2018) and Caselli and Reynaud (2020) find that national-level fiscal rules do not significantly improve fiscal balances after accounting for countries' existing degrees of fiscal responsibility. Supranational-level fiscal rules, such as those in the European Union (EU), have also disappointed, with Blanchard et al. (2021) writing that "there is a wide consensus among economists and policymakers in the European Union that the fiscal rules have not been very successful" even though the rules have been significantly reformed multiple times. The ineffectiveness of these rules has contributed to growing dissatisfaction with rule-based fiscal governance generally, with some scholars recently proposing alternative governance approaches.

The main contributions of this chapter are as follows: First, I categorize and synthesize the main critiques of rule-based fiscal governance. While an extensive literature details the drawbacks of fiscal rules and offers proposals for reform, much of it does so from a narrow perspective. Many of the studies such as that of Lledo et al. (2018) focus on technical elements of rule design, some such as that of Clift (2022) emphasize the role of partisan politics in rule-making and rule implementation, and others such as that of Drazen (2004) highlight credibility problems with rules. However, without explicitly considering the main challenges for rule-based governance together, reform proposals are likely to be ineffective.

Second, I evaluate the recent proposal of Blanchard et al. (2021) to implement "fiscal standards" in the EU as an alternative to fiscal rules. Their critique of rules has merit, but I argue that fiscal standards present additional governance challenges at both the national and supranational levels while still being largely subject to the same critique.

Third, I examine the work of James Buchanan and Richard Wagner on fiscal rules. I outline their rule proposal and explore how it both differs from modern proposals and illuminates a path for reform. Although Buchanan and Wagner's work is rarely cited in the modern literature on fiscal rules, it remains relevant for current debates around fiscal governance and provides a framework for analyzing recent historical experiences with rules.

THE REASON OF (FISCAL) RULES

Fiscal rules have surged in popularity since 1990, and more than 105 countries now have at least one rule in effect (Davoodi et al. 2022). The main component of these rules is typically a numerical limit on an aggregate fiscal variable such as the deficit, public revenue, public expenditure, or the debt itself. In the EU, for example, the 1997 Stability and Growth Pact (SGP) includes both a deficit limit of 3 percent of GDP and a debt limit of 60 percent of GDP that currently still applies to all member countries.

The potential usefulness of fiscal rules is widely recognized by scholars. As Drazen (2004) explains,

> The main argument for fiscal rules is the bias towards positive government budget deficits we observe in many countries. That is . . . the attraction of rules is that by constraining policymakers, they will reduce or eliminate the tendency towards budget deficits.

Fiscal rules are thus a tool to "correct policymakers' incentives by raising the costs of excessive deficits, as noncompliance triggers reputational and electoral costs and, in some cases, sanctions" (Eyraud et al. 2018).

Buchanan (1997) argues that these incentives arise because present voters do not fully reckon with the genuine opportunity cost of government borrowing, as government borrowing lacks the assigned liability present with individual borrowing. He explains that

> The owner of a government bond holds a claim against the general tax base of the political community, not against the income or assets of some identified person or group. There is no effective presence of future period taxpayers in current

> period political choice settings, a presence that might exert some rough balance into the fiscal cost-benefit calculus. (Buchanan 1997, 121)

Thus, politicians' ability to spend without levying additional taxes helps create a "fiscal illusion" in which the costs of public policies appear less than they truly are, increasing current voters' demand for public spending and generating a "regime of fiscal deficits as a necessary consequence of fully rational responses of political agents to the demands of their constituents" (ibid., 122). Even if there were responsible politicians who recognized the harms of deficits and made unpopular decisions to balance the budget, not only would they likely get voted out, but future coalitions may also roll back any progress that was made (ibid., 122). Therefore, fiscal rules could ensure both present and future fiscal responsibility.

However, fiscal rules in practice routinely suffer from design weaknesses such as accounting loopholes, vaguely defined escape clauses, opaque measurement and projection methodologies, and a lack of independent compliance monitoring. As a result, many rules have been changed, circumvented, or broken, severely hampering their effectiveness (Reuter 2015). To capture the prevalence of weak design features across countries, Schaechter et al. (2012) construct an index of fiscal rule design strength based on a variety of design features, including the legal basis of the rule, the existence of correction mechanisms and sanctions, and the independence of any monitoring and enforcement bodies. The index ranges from zero (weakest) to one (strongest), where the average rule's score was only 0.29, with just five countries' rules scoring 0.8 or above. Therefore, by this measure at least, most fiscal rules at the time were weakly designed. While the index is based only on design rather than implementation, it is consistent with recent empirical studies that suggest fiscal rules typically have limited, if any, effects on national fiscal balances (Heinemann et al. 2018).

CHALLENGES FOR MODERN FISCAL RULES

Designing fiscal rules is a daunting task, as there seem to be many features that a "good" rule should have. Kopits and Symansky (1998) propose eight desirable features that include simplicity, ease of monitoring and enforcement, ease of operationalizing the rule into the budget process, and effectiveness in ensuring long-term debt sustainability. Debrun et al. (2018) advocate for a trio of features with similar themes: "simplicity to facilitate communication and anchor expectations about the financial sustainability of future fiscal policies, flexibility to accommodate temporary changes in fiscal policy when desirable, and enforceability to inflict tangible costs to financially reckless governments." However, these features may conflict with each other and necessitate trade-offs. For example, it may seem prudent to delineate allowable fiscal policy responses for various kinds of negative shocks, but doing so comes at the cost of simplicity.

The trade-off between flexibility and simplicity has been highly relevant for the evolution of the EU's fiscal rules. Debrun et al. (2018) explain that:

> The original [EU] arrangement based on a deficit cap of 3% of GDP and a debt ceiling of 60% of GDP gradually morphed into a maze of potentially conflicting and overlapping benchmarks . . . In a nutshell, simplicity was sacrificed to maximize flexibility while enhancing enforceability, which ultimately undermined the rules' capacity to guide fiscal policy."

Despite these design challenges, most fiscal governance reform proposals remain grounded in the current rule-centered paradigm of a numerical limit on one or more fiscal aggregates. The proposals generally focus on enhancing rule simplicity and creating supporting fiscal institutions such as "fiscal councils" to assist in rule implementation and enforcement (Medas et al. 2022).

First Challenge: Knightian Uncertainty

While a great deal of research focuses on how to best balance simplicity, flexibility, and enforceability, Blanchard et al. (2021) argue that

> The most important argument against fiscal rules . . . is not that getting the trade-offs right would require even more complexity. Rather, it is that economists would be incapable of defining any rule that gets the trade-offs right ex ante even when given a free hand in making the rules as complex as desired. The reason for this is "Knightian uncertainty": many relevant contingences, the probabilities associated with them, and the right way to map them into a rule, are impossible to identify ex ante.

This insight reveals several related problems for rule-centered fiscal governance. First, because the future is inherently uncertain, there are an infinite number of possible contingencies; therefore, any fiscal rule is necessarily an incomplete contract. Many relevant contingencies can certainly be identified based on theory and experience, but policymakers cannot know their respective probabilities of occurrence ex ante, and so the expected benefits of creating plans to respond to them are uncertain. This is especially problematic given that more detailed response plans come at the cost of more complexity. Also, even if the contingencies and their probabilities of occurrence were known, mapping responses onto a rule is not a trivial matter. The proper way to adjust a rule to allow the "optimal" amount of flexibility while still imposing reasonable limits will not be immediately obvious, especially if political and economic conditions differ from those that prevailed when the rule was written. For example, the debt burden and tax base evolve over time, and the ability of monetary policy to effectively complement fiscal policy may also be limited if countries have reached their "fiscal limit" in the sense that they can no longer raise additional tax revenue (Leeper and Walker 2011).

Because every fiscal situation or shock is going to be different and occur under unique circumstances, it may seem prudent to implement a rule with a conservative limit that compensates for the uncertainty regarding the current sustainability of finances, the possibility of negative shocks, and other factors. However, Blanchard et al. caution that

> While "conservative" may sound good, it implies that in most states of the world, such a rule would be excessively restrictive in constraining fiscal policy in its stabilization function. Conversely, a rule that is calibrated to allow adequate space for stabilization policy would have to give countries so much free reign to create debt that they could easily end up in the danger zone. One way or the other, rules that attempt to codify the trade-off between debt risks and stabilization benefits of fiscal policy ex ante will get it wrong. (2021, 215)

In other words, rules will either be too tight or too loose, and a rule that is too tight at one point in time may be too loose at another due to changes in real interest rates and other relevant variables. Additionally, how to judge whether a rule is too tight or too loose is likely to be the subject of political and economic contestation, especially since a variety of fiscal policy goals and approaches could reasonably be argued for. Clift (2022) notes that "Fiscal doctrine tends to be invoked in ways that intimate the existence of a single unanswerable body of fiscal policy wisdom. This jars with the politics of economic ideas and the relatively broad spectrum of respectable fiscal thinking." Fiscal governance has increasingly been seen as a technocratic enterprise based on principles of sound fiscal policy, but while the consensus goal of a fiscal rule is to promote "fiscal responsibility," there are many different conceptions of what this practically implies. Some economists like Buchanan support a balanced budget rule, while others believe a deficit rule in the realm of 3 percent of GDP is sufficient. Some believe that capital investment should be shielded from budget cuts, while others believe doing so is unnecessary. The practical objectives of fiscal policy are disputed, unlike the objectives of monetary policy. Mathieu and Sterdyniak (2013) note that

> The objective of monetary policy is rather clear: maintaining low and stable inflation . . . The issue is more delicate for fiscal policy: should it target full employment or the equilibrium of public finances, and how to define the latter?

> What is an optimal fiscal policy? Can rules allowing . . . optimal fiscal policy in permanence be defined?

The features and objectives thought to constitute an "optimal" fiscal rule have changed over time and will likely continue to do so. Clift (2022) documents that fiscal rules in Britain have evolved significantly since their introduction in the 1990s. While they initially focused on balancing fiscal prudence with increasing capital investment and were implemented as general principles, they evolved along with EU rules to become more focused on specific numerical targets. The 2008 Global Financial Crisis then prompted a tightening of the targets amid worries about debt sustainability; however, these changes, many subsequent modifications, and their implementation were the result not only of evolving economic ideas but also partisan politics.

Second Challenge: Political Discretion

In addition to technical design decisions amid Knightian uncertainty, political factors also affect fiscal rules in many important ways. For example, Clift (2022) documents that the New Labour Party's introduction of fiscal rules in Britain was "driven primarily by a yearning for greater economic credibility." The rules were chosen to embody a new policy of "constrained discretion" that was intended to restore trust in the party's ability to effectively manage the economy. The rules were largely successful, but facing strong public demand to increase spending, politicians and bureaucrats repeatedly employed creative methods to evade the rules' constraints, exploiting the room for discretion in the application of the rules' components. For example, in 2005, the Chancellor of the Exchequer "retrospectively altered the UK cycle's start from 1997 to 1999," highlighting the cycle's "inherent uncertainty and contestability" and drawing attention to the "flexibility and interpretive leeway inherent within fiscal rules regimes" (Clift 2022). As a former Treasury official explains, gauging the economic cycle is

> a very approximate art. And when you've got those approximations, you are going to have political desire. If we chose that date rather than that date, that generates more revenue for us to use . . . the bias for the politicians is towards taking certain interpretations that implies things are better. (Clift 2022)

The implementation of fiscal rules inevitably leads to fiscal maneuvers for political advantage.

One way to punish and curtail these maneuvers is through monitoring and reputational effects. If voters discover that politicians and bureaucrats are acting in opposition to the spirit of the rules or are misleading them about the true state of the country's finances, they can hold them accountable to some degree through elections or other formal means. However, even though Britain's Office of Budgetary Responsibility (OBR)

> has a track record of puncturing [such] façade[s], showing the Chancellor's workings to unearth sharp practices and highlight shenanigans . . . most people do not read long OBR reports, and *apparent* fiscal rule observance—a headline claim or a line in a budget speech—is what "counts" politically for economic credibility. (Clift 2022)

Surprisingly, the index from Schaechter et al. (2012) ranks Britain's fiscal rules as some of the strongest, underscoring the severity of problems with fiscal rule implementation globally.

The complexity of modern fiscal rules has created similar problems with political accountability in other countries as well. Even if a detailed analysis of a rule was publicly available—perhaps put online by an independent news or research organization—there would still be a significant cost to reading and understanding the analysis. Schuknecht (2004) notes the superficial character of public discussion around the fiscal rules in the EU's Stability and Growth Pact (SGP):

> The public in particular only seems to take notice of issues that relate to easily understandable, simple, clear criteria as this is more compatible with high monitoring costs. One can observe that the public debate on the SGP does not focus on the intricacies of cyclical adjustment but only on the 3% deficit limit—one single number!

Thus, many voters will remain rationally ignorant of a rule's finer details, reducing the probability of external enforcement, especially in nontransparent political environments.

Third Challenge: Political Commitment

The tendency of politicians to exploit discretion and selectively enforce or even change fiscal rules highlights the difficulty of commitment in this context. As discussed previously, deficits can arise from the rational decisions of politicians to cater to voters' demands, which are a common justification for imposing fiscal rules. However, since fiscal rules are political artifacts, politicians are the ones designing their own constraints. Given this fact, Drazen (2004) poses a natural question: "More generally, how can it be made credible that existing laws will not be changed whenever current circumstances make it convenient to do so?"

One strategy is to take a constitutional approach to fiscal rules and thereby increase the costs of changing them. As Drazen (2004) summarizes:

> A promise to follow through on a certain action may be made credible by enacting it into a law which itself is difficult to undo, that is, by "constitutionalizing" it . . . Effective commitment follows from the extreme difficulty in changing a law once it is given constitutional status.

However, while a constitutional approach may greatly enhance commitment, it is far from a guarantee of an effective rule, as the rule being committed to may be flawed in multiple important ways. For example, a rule may have many state-contingent elements, making it difficult to determine whether the rule has been broken if the relevant states are not well-defined. Therefore, "The difficulty of verifying whether the government has abided by a numerical fiscal restriction in itself suggests that to be credible, numerical fiscal policy rules must be simple" (Drazen 2004). But even a simple constitutional rule could be ineffective. For example, the relevant fiscal variables may be vaguely specified, or the numerical limits of the rule may be too lenient. These features are potentially more likely with constitutional fiscal rules specifically for two reasons: First, the rule's design may come under relatively more scrutiny, making consensus less likely; second, politicians may prefer more flexibility to avoid having to amend the rule—and thus the constitution—in the future. These reasons may be less relevant in countries where the constitution is easier to amend, but that also implies the constitution is less useful as a commitment device.

FISCAL STANDARDS AS AN ALTERNATIVE TO FISCAL RULES

Given the challenges of rule-based fiscal governance, Blanchard et al. argue that the EU should move away from fiscal rules altogether:

> [We need] an alternative approach . . . one that looks at each case individually taking into account country and context specificities and comes to a judgement on whether fiscal policy needs to be adjusted. Rather than attempting to codify the tradeoff between debt risks and output stabilization ex ante, this trade-off would be evaluated continuously, based on all information available at the time. Fortunately, such an approach exists: the legal literature refers to it as a standard as opposed to a rule. In the supranational context of the EU, it would not be easy to implement. But unlike fiscal rules, it stands a chance conceptually. (2021, 215–216).

They explain that the main difference between a rule and a standard is in "the degree to which legal content is defined ex post, at the point of application, rather than ex ante" (ibid., 216). For example, the legal content of a standard vehicle speed limit is defined ex ante—you are either in compliance with the limit or not based on predefined criteria. In contrast, the legal content of a hypothetical requirement for drivers to not drive at an "excessive speed" would be determined ex post "based on social norms and legal precedent" (ibid., 216). In the context of fiscal rules, they note that

> "Standards and rules are commonplace in national and EU law. In the present EU fiscal framework, paragraph 1 of Article 126 of the Treaty on the Functioning of the EU (TFEU), "Member States" shall avoid excessive government deficits' constitutes a pure standard, while the requirement that countries with a structural balance below -0.5% of GDP must increase it by at least 0.5 percentage points of GDP every year . . . constitutes a pure rule. (ibid., 216)

As a proof of concept for the expanded use of fiscal standards, Blanchard et al. cite the national-level case of New Zealand.

Fiscal Standards in Practice

New Zealand's fiscal framework was introduced as part of its Fiscal Responsibility Act of 1994 and is written in terms of "principles of responsible fiscal management" that are comparable to fiscal standards. As explained in New Zealand Treasury (2019), the principles include objectives to

- "Achieve and maintain prudent public debt levels."
- "Ensure that, on average, Crown operating expenses do not exceed Crown operating revenue."
- "Achieve and maintain levels of Crown net worth to provide a buffer against shocks."
- "Manage fiscal risks facing the Crown prudently."
- "Consider the likely impact of fiscal strategy on present and future generations."
- "Have regard to the interaction between fiscal policy and monetary policy."

New Zealand explicitly rejected fiscal rules because, among other reasons,

> A legislated fiscal rule will not necessarily reflect the government of the day's assessment of what constitutes good fiscal policy . . . For example, a limit on Crown borrowing could require a government to cut spending even if the evidence suggests that doing so would have negative consequences for economic growth or living standards more generally. (New Zealand Treasury 2015)

While establishing a causal relationship between a fiscal governance framework and fiscal outcomes can be difficult given endogeneity problems, New Zealand's fiscal health has undoubtedly improved since the Act was passed, with its debt-to-GDP ratio falling from roughly 50 percent in 1994 to 16 percent in 2007 (IMF 2023). Though the ratio has risen significantly since 2007, New Zealand remains in a position of relative fiscal health and stability.

Although fiscal standards can clearly be part of an effective fiscal governance framework, an important question for widespread adoption at either the national or supranational level is how to determine such vague concepts as "prudent" debt levels. Blanchard et al. (2021) argue that in the absence of a guiding body of case law, "deficits are to be considered excessive when debt does not appear to be sustainable with high probability, conditional on current and projected policies" and that the primary tool of assessing whether debt is sustainable or not should be "Stochastic Debt Sustainability Analysis" (SDSA). They explain that

> Conceptually, [an SDSA] would generate a distribution of paths of the debt ratio (sometimes called a 'fan chart'), based on forecasts for the drivers of the debt dynamics, which are themselves stochastic: the path of primary balances; one-off liabilities, for example, related to aging or the retirement system; and growth, interest rates and the maturity structure of the debt. The forecasts would also take into account the policy intentions of the authorities, as well as the interactions between growth and fiscal policies. The result would be a distribution for the debt ratio n years out, for the actual primary balance and for the debt stabilizing primary balance, conditional on expected policies (but allowing for uncertainty about how these policies would affect the economy). (Blanchard et al. 2021, 218)

A country would then be considered in compliance with a fiscal standard prohibiting excessive deficits, for example, if its deficits were compatible with future debt sustainability with a certain probability. Blanchard et al. admit that SDSA is extremely technical and that "a notoriously difficult aspect is to capture linkages between the various forecasts, such as feedback from the debt level to the interest rate," but they maintain that "whatever the failing of these models, they are vastly superior, as a predictor of debt distress, to the simple debt ratios that underlie the current EU fiscal framework" (ibid., 219). No single debt-to-GDP ratio will be an accurate reflection of the "safe" or "sustainable" level of debt over time for one country, much less for multiple countries. Therefore, they argue that policymakers must account for country and context-specific factors to avoid fiscal policy that is unnecessarily tight or dangerously loose.

Challenges for Fiscal Standards

The complexity of the models underlying SDSA creates significant challenges for fiscal standards. The intricate and conditional interrelationships between model variables such as debt, interest rates, and economic conditions—both domestically and globally—are uncertain and theoretically contested. Even if economists use historical data to guide their assumptions, the variables' interrelationships may evolve in unexpected ways, creating more doubt about the precision and validity of the model's results. One might counter that this is a reason why fiscal standards and SDSA are superior—new developments can be quickly incorporated into sustainability analyses, which in turn can inform policy recommendations. However, judging whether developments are temporary or permanent is difficult, if not impossible, and Wyplosz (2023) argues that "the assumption [in SDSA] that future uncertainty will be similar to past uncertainty is dubious at best." This challenge is especially relevant for sustainability analyses that necessarily forecast years or decades into the future, and it is compounded by problems of measurement. As discussed previously, many relevant economic concepts such as the business cycle and potential GDP are notoriously difficult to define and measure. This raises "a natural question [of] how each measure's uncertainty is combined with the uncertainty of DSA" (Wyplosz 2023). Blanchard et al. (2021) concede that certain modeling choices will be unsatisfactory to some, but they argue that such sustainability analyses remain the only conceptually sound approach and that their complexity is unavoidable given the complexity of the world. However, I argue that the complexity of SDSA has significant implications for the communicability and credibility of adjustment requirements that Blanchard et al. fail to sufficiently reckon with.

One possibility is that because SDSA and the methodological debates surrounding it are highly technical, "the details [of an SDSA] may be overlooked by policymakers and observers and accepted without proper analysis" (Wyplosz 2023). Alternatively, and perhaps more likely, policymakers and citizens may *object* to consolidation requirements for similar reasons. An important advantage of numerical fiscal rules is that they *can* be simple and straightforward, facilitating transparency and effective communication about the rules' mechanisms and how they help to achieve fiscal goals. As SDSA is far more complex, both economists and policy advisors may struggle to justify its use and communicate findings, lowering support for any resulting policy recommendations that impose short-term costs such as cutting spending or raising taxes. Additionally, many politicians who prioritize staying in office would want to exploit justifications for rejecting requirements that would necessitate such consolidation. Politicians could argue that the authors of an SDSA underestimated future growth rates, failed to sufficiently incorporate the effects of intended future policies, or were inconsistent with past analyses of their country and/or other countries. If these or other objections are raised, the process of adjudicating the dispute becomes particularly important. Dani et al. (2021) argue that the proposal of Blanchard et al. (2021) to delegate adjudication responsibilities in the EU to the EU Court of Justice is problematic because the judges would lack relevant technical expertise. The judges would also have to balance the testimony of expert authorities against other factors and do so without legal precedent, regardless of whether this is undertaken in a "specialized chamber" created explicitly for such cases.

Regardless of adjudication procedures, a conceptual problem with SDSA remains: it relies heavily on discretion, which will inevitably generate recommendations that are too tight or too loose. One source of discretion is the modeling assumptions of SDSA, which even mainstream economists disagree about (Wyplosz 2023). Another source is the choice of probability at which debt is considered unsustainable with "high probability" and thus in need of corrective adjustment. Blanchard et al. (2021) suggest requiring adjustment if debt is unsustainable with an estimated probability of 5 percent or more, but they implicitly acknowledge that the optimal probability is not obvious ex ante. Additionally, if a country needs to adjust, the details of the adjustment are also subject to discretion. Blanchard et al. (2021) suggest that the speed of adjustment should factor in "risks to sustainability, the state of the economic cycle and the capacity of monetary policy to offset the contractionary impact of adjustment on the European Union as a whole," but the appropriate weights to put on each of these variables are unclear, and the high degree of discretion such decisions would require has generated preemptive pushback from Germany and other EU member countries (Strupczewski 2023). Therefore, while fiscal standards could theoretically mitigate the downsides of fiscal rules' relative inflexibility, they cannot conceptually solve the "goldilocks problem" of ensuring fiscal policy that is neither too tight nor too loose. This is true of every fiscal governance framework, but the challenges of fiscal standards are significant, and enforcing compliance would remain difficult.

The problem of enforcement has widely been recognized as one of the biggest challenges for fiscal governance at both national and supranational levels, and this would likely remain true under fiscal standards. At the national level, vaguely defined terms or principles of fiscal responsibility would create room for the same types of politically advantageous fiscal maneuvers that have plagued rule-based fiscal governance systems, even if the fiscal standards were constitutionalized. At the supranational level, member countries might object to requirements for fiscal consolidation based on SDSA and initiate unprecedented adjudication procedures overseen by institutional bodies ill-suited to the task, thereby damaging the credibility of fiscal standards. While the EU's current fiscal rules struggle with credibility, it is far from obvious that fiscal standards would be a significant improvement as the centerpiece of a fiscal governance framework. Following Buchanan and Wagner (2000), I argue that reforming rules to be simpler and more enforceable is more likely to improve fiscal outcomes than a wholesale shift to fiscal standards.

BUCHANAN AND WAGNER'S FISCAL RULE PROPOSAL

James Buchanan and Richard Wagner have been among the most ardent supporters of rule-based fiscal governance. They argue that appropriate fiscal rules could prevent the deficits that commonly arise from "ordinary" politics—rational and self-interested politicians satisfying voter demands for more spending with less taxation. While some scholars have questioned Buchanan and Wagner's theory of deficit emergence, alternative theories also emphasize the role of political factors and generally arrive at a similar conclusion: a fiscal rule may be necessary to prevent further deficits. I argue that Buchanan and Wagner's work contains numerous insights that show both why most fiscal rules have failed and reveal a path for reforming them.

Qualities of Effective Rules

Buchanan and Wagner repeatedly emphasize that fiscal rules must be implemented at the constitutional level, or at the highest legal level possible. Rules at lower legal levels are vulnerable to the whims of the legislature, but changing the constitution is typically a complex and lengthy process that requires a high degree of political support. Therefore, only a constitutional rule—one that is "external and superior"—constitutes an effective commitment (Buchanan and Wagner 2000, 182).

However, a fiscal rule's constitutional status does not guarantee effectiveness, and Buchanan and Wagner identify three general qualities that effective constitutional rules must possess. The first quality is sufficient simplicity, such that the rule is "capable of being understood by members of the public" (ibid., 183). The second quality is that the rule "must be capable of offering clear criteria for adherence and for violation. Both the politicians and the public must be able readily to discern when the rule is being broken" (ibid., 183). The third quality is the one that they deem most important: "The fiscal rule must reflect and express values held by the citizenry, for then adherence to the precepts of the rule may, to some extent, be regarded as sacrosanct" (ibid., 183). In summary, "these qualities add up to a requirement that any effective budgetary rule must be understood to 'make sense' to the ordinary voter both in terms of technical detail and in the goals they seek to advance" (ibid., 183).

The need for simplicity and enforceability is largely echoed in the modern literature on fiscal rules, but Buchanan and Wagner depart in at least two important ways. First, they de-emphasize flexibility because they believe it can compromise a fiscal rule's status as a rule, in the sense that a rule must demand strict adherence. Second, they emphasize the need for congruence between fiscal rules and the values of citizens. I argue that these departures are highly relevant for debates around reforming fiscal rules and deserve more attention.

Flexibility and Real versus Pseudo Rules

Throughout their discussion of rules, Buchanan and Wagner make their wariness toward flexibility clear. For example, they write that an escape clause allowing for the temporary suspension of a rule's limits—a common flexibility feature in modern rules—must be incorporated in any rule proposal only because of "political reality" given widespread concerns that the rule might exacerbate the negative economic effects of wars, recessions, or other national emergencies (ibid., 184). While Buchanan and Wagner are skeptical of these concerns, arguing that a rule would create a stabilizing force for the economy and an anchor for agents' expectations, they nonetheless choose to include an escape clause in their proposal, albeit with carefully chosen constraints to reduce the potential for abuse. The clause can only be activated in a national emergency "as declared by two-thirds of both houses of Congress, and approved by the president," and an activated clause expires after a year, requiring reauthorization for further use (ibid., 188). While flexibility is emphasized in modern discussions about fiscal rules and some measure of it may be desirable, too much flexibility risks neutering a rule and rendering it so rarely binding as to be irrelevant. Therefore, the central focus of Buchanan and Wagner's proposal is ensuring that the rule is a hard constraint and limiting opportunities for evasion plays an important role in accomplishing that goal.

To motivate some of Buchanan and Wagner's emphasis on hard constraints and limited flexibility, I briefly consider the monetary rule context and specifically the distinction that Selgin (2016) makes between what he calls "real" and "pseudo" monetary rules. Selgin defines a "real rule" as a rule that is strictly enforced and that endures (or is expected to endure for the foreseeable future) (2016, 282). Any other rule is a "pseudo rule" that serves as a mere guide to monetary policy conduct at best and a destabilizing source of uncertainty at worst. In this framework, Buchanan and Wagner advocate for what could be called a "real" fiscal rule, especially regarding enforcement. Just as Buchanan and Wagner argue in the fiscal rule context, Selgin argues that a constitutional amendment is the only institutional device

> capable of providing for anything like the strict enforcement that a real monetary rule requires. [Other] devices, in contrast, can serve only as the basis for pseudo monetary rules, for none offers any reliable assurance that a 'prescribed guide for the conduct of monetary policy' will actually be heeded. (2016, 282)

By this criterion, most fiscal rules in effect today are pseudo rules.

Robustness and Four Dimensions of Rule Flexibility

Buchanan (1997) notes that a common criticism of a constitutional balanced budget rule is that while such a rule may ensure strict enforcement, flexibility would be too limited, which would then make noncompliance inevitable and potentially even warranted, violating the endurance criterion. Selgin confronts similar criticisms and argues that a constitutional rule can endure, but to do so, it must be "robust" in the sense that its strict enforcement "is not likely to be the cause of such regret as might lead to its frequent revision or abandonment" (2016, 287). Robustness is an elusive quality given the time-inconsistency of fiscal politics. If politicians agree initially on a rule, but unpopular fiscal consolidation is eventually required to comply, then they may renege to avoid the ire of their respective constituencies. However, while Buchanan and Wagner's proposed fiscal rule would be stricter than most that are currently in force, I argue that it includes at least four main features that create multiple dimensions of flexibility and encourage a higher degree of robustness than many might associate with a constitutional balanced budget rule.

The first feature is the aforementioned escape clause that reduces the temptation to break the rule in a national emergency. While Buchanan and Wagner believed a rule could help stabilize the economy in an emergency, they were skeptical of the practical need for an escape clause apart from political considerations, including an escape clause that does make a rule more flexible and arguably more likely to endure.

The second feature is that compliance would be determined based on ex ante projections of federal outlays and revenues (Buchanan and Wagner 2000, 187). Buchanan (1997) frames this feature primarily as a response to criticisms that mandating budget balance ex post could exacerbate the business cycle if a negative shock were to hit during the fiscal year and the government is forced to enact some combination of tax increases and spending cuts. If compliance is determined *ex ante*, as long as *projected* outlays and revenues are equalized, then the government would not be in violation of the rule if *actual* outlays and revenues end up unequal (in either direction).

This compliance methodology also encourages robustness by ensuring that well-meaning politicians who sincerely try to comply will virtually always be successful. Selgin points out that in the monetary context, even if there were strong sanctions for breaking a rule, if the target variable is not under the monetary authority's direct control (e.g., the inflation rate), then strict adherence cannot be expected (2016, 287). In the context of ex ante projected budget balance, this would not be a significant concern if tax revenue projections are provided sufficiently ahead of time, since projected outlays are under the direct control of the government. If politicians fail to reduce projected outlays enough to equal projected revenue, Buchanan and Wagner (2000) recommend an automatic adjustment mechanism that sufficiently reduces outlays to enforce compliance. No third-party compliance bodies would be necessary because enforcement is mechanical and institutionally mandated.

The third feature is one of omission—namely, that there are no requirements for *how* the rule must be complied with (Buchanan and Wager 2000, 184). To eliminate a deficit, any adjustment of outlays or revenues may be employed. Many countries have secondary rules that require action on one variable or the other (typically outlays) to assist in the short-term operationalization of a primary rule such as a deficit rule. However, while potentially helpful, such rules are not strictly necessary, make fiscal governance more complex, and may lead to unnecessary conflict in the process of rule compliance. Limiting the paths to compliance increases the likelihood of the rule being broken and thus reduces robustness.

An additional benefit of omitting secondary operational rules is that many sizes of government and allocations of public spending can comply with the rule. Given that the projected budget is balanced, both the amount of spending and how it is allocated are still subject to the political process, though presumably with more "conscious and careful weighting of benefits and costs" (ibid., 185). This political flexibility relates to what Buchanan (1997) calls an "essential distinction" between procedural and substantive rules. Buchanan defines procedural rules, intuitively, as those that act "on the *procedures* through which participants are allowed to reach and to carry out decisions," and he defines substantive rules as those that act "directly on the outcomes that any such decisions might describe." He argues that a constitutional balanced budget rule is (perhaps counterintuitively) *procedural* because it "lays out a new rule for making fiscal choices; it does not lay down guidelines for what these choices might be." This distinction matters to Buchanan on a normative level because he believes that only procedural rules are appropriate for inclusion in the constitution, and he criticizes the substantive components of the constitutional balanced budget amendment that was nearly adopted in the United States in 1995. Indeed, he writes that those components "clearly represented an attempt to introduce substantive direction as to how the federal budget was to achieve and maintain balance," which explains why they were widely denounced as an attempt to constitutionalize a specific economic ideology (Buchanan 1997). On a positive level, by allowing flexibility for the political process to decide the amount and relative allocation of spending, one may reduce the likelihood that strict enforcement of a constitutional balanced budget rule will lead to calls for revision or abandonment. This is especially true over the long run, during which a country's support for various substantive components of a fiscal rule would almost certainly evolve.

The fourth feature is the extended transitionary period during which the rule gradually takes effect. Buchanan and Wagner's proposal specifies that the rule would be implemented over a period of five years, with a mandatory 20 percent annual deficit reduction (Buchanan and Wagner 2000, 188). A gradual transition can help raise the necessary political support to pass the rule because it provides time to negotiate any structural fiscal reforms that are needed to comply with the rule. The transition also serves to "minimize disruptions in established expectations of citizens, whether as program beneficiaries, taxpayers, or their political agents" (Buchanan 1997).

While not a part of the rule proposal in Buchanan and Wagner (2000), a related strategy for constitutional change in Buchanan's work that is highly relevant for fiscal rules is lagging the process of transition itself. Buchanan (1994) notes that in the United States, even constitutional fiscal rule proposals with long transition periods had generally failed to garner much public support. He argues that

> The transitional evidence seems clear that persons are unwilling to trade off the current or short-term utility losses that any shift toward a balanced-budget regime would involve in exchange for the future period utility gains that would ensure from the removal of the interest charges (or any part thereof) from future period income.

But this need not be the end of the story, as Buchanan proposes that lagging the transition would "enable individuals to escape from the pressures on their choice calculus by the immediacy of the promised utility losses consequent on the enforcement of the constraint." He writes that a hypothetical example would be "a constitutional amendment to be approved in 1993, to commence to be implemented in 1996, with final achievement of budget balance by 2002"—a temporal structure which he speculates might help secure general support for a rule. The temporal gap created by the lag can help overcome the present bias of agents and encourage a more long-term perspective.

The implementation of Germany's constitutional debt limit represents a case study of how both a lag and an extended transition could work. Germany's rule was approved in 2009 and began a gradual implementation in 2011, with the transition period lasting until 2016 for the national government and 2020 for the state governments (Feld and Reuter 2021). Discussing the

German rule, Janeba (2012) notes that a lag in combination with an extended transition makes a constitutional fiscal rule more palatable to both voters and politicians. Indeed, he argues that

> Political opportunism is likely to be one important reason for the delay between the legislative act and the effective implementation of fiscal rules. The costs of adjustment are passed on to future policymakers, who may differ from today's ones, and possibly to future generations or individuals who are not politically active today.

The delay in confronting these costs provides some measure of protection to current politicians, as a politician who "is forced by a balanced budget constraint to reject various claimants" may well be voted out, especially if voters are accustomed to fiscal largesse (Buchanan and Wagner 2000). On a general level, while the lagged and gradual implementation entails a weaker fiscal adjustment in the short term, it may be a necessary feature for a rule—especially a constitutional one—to garner enough public and political support to be implemented at all.

Rules as Symbols and Reflections of Values

Discussing fiscal rules in relation to the values of citizens is rare in the modern literature on rules. However, not only do Buchanan and Wagner explicitly argue that fiscal rules should reflect and express the values of citizens, but they also assert that this quality is the *most* important of the three qualities that they enumerate, "for then adherence to the precepts of the rule may, to some extent, be regarded as sacrosanct" (Buchanan and Wagner 2000, 183). In other words, while a constitutional rule is typically the strongest *political* commitment possible, the rule may still not be binding in practice if it is misaligned with voters' values. For example, breaking fiscal rules is a common occurrence: Reuter (2019) finds that for fifty-one national fiscal rules in force in EU member states from 1995 to 2015, the average compliance rate across all rules and countries was only around 50 percent, and Eyraud et al. (2018) indicate that similar compliance struggles exist outside of the EU as well.

If these rules had been part of the countries' respective constitutions, compliance rates would have likely been higher. However, it is nontrivial to implement such a constitutional rule, perhaps indicated by the fact that a select few countries have one. Drazen (2004) explains that

> Giving a provision constitutional status is meant to give it a permanence it would not otherwise have. In fact, the use of constitutional fiscal rules to achieve fiscal discipline may be seen as meant to send the signal that fiscal discipline

> is seen as an important or basic goal of society . . . "Constitutionalizing" a law sends the signal that a society sees the law as one not "to be tampered with."

Indeed, the few countries with constitutional rules empirically tend to have a preexisting proclivity for fiscal responsibility that a constitutional rule merely crystallizes—fiscal responsibility is seen as a "basic goal of society" and rules in accordance with achieving that goal are thus deemed by citizens as appropriate for constitutional inclusion. In Buchanan and Wagner's words, a constitutional rule specifically "makes sense" to them.

One country where this appears to be the case is Germany, which has become well-known for its cultural attitudes toward fiscal responsibility. The "black zero"—representing a balanced budget—has acquired widespread symbolic significance in German culture and is often referenced in speeches and debates related to fiscal issues. Schulteis (2023) argues that

> The longtime fixation on the black zero illustrates the extent to which a dislike for debt is deeply ingrained in German politics and society . . . many people rent rather than buy homes, credit cards are less widely used, and saving money is seen as a virtue . . . This attitude is even reflected linguistically: The word for debt, Schuld, literally means "guilt."

Others point out that the economic history of Germany likely contributed to the development of this attitude, as Germany experienced hyperinflation in the 1920s and the government encouraged saving and frugality to help recover from World War II (Schulteis 2023).

Germany's debt increased throughout the second half of the twentieth century (partially due to unification and other historical factors), leading to heightened public concern about debt sustainability. This concern eventually resulted in Germany adding a "debt brake" to the country's constitution (*Grundgesetz*) in 2009, which limits the structural deficit to 0.35 percent of GDP. The constitutional nature of the debt brake is an important feature. The *Bundesverfassungsgericht* (Constitutional Court) is powerful in German politics, and "the constitutionality of any political action taken therefore plays an important role in practically all political debates" (Thiele 2015). Noncompliance with the debt brake would have significant political and social consequences, especially given the broad support for the debt brake among German citizens—Hayo and Neumeier (2016) conducted a survey of 2000 representative citizens and found that 61 percent of respondents support the debt brake while only 8 percent opposes it.

Another country with a strong culture of fiscal responsibility is Switzerland, whose fiscal rule was added to the country's constitution in 2001 by popular vote with 85 percent support. Switzerland's federalist system with direct democracy presented minimal obstacles to rule adoption, especially since voters had experience with fiscal rules at the cantonal level and were worried about increased debt levels after recessions in the late 1980s and early 1990s (Merrifield and Poulson 2016). Beyond its constitutional basis, the practical elements of the rule are strikingly similar to what Buchanan and Wagner recommend and are perhaps even stricter. The rule mandates a (structural) balanced budget determined by ex-ante projections; any ex-post deficits are recorded in a notional account that must be paid off if it exceeds 6 percent of expenditures, and it includes an escape clause that can only be activated by a legislative supermajority in extraordinary circumstances (Davoodi et al. 2022). Interestingly, the description of the rule by Switzerland's Federal Department of Finance (FDF) emphasizes that while the rule is stringent and binding, it is still flexible due to its escape clause and measures to account for the business cycle, with the endurance of the rule through both the 2008 Global Financial Crisis and the Covid pandemic serving as a testament (FDF 2023). Minor adjustments have been made to the rule to extend the deadline for paying back debt accrued during the pandemic, but Switzerland's fiscal position remains perhaps the strongest in Europe.

Other countries in Europe have adopted constitutional rules, partially due to various requirements and recommendations in the EU's "Fiscal Compact" (Davoodi et al. 2022). However, while some constitutional provisions are designated as "fiscal rules" in datasets, such designations may belie their true nature. For example, Italy's constitutional fiscal rule "introduces the principle of a balanced budget in structural terms," but the "details and implementation principles" were left to the legislature to specify (Davoodi et al. 2022). Such rules are subject to the concerns about commitment and enforcement that Buchanan, Wagner, Selgin, and others have raised.

Despite these shortcomings, historical evidence suggests that even a weak constitutional rule may form a foundation for stronger constitutional rules in the future. Germany's debt brake replaced a constitutional but largely ineffective balanced budget rule that had been in place since 1949 (Thiele 2015). Peru passed a new constitution with a balanced budget rule in 1979 that was largely ignored for over a decade until constitutional reforms in 1993 clarified the rule and removed loopholes, resulting in consistently balanced budgets thereafter (Amick et al. 2019). In the 1990s, Switzerland's constitution included "the principle that the 'shortfall in the Confederation's statement of financial position must be paid off,'" but "the required debt reduction remained a dead letter" because politicians repeatedly came up with justifications for deferring it (FDF 2023).

The preexistence of constitutional fiscal rules relates to a broader question of where preferences for strong fiscal rules come from. As implied throughout this section, one origin of these preferences may be historical experiences with fiscal crises. Discussing fiscal reform broadly, Urrutia et al. (1989) argue that the present benefits of deficits may seem to outweigh potential future costs "unless people have suffered from severe inflation in the preceding years and have a good understanding of the costs of fiscal deficits." Thus, it makes sense that, as Leeper (2016) succinctly puts it, "fiscal crises spawn fiscal rules." However, only a few of the many countries that have experienced fiscal crises have *strong* fiscal rules. Other factors such as culture, political institutions, and political leadership are also important and worthy of further study to better understand how binding fiscal rules can be harmonized with citizens' values to encourage rule compliance and endurance.

CONCLUSION

Fiscal rules are not a perfect solution to debt problems at either the national or supranational level. Their historical record is decidedly mixed, and designing rules that are simple, flexible, binding, and insulated from political manipulation has proven difficult. However, proposed fiscal governance alternatives such as fiscal standards have many problems of their own. Using SDSA or similar methods to assess whether debt is "sustainable" inserts highly technical methodological debates into fiscal politics, thereby hindering communication with stakeholders and damaging the credibility of any adjustment requirements. Additionally, fiscal standards using SDSA would involve significant discretion at multiple levels of implementation, creating opportunities for politically motivated objections. Dani et al. (2021) reject the idea of fiscal standards and argue that

> instead of cloaking discretion, wrapping it up in legal norms or legal standards combined with contestable numerical indicators produced through tools such as SDSA, we need to frame it in the only way which is at the same time feasible and legitimate: democratic politics.

Focusing on democratic politics necessarily raises questions of enforcing any fiscal governance mechanisms in effect. Drazen (2004) argues that rules often do not work because "they don't address the case of fiscal bias; they attach no real costs to deviating from the rules; they attach no real costs to changing the rules." The constitutional approach that Buchanan and Wagner advocate for could greatly improve the effectiveness of fiscal rules primarily by enhancing enforceability, especially if the rules are simple and can be understood and monitored by citizens. Buchanan (1997) acknowledges that a fiscal rule "will not, directly, reduce or eliminate the pressures brought to bear on fiscal decision makers" and that politicians will try to avoid rules' constraints in various and creative ways, but he maintains that this "does not, however, support the conclusion that such a rule would not succeed in imposing fiscal constraint." A few countries like Germany and Switzerland have adopted effective constitutional rules similar to what Buchanan and Wagner recommend, and including features such as a lagged and gradual transition in constitutional rule proposals could help raise political support in other countries. Even though widespread adoption of constitutional fiscal rules remains unlikely, identifying why some fiscal rules have failed and why others have succeeded is an important step toward successful reform.

REFERENCES

"A Guide to the Public Finance Act." 2019. New Zealand Treasury. https://www.treasury.govt.nz/sites/default/files/2019-11/guide-pfa-2019.pdf

Amick, Joe, Terrence Chapman, and Zachary Elkins. 2020. "On Constitutionalizing a Balanced Budget." *The Journal of Politics* 82 (3): 1078–96.

"An Introduction to New Zealand's Fiscal Policy Framework." 2015. New Zealand Treasury. https://www.treasury.govt.nz/publications/guide/introduction-new-zealands-fiscal-policy-framework#how-does-our-fiscal-policy-framework-operate

Blanchard, Olivier, Alvaro Leandro, and Jeromin Zettelmeyer. 2021. "Redesigning EU Fiscal Rules: From Rules to Standards." *Economic Policy* 36 (106): 195–236.

Buchanan, James M. 1994. "Lagged Implementation as an Element in Constitutional Strategy." *European Journal of Political Economy* 10 (1): 11–26.

———. 1997. "The Balanced Budget Amendment: Clarifying the Arguments." *Public Choice* 90 (1/4): 117–38.

Buchanan, James M., and Richard E. Wagner. 2000. *Democracy in Deficit: The Political Legacy of Lord Keynes*. Indianapolis, IN: Liberty Fund.

Caselli, Francesca, and Julien Reynaud. 2020. "Do Fiscal Rules Cause Better Fiscal Balances? A New Instrumental Variable Strategy." *European Journal of Political Economy* 63 (June): 101873.

Clift, Ben. 2022. "Technocratic Economic Governance and the Politics of UK Fiscal Rules." *British Politics* 18: 254–278

Dani, Marco, Dario Guarascio, Joana Mendes, Augustin Jose Menendez, Harm Schepel, and Mike Wilkinson. 2021. "What Blanchard Gets Wrong: The Puzzling Persistence of Managerialism in EU Fiscal Governance." *EUROPP* (blog). 2021. https://blogs.lse.ac.uk/europpblog/2021/03/25/what-blanchard-gets-wrong-the-puzzling-persistence-of-managerialism-in-eu-fiscal-governance/

Davoodi, Hamid, Paul Elger, Alexandra Fotiou, Daniel Garcia-Macia, Andresa Lagerborg, W. Raphael Lam, and Sharanya Pillai. 2022. "Fiscal Rules at a Glance: An Update 1985–2021." Washington, DC: International Monetary Fund.

Debrun, Xavier, Luc Eyraud, Andrew Hodge, Victor Lledo, and Catherine Pattillo. 2018. "'Second-Generation' Fiscal Rules: From Stupid to Too Smart." *VoxEU*.

Org (blog). May 22, 2018. https://voxeu.org/article/second-generation-fiscal-rules-stupid-too-smart

Drazen, Allan. 2004. "Fiscal Rules from a Political Economy Perspective." In *Rules-Based Fiscal Policy in Emerging Markets*, edited by George Kopits, 15–29. London: Palgrave Macmillan UK.

Eyraud, Luc, Xavier Debrun, Andrew Hodge, Victor Lledo, and Catherine Pattillo. 2018. "Second-Generation Fiscal Rules: Balancing Simplicity, Flexibility, and Enforceability." *Staff Discussion Notes* 18 (04): 1–39.

FDF, Federal Department of Finance. n.d. "The Debt Brake." Accessed September 11, 2023. https://www.efd.admin.ch/efd/en/home/finanzpolitik/die-schuldenbremse.html.

Feld, Lars P., and Wolf Heinrich Reuter. 2021. "The German 'Debt Brake': Success Factors and Challenges." *Freiburger Diskussionspapiere zur Ordnungsökonomik*, No. 21/10. Albert-Ludwigs-Universität Freiburg, Institut für Allgemeine Wirtschaftsforschung, Abteilung für Wirtschaftspolitik und Ordnungsökonomik, Freiburg i. Br.

Hayo, Bernd, and Florian Neumeier. 2016. "The Debt Brake in the Eyes of the German Population." *International Economics and Economic Policy* 13 (1): 139–59.

Heinemann, Friedrich, Marc-Daniel Moessinger, and Mustafa Yeter. 2018. "Do Fiscal Rules Constrain Fiscal Policy? A Meta-Regression-Analysis." *European Journal of Political Economy* 51 (January): 69–92.

IMF. 2023. "Global Debt Database—Central Government Debt." 2023. https://www.imf.org/external/datamapper/CG_DEBT_GDP@GDD

Janeba, Eckhard. 2012. "Germany's New Debt Brake: A Blueprint for Europe?" *FinanzArchiv* 68 (4), 383–405.

Kopits, George, and Steven Symansky. 1998. *Fiscal Policy Rules*. Occasional Papers. Washington, DC: International Monetary Fund.

Leeper, Eric. 2016. "Should Central Banks Care About Fiscal Rules?" w22800. Cambridge, MA: National Bureau of Economic Research.

Leeper, Eric M., and Todd B. Walker. 2011. "Fiscal Limits in Advanced Economies." *Economic Papers: A Journal of Applied Economics and Policy* 30 (1): 33–47.

Lledo, Victor Duarte, Paolo Dudine, Luc Eyraud, Victor Duarte Lledo, and Adrian Peralta-Alva. 2018. *How to Select Fiscal Rules: A Primer*. Washington, DC: International Monetary Fund.

Mathieu, Catherine, and Henri Sterdyniak. 2013. "Do We Need Fiscal Rules?" *Revue de l'OFCE* 127 (1): 189–233.

Medas, Paulo, W. Raphael Lam, Daniel Garcia-Macia, Alexandra Fotiou, Andresa Lagerborg, Paul Elger, Xuehui Han, and Hamid Davoodi. 2022. "Fiscal Rules and Fiscal Councils: Recent Trends and Performance during the COVID-19 Pandemic." *IMF Working Papers* 2022 (011): 1–40.

Merrifield, John, and Barry Poulson. 2016. "Swedish and Swiss Fiscal-Rule Outcomes Contain Key Lessons for the United States." *The Independent Review* 21 (2): 251–74.

Reuter, Wolf Heinrich. 2015. "National Numerical Fiscal Rules: Not Complied With, but Still Effective?" *European Journal of Political Economy* 39 (September): 67–81.

———. 2019. "When and Why Do Countries Break Their National Fiscal Rules?" *European Journal of Political Economy* 57 (March): 125–41.

Schaechter, Andrea, Tidiane Kinda, Nina Budina, and Anke Weber. 2012. "Fiscal Rules in Response to the Crisis: Toward the 'Next-Generation' Rules: A New Dataset." *IMF Working Papers*, 2012/87. Washington, DC: International Monetary Fund.

Schuknecht, Ludger. 2004. "EU Fiscal Rules: Issues and Lessons from Political Economy." Working Paper Series 421. European Central Bank. https://econpapers.repec.org/paper/ecbecbwps/2004421.htm

Schulteis, Emily. 2023. "Post Pandemic and Russia's Invasion, Germany Debates Debt Brake, Spending to Confront New Fiscal Policy Challenges." *Foreign Policy*, 2023. https://foreignpolicy.com/2023/06/13/germany-debt-break-black-zero-spending-economics-climate-war-scholz/

Selgin, George. 2016. "Real and Pseudo Monetary Rules." *Cato Journal* 36 (2): 279–96.

Strupczewski, Jan. 2023. "Germany, France Clash over Reform of EU Fiscal Rules, Deal Seen by End-2023." *Reuters*, June 16, 2023, sec. U.S. Markets. https://www.reuters.com/markets/us/germany-france-clash-over-reform-eu-fiscal-rules-deal-seen-by-end-2023-2023-06-16/

Thiele, Alexander. 2015. "The 'German Way' of Curbing Public Debt." *European Constitutional Law Review* 11 (01): 30–54.

Truger, Achim, and Henner Will. 2013. "The German 'Debt Brake': A Shining Example for European Fiscal Policy?" *Revue de l'OFCE* 127 (1): 153–88.

Urrutia, Miguel, Miguel Urrutia Montoya, Shin'ichi Ichimura, and Setsuko Yukawa. 1989. *The Political Economy of Fiscal Policy*. Tokyo: United Nations University Press.

Wyplosz, Charles. 2023. "The European Commission's Expenditure Benchmark." Centre for Economic Policy Research (CEPR) Working Papers (121).

Chapter 5

"Human Wisdom"

What Plato Can Teach Us about Technocracy

Eryn Rozonoyer

This chapter will take up an old question, but one worth revisiting: to what extent should political power be placed in the hands of experts? That is to say, does the possession of expertise give one a right to political power? This is not a ridiculous question; of course, in many areas of life, we often seek out expertise and rely on it. Wouldn't you rather place your health in the hands of an expert doctor rather than a quack? When driving over a bridge, doesn't it give you peace of mind to think that that bridge was made by a skilled civil engineer rather than an unskilled one? Why should politics be the one arena in which those who lack expertise are thought to be just as worthy to participate as those who have it? The belief that the best rule is the rule by experts, that is, by those who possess *techne* (often translated as "art," "skill," or "craft"), has long been known as technocracy, and the fact that there is something that intuitively makes sense about technocracy is a challenge that democracy must tackle if it is to defend itself as the best form of political rule.

The challenge of technocracy has appeared in different guises throughout American history. Often, its most appealing form is something that might be termed managerial politics, administrative centralization (as Alexis de Tocqueville put it), or bureaucratic administration (as Vincent Ostrom put it). This approach sees politics as something that can be engineered and managed, and thus requires the expertise of those with the appropriate engineering and managerial skills. One can see the influence of this approach in many moments of American history. For instance, in the Progressive Era, during which Americans grappled with widespread corruption and crony capitalism that attended accelerating industrialization, the idea of reforming politics according to a new expert vision became appealing to many. The

Progressives faced a dilemma in the tension between their faith in expertise and their faith in direct democracy.

Woodrow Wilson, the father of modern public administration, might be considered a seminal example of the Progressive preference for expert management in politics. As the Princeton Chair of Jurisprudence and Political Economy, Wilson expressed his hopes for how the government could contrive general welfare "by a hundred and one limitations of the power of unscrupulous or heartless men to out-do the scrupulous and merciful in trade or industry," as he wrote in his textbook, *The State* (Wilson 1918, 65). In "The Study of Administration," Wilson famously described the polity as a sort of machine. Good government is a matter of "putting in new boilers," "new running parts," and fixing "old wheels and joints and valves" (Wilson 1887, 216). Politics, then, would be an engineering project, and those most suited to undertake the task would be those trained in the *techne* of political engineering: a vast bureaucracy of administrators tasked with keeping a complex industrial nation running smoothly.

In more recent times, the question of the role of expertise has resurfaced in the American consciousness. We wonder whether things would not be going better for us if we just trusted the experts to guide policy instead of holding onto more purely democratic ideals. Many might point to the 2016 and 2020 presidential elections as catalysts for Americans to begin to doubt self-government, or at least events that revealed how deeply this doubt had begun to creep. In February 2020, the Pew Research Center found that only 34 percent of Americans expressed "trust and confidence in the wisdom of American people in making political decisions." "As recently as 2007," Pew goes on to say, "that balance of opinion was almost the reverse, with 57 percent confident and just 42 percent not confident in their fellow citizens." Furthermore, it appeared that many Americans saw politicians as constituting a class separate from themselves rather than as representatives of their interests: 74 percent "say elected officials don't 'care what people like me think' and put their own interests first" (Dimock 2020).

The coronavirus pandemic was another event that caused deep divisions when it comes to trust in the experts that play a role in governmental decision-making. The pandemic occasioned an opportunity to evaluate whether scientific experts should be trusted to advise good policy decisions. Trust in these experts has split widely along partisan lines. The Pew Research Center found in February 2022 that "Among Democrats and Democratic-leaning independents, nine-in-ten express either a great deal (44%) or a fair amount (46%) of confidence in medical scientists to act in the public's best interests," while among Republicans, "Just 13% have a great deal of confidence in scientists" (Kennedy et al. 2022). However, even prior to the coronavirus, the partisan divide was strong. Pew found in 2019 that "Most Democrats (73%) believe scientists should take an active role in scientific policy debates. By contrast, a majority of Republicans (56%) say scientists should focus on establishing sound scientific facts and stay out of such policy debates" (Funk et al. 2019).

We hear a lot about the polarization of America, and the tension between those who prefer to trust experts when it comes to political decision-making versus those who demand unadulterated representation of the will of the people appears to play a large role in this polarization. On the one hand, some worry that as trust in institutions and even science itself erodes, the country is in danger of being hijacked by a backward and uneducated minority that inexplicably denies objective truths and selfishly seeks to assert its own partisan interests at the expense of the common good. Others believe that America faces a hostile takeover by a privileged, credentialed upper class who, on the basis of their "expertise," claim that they alone hold the knowledge necessary to run society, thereby denying that the people are capable of self-governance. It appears, at this point in history, that the question of the role of expertise in politics has become a critical point of contention among Americans. The challenge of technocracy, then, must be addressed head-on.

LITERATURE REVIEW

Much has been written about the role of expertise in political rule and about the question of technocracy. In various journals and online publications, articles both about democracy's inferiority to technocracy and about the danger of technocracy are published with some regularity. However, in recent years, especially since 2016, some successful books have appeared that call for an increased role for expertise in American politics. For instance, Tom Nichols' 2017 book *The Death of Expertise* laments what the author sees as the undermining of experts' reputation in the court of American public opinion. In his conclusion, Nichols blamed "all of the other dysfunctions" of American politics on "the abysmal literacy, both political and general, of the American public" (Nichols 2017, 216). Nichols gives many reasons why the trust of the American public in experts has collapsed, including grade inflation, an oversaturation of information stemming from the internet, and low-quality journalism. All these things, in his estimation, led to such political catastrophes as the 2016 presidential election. In Nichols's mind, the situation is grim: "Citizens of the Western democracies, and Americans in particular, no longer understand the concept of democracy itself" (Nichols 2017, 231).

The year before, Jason Brennan's 2016 book *Against Democracy* had gone even further, proposing that the American democratic political order should be eschewed in favor of "epistocracy," which would be a system of government in which only citizens who could prove they are "informed" would be allowed to vote (Brennan 2016, x). The book made a small stir, although reviewers generally recognized that Brennan's ideas could not simply be put into practice but remained a distant possibility. The obvious problems that would arise from implementing any kind of voter qualification test are not thoroughly examined in the book, but Brennan's basic point seems to be that the vast majority of people (whom he deems "hobbits and hooligans") are too uninformed about politics, either through apathy or through extreme partisanship, to be qualified to take part in government by voting. He implies that we should instead be ruled by those he calls "vulcans," who possess the intelligence and level-headedness to truly understand politics (Brennan 2016).

There has also been a recent interest in examining alternatives to liberal democracy which rely on meritocratic systems to place those with specialized knowledge in charge. For instance, Tongdong Bai's 2019 book *Against Political Equality*, Daniel Bell's 2015 book *The China Model*, and Joseph Chan's 2013 book *Confucian Perfectionism* all point to Confucianism as the root of a model of governance that can give power to the best members of society. These books wonder whether an infusion of Confucian-esque rule by experts might improve liberal democracy. As Bai puts it, Confucius sought a different ground for political legitimacy than "some sort of divine right of the king," which turns out to be a kind of competency (Bai 2020, 34). As the dust jacket summarizes, "Confucianism would give more political decision-making power to those with the moral, practical, and intellectual capabilities of caring for the people" (Bai 2020).

On the other hand, plenty of books have also been released that express skepticism about or seek to place limits on rule by experts. Roger Koppl's 2018 *Expert Failure* develops a theory of political expertise influenced by the study of economics. Koppl proposes that expertise fails to be useful when experts obtain a monopoly on authority. Instead, Koppl envisions expertise as a complex web in which different experts have different knowledge (due to specialization) and therefore must work according to a "division of labor" (Koppl 2018, 10). The result should be competition in a marketplace of experts, which in part takes the form of the possibility of opposing expert opinions coexisting, as well as a limitation on experts' political power. In a similar vein, Jeffrey Friedman's *Power Without Knowledge: A Critique of Technocracy* argues that technocracy has a fatal flaw due to a knowledge problem; technocrats are unable to fully account for and predict the way the people will make choices and behave. In order for technocracy to work even according to its own principles, argues Friedman, technocrats must possess an incredible amount and variety of information about the political problems that need solving. Such information cannot simply be presumed to be readily available—especially because, in Friedman's view, people are, in an essential way, unpredictable to each other due to "ideational heterogeneity" (Friedman 2019, 27).

The current chapter will not directly enter into the debate about whether liberal democracy is the best regime, as does *Against Democracy* or the books about China's alternative meritocratic model. Nor will it directly seek to evaluate the current problems with the American public's approach to politics, as does *The Death of Expertise*. This chapter seeks to engage the question of the role of expertise in politics in a different way. First of all, the chapter will focus on the theoretical or philosophical question of the legitimacy of the claim that the possession of some kind of knowledge qualifies one to rule, as well as what kind of knowledge that might be. The chapter will approach this question by way of the thought of Plato and will contribute to the conversation about the role of expertise in politics by highlighting Platonic ideas that have not yet been addressed by the important recent literature on the modern technocratic problem. In doing so, it will enter into dialogue with books like *Expert Failure* and *Power Without Knowledge* in an attempt to identify what kind of knowledge would be necessary for ruling experts to possess.

Why approach the question of the rule of experts through Plato? Many who write about technocracy point a finger at Plato as the originator of the whole idea. Plato's description of the "philosopher king" in the *Republic* often appears to be a simple recommendation of technocracy as the best regime. The prevalence of this reading of Plato can certainly be traced in part to Karl Popper's *The Open Society and Its Enemies*. Popper paints Plato as a proponent of a "closed society," a totalitarian regime in which the philosopher would suppress freedom (Popper 2020, Volume I). Popper takes Plato's Socrates' description of "kallipolis" as a prescriptive political program. Many have since agreed with Popper that Plato encouraged a proto-technocratic political order that is antithetical to liberal democracy and destructive of freedom.

Although Popper's condemnation of Plato as a totalitarian technocrat has been widely disseminated throughout the intellectual sphere, conversations about what Plato believed about technocracy, and conversations about the role expertise should play in politics in the modern world remain almost entirely separate. Returning to examine what Plato actually says in the *Republic* about the rule of the philosopher king—not just what Popper or other scholars attribute to him—might shed light on the root of the claim to rule that experts might possess, and therefore be germane to the question of modern technocracy. Plato might help us think through what exactly it would mean to possess the knowledge that would make one fit to have political power. Although the political world has obviously changed drastically since Plato's time, and this chapter certainly does not seek to make a case that Plato's ideas are any sort of precursor to or guide for how modern liberal democracies operate, those who wish to contribute to the modern debate about technocracy will need to think through the same things that Plato thought through. Whereas other recent work often seeks to diagnose and solve problems in modern politics or to compare technocratic and democratic regimes, my chapter proposes that preliminary work is first necessary: a return to directly face the question of what sort of expertise would make one fit to rule.

PLATO'S "TECHNOCRACY"

In his *Republic*, Plato famously describes the "philosopher king," who ascends from the cave of ignorance to glimpse the sun of the Good, and then "must be compelled, each in his turn, to use it as a pattern for ordering the city, private men, and themselves for the rest of their lives" (Plato 1968, 219). Apparently, Plato's answer to the question of who should rule is technocratic; the philosopher should rule because of the knowledge he possesses. This notion of the "philosopher king" is often credited as a quintessential example of rule by experts. My purpose is to find out what can be learned from Plato about the challenge of technocracy. What exactly did Plato hope for when he dreamed up philosopher kings? Was it what we all hope for when we believe experts can fix our politics?

To find out what kind of expertise the philosopher king has, we must find out who he is. Socrates describes philosophers and philosophy at length in various parts of the book, but the most famous image of the philosopher is the one presented in the famous allegory of the cave. In the cave, all men dwell in darkness, bound so that they must look at shadows projected onto a wall by the light of a fire. Having never seen anything else, they mistake these shadows for real objects. The philosopher is the one who escapes the cave and ascends to the upper world. In this bright upper world, illuminated by the sun, he is at first unable to see anything, but when his eyes adjust, he is able to see not merely shadows, but "things themselves." Eventually, he is even able to "make out the sun" (ibid., 195). This sun is an allegory for the Idea of the Good. Seeing the Good is what sets the philosopher apart from all other men and makes him capable of ordering the city. Knowledge of the Good, then, is what makes him fit to rule.

The Idea of the Good in the *Republic* is highly enigmatic. It is the culmination of the puzzling theory of forms. The Good has to do with the question of why things are what they are: what makes the universe intelligible. Eventually, because the forms are inadequate to answer this question, Socrates must go behind the forms to something beyond being itself, to the Idea of the Good, which is "what provides the truth to the things known and gives the power to the one who knows," and also is "the cause of knowledge and truth" but is different from either knowledge or truth, and "must receive still greater honor" than either (ibid., 189). Evidently, the content of the Good cannot simply be expressed, but whatever this Good might be, it somehow provides a "pattern" according to which the philosopher must rule the just city.

On the surface, Plato apparently thinks that the ideal city would be ruled by an elite king with specialized knowledge that makes him and only him fit to rule. But what conclusions can we draw from the complicated picture of the Good in the *Republic*? The specialized knowledge that justifies the rule of the philosopher-king is not any particular body of information, but a glimpse of the Good itself. As we have seen, the Good is not one subject among many, but the pattern that underlies all reality. Its relation to politics seems to be that it provides something like a vision that one must have in mind when practicing statecraft. In other words, it provides a vision of the goal or end of politics. This leads us to wonder: is the political knowledge imparted by a glimpse of the Good analogous to the kind of knowledge practitioners of other *technai* possess? The philosopher's right to rule is based on his vision of the Good, but is that the same thing as possessing political *techne*? Is politics indeed a *techne* at all?

The *Republic* seems to suggest that the knowledge prerequisite for "perfectly just" politics is not knowledge specific to politics. Knowledge of how to rule, then, does not seem to consist of a set of skills or facts that can be taught, as is the case with other *technai*. The knowledge of how to rule does not stand on its own but is grounded in knowledge of the Good. If one goes to medical school and learns all the knowledge and skills needed to become a doctor, one may become a good doctor, even without knowledge of non-medical subjects, but being a good ruler is not simply a matter of learning knowledge and skill in politics. Statecraft cannot be learned on its own without making reference to the Good.

Another Platonic dialogue, the *Apology*, sheds more light on the relationship between politics, philosophy, and *techne*. The *Apology* is Socrates' defense of his life of philosophy before the Athenian assembly; thus, it provides a look at who the philosopher might be in reality, not just in speech. In the *Apology*, Socrates does not describe transcending the rest of mankind by acquiring an elite knowledge as does the philosopher in the allegory of the cave. Rather, he considers himself to have spent his life honing a certain "human wisdom" (Plato 1980, 9). This human wisdom apparently consists not of any body of facts, but rather Socrates' knowledge of his own ignorance. He hones this wisdom by interviewing those who are esteemed as wise, as he is on a constant search to find someone wiser than himself. But invariably, all the people he talks to believe themselves to know more than they actually do. Since Socrates, who claims to know nothing, is at least aware of the limits of his knowledge, he has to conclude that these other people are not wiser than he: his "human wisdom," which makes him wiser than others, is his knowledge of his limitations.

Among the people Socrates describes interviewing in the *Apology* are the *hierotechnes*: the possessors of *techne*. Socrates acknowledges that these experts do possess some knowledge—knowledge of their craft—but he is dismayed to find that "on the strength of their technical proficiency they claimed a perfect understanding of every other subject, however important, and I felt that this error more than outweighed their positive wisdom" (ibid. 8–9). The "positive wisdom" that these experts possess is knowledge of their specific *techne*. The doctors do possess knowledge of medicine, the carpenters possess knowledge of carpentry, the cobblers possess knowledge of shoemaking, and so on. But the knowledge involved in each of these *technai* is limited to knowledge of the means necessary to achieve a certain end. The doctors know how to achieve good health, the carpenters know how to build a good house, the cobblers know how to make good shoes. Thus, technical knowledge is limited to knowledge of means; the end at which those means aim is implied in the *techne* itself. The mistake the *hierotechnes* make in the *Apology* is to think that this knowledge of means is broader than it actually is. They fail to see that their *techne* makes up only a part of their society; in claiming "perfect understanding of every other subject, however important," they overestimate the domain of their knowledge and lose the awareness of its partialness. Thus, practitioners of medicine, carpentry, or shoemaking, for instance, might consider that because they know how to produce good health, a good house, or a good pair of shoes, they also know how to solve problems in other domains of human life. Socrates' "human wisdom" is clear-sightedness about the limits of different types of knowledge, never mistaking knowledge of a part of the whole for the complete knowledge of all things that would only come by glimpsing the Good.

We might use the *hierotechnes*' lack of humility about their wisdom to consider the nature of politics and political wisdom. In some sense, politics *is* like a *techne*. Each *techne* strives toward some end: to make the house or bridge or shoe or health of the patient or whatever is being crafted as good as it can be. Politics is also oriented toward an end. But the end toward which politics aims, at least according to Plato, is to make the polity as good as it can be. In other words, politics aims at the good of the whole—the whole that is made up of the sum of all the people in a polity. But what could possibly justify saying that we know what is good for people? Other *technai* might be self-justifying in this sense; expertise in the *techne* of medicine or carpentry or cobblery makes one able to know what good health or a good house or a good shoe is. However, politics is not like this because the polity is not like health or houses, or shoes. The good of the polity, what is good for people, is not any partial good like the goodness of a good shoe or bridge, but the Good itself—partial knowledge of the Good is not enough. A shoe can be good, indeed very good, and thus reflect the Good, but this will always be a partial reflection because the goodness of the shoe is subordinate to some higher good. Cobblers aim at making good shoes for the sake of the higher aim of those shoes being used for the purposes of those who wear them. What, then, is the point of doing politics well? What exactly is the goodness of the good polity?

A good polity is a polity where people can live well; that is, politics is for the sake of the Good itself. Politics is inextricably linked to the question of what is good for human beings. This is why the truly just ruler must glimpse the Good as such; it is sufficient for the *hierotechnes* to gain only specialized, incomplete knowledge. The uncritical assumption that politics is a *techne* just like any other—and thus that the best polity can be engineered by those with the greatest expertise—does not recognize the difficult problem that is unique to politics. Unlike other *techne*, politics must have an immediate rather than a mediated relationship to the Good, since it must ultimately aim at what is good for people and thus what is good as such, rather than some partial goodness like the goodness of a good shoe.

People hold onto the hope that some sort of expertise is what justifies rule, and thus that all our political problems could be solved if only the right experts were in charge. In the *Republic*, Socrates takes this ordinary view seriously and carries it to its logical end. If some sort of knowledge is ultimately what justifies political rule, this knowledge must be nothing less than knowledge of the Good: the "cause" of all knowledge and truth. All existing polities fall short of this standard, because, despite what Socrates tells Glaucon, knowledge of the Good is not as simple as ascending from a cave and seeing the sun but is the culmination of the highest human excellence: something we can approach asymptotically but never pin down in our grasp. How then can we hope for technocracy?

Politics portrayed as a *techne* and thus as a matter of expertise therefore encounters something of a knowledge problem: it requires knowledge of the Good to justify itself, but the logic of its own principles cannot be used to discover the Good. Politics must look to something outside itself to ground itself. In Plato's view, this is philosophy, which turns men toward the Good even if all it ever really provides is a "human" wisdom about one's own ignorance. Yet political expertise would not be political expertise if it did not include knowledge of what legitimates political rule. It is not the political expert, but the Socratic philosopher who claims to lack political expertise, that can provide this. Thus, the impossibility of expert rulers giving an account of the knowledge on which their rule would be justified is the rock on which technocracy flounders. The "expertise" they would truly need to make rule by experts self-consistent would not be a body of knowledge or skills, but the never-ending project of human virtue. Lack of knowledge about the Good precludes the possibility of a science or *techne* of politics and puts a thorn in the side of those who would advocate for solving political problems by treating the polity as something that can be engineered or managed by those with specialized knowledge. Hayek remarked, "The curious task of economics is to demonstrate to men how little they really know about what they imagine they can design" (Hayek 2011, 76). A thorough understanding of Plato brings us to a similar sentiment: politics done properly would involve an education in the Good, and thus the cultivation of a certain human wisdom—that is, knowledge of our own ignorance.

THE MODERN DEBATE ABOUT TECHNOCRACY

What can the contemporary debate between technocrats and populists learn from Plato? Is there in fact anything that modern representative democracies can learn from an ancient Greek who could never have conceived of the course that the history of politics would take? It is, of course, tempting to treat Plato's political philosophy as a mere museum piece and to presume that the progress of history has rendered the world of Plato, and thus the thought of Plato, obsolete. But if we are to read Plato charitably, granting that in spite of his antiquity, his thought may in fact be at least partially right, we are compelled to consider the possibility that his political thought directly bears on contemporary politics. This is because if Plato is right and politics is ultimately concerned with the Good, and if the question of the Good must remain open, by definition, as previously indicated, the core of politics as the question of the Good is the same in ancient times as it is today. In other words, although the political regimes described in the *Republic* may look nothing like our modern representative democracies, all political orders are fundamentally similar insofar as they must ask the question of the Good. This means that ancient technocracy and modern technocracy may be susceptible to the same problems. Even though today's technocratic movements have arisen out of representative democracies, inasmuch as they also claim that specialized knowledge confers the right to political power, they fall prey to the same knowledge problem as the apparently technocratic philosopher king of the *Republic*.

However, to apply Plato's insights to the modern case for technocracy, the modern alternatives to technocracy must be considered. Today, technocracy is often contrasted with populism. Although, as we have seen, a careful analysis of Plato's thought points away from technocracy, this does not mean that Plato would favor the claims of modern populists. The modern debate between technocrats and populists centers around the question of whether we should look to the knowledge possessed by experts or to the "will of the people" in order to solve political problems. This is not a question about what is truly good for human beings or for the polity; it is a question about means, not ends. We do not spend so much time wondering what politics should be doing, but rather wonder which people we should turn to in order to get it done. In this way, both technocrats and populists miss Plato's argument for a continual awareness of our ignorance about the Good. Both sides miss the manner in which politics, unlike other techne, must always concern itself with ends rather than means.

Thus, the populist answer to technocracy does not arise out of a sober understanding of Plato's wisdom about the connection between politics and the Good, and we should not run from technocracy into its arms. The populists who rally against modern technocracy can learn from Plato as well. Rather than directly asking what is good, populists focus on the question of how the people might be represented: in doing so, they become absolutists about the unity of the people who are represented. Whether a leader represents "the people" becomes conflated with whether that leader does good politics. As Jan Werner-Muller puts it:

> In addition to being antielitist, populists are always *antipluralist* . . . The claim to exclusive representation is not an empirical one; it is always distinctly *moral.* When running for office, populists portray their political competitors as part of the immoral, corrupt elite; when ruling, they refuse to recognize any opposition as legitimate. The populist logic also implies that whoever does not support populist parties might not be a proper part of the people—always defined as righteous and morally pure. Put simply, populists do not claim "We are the 99 percent." What they imply instead is "We are the 100 percent." (*What is Populism*, 3)

In other words, populism, in trying to avoid the error of technocracy, which claims that the right to rule is founded on the possession of specialized knowledge, proposes instead that the right to rule is founded on representation of the people. As technocrats justify their position with the implicit assumption that expert rule will result in the best political outcomes, so do populists justify their position with the implicit assumption that the best political outcomes will be achieved when the people are most properly represented because the people are the best source of solutions. Neither asks: "what is truly good?"

What technocrats and populists have in common, then, is first that they both support their preferred political orders with the logic that some group (either experts or the proper representatives of "the people") has the legitimate right to rule because they are the ones suited to produce the best political outcomes. We still choose our preferred political orders because we believe that, in some sense, they are the "best regime," and see the legitimacy of political rulers—that is, the answer to the question "who should rule?"—as founded in their capacity to produce the best regime. But these questions have changed in our age insofar as they have become unmoored from the question "what is good?" This can be seen in the second characteristic that populists and technocrats have in common: neither of them can suffer competing views about what is good to be considered legitimate. Technocrats, in believing that they possess specialized knowledge that others lack, cannot justify listening to those who disagree with them. If only experts possess the knowledge necessary to rule, the only voice justifiably allowed in the public square is that of the experts. Similarly, in believing that the people are the ultimate foundation both of legitimate political power and of political judgment, populists "refuse to recognize any opposition as legitimate," as Werner-Muller puts it. In failing to truly ask the question "what is good?"—that is, in failing to acknowledge our ignorance about the answer to this question and instead treating it as already answered—both technocrats and populists are antipluralists.

Plato's lesson about the impossibility of classifying knowledge of what is truly good with other types of knowledge—and thus his implied admonition for humility about our ignorance of what is truly good—condemns not only technocracy but the entire contemporary debate between technocrats and populists. Plato is insistent in the *Republic* that the question "what is good?" appears at the very center of the best political regime as its guiding force. Yet we are tempted, in our age, to forget this question or uncritically identify it with other things. We conflate knowledge of the Good with expertise in other *techne*, or we conflate knowledge of the Good with being a member of "the people." In losing track of the question about what is truly good and the role it plays in politics, we also lose the humility that would come with an awareness of our ignorance about this question.

WHAT IS TO BE DONE?

If Plato teaches that politics must always have before it the question "what is good?" but never lose sight of man's ignorance of the answer to that question, how is politics to be conducted? One takeaway must be that the kind of antipluralism found in both technocracy and populism, which stems from an unthoughtful assumption that the Good is already known and thus differing views cannot be tolerated, must be abandoned. A modern political order that reflects Plato's ancient wisdom about the Good must reopen the question of the Good by allowing for those with differing answers to this question to interact and negotiate with each other. This is, of course, not what Plato actually recommends in the *Republic* or in other dialogues; however, Plato's dialogues are dialogues, not treatises or prescriptive arguments; their purpose is to shed light on philosophical questions rather than to recommend policy. As we have seen, Plato does not only advocate for rule by a philosopher king but he also implies that the ideal philosopher-king regime is impossible in reality.

Given that we cannot institute a philosopher king with true knowledge of the Good, how do we foster both inquiry into the question of the Good, and knowledge of our ignorance of the Good in modern politics? What is the alternative to the antipluralist tendencies of both technocracy and populism? I do not wish to suggest that the answer is moral relativism or Isaiah Berlin-style pluralism. Rather, there must be a shift in the way we think about solving political problems that emphasize intellectual humility and reject the idea that a single center of power can know and administer the Good for the whole polity.

In *Technopopulism*, Christopher J. Bickerton and Carlo Invernizzi Accetti find that there is a "deep affinity" between populism and technocracy "which consists in the fact that they are both unmoored from the representation of specific values and interests within society and therefore advance an *unmediated concept of the common good*, in the form either of a monolithic conception of 'the popular will,' or the specific conception of political 'truth' technocrats claim to have access to" (2021, original italics). As Bickerton and Accetti see it, the version of the Good that populism and technocracy consider is identified with "a monolithic conception of 'the popular will'" or "the political 'truth' technocrats claim to have access to" respectively. If populists do not distinguish the popular will from the common good, and if technocrats do not distinguish expert truth from the common good, they must have conflated means with ends. Bickerton and Accetti do not explicitly draw this conclusion, but they contrast the "unmediated" version of the Good advanced by populism and technocracy with "specific values and interests within society." They further argue that neither technocracy nor populism is aligned with "the traditional conception of party democracy as a system of 'regulated rivalry' between competing social interests and values that are all in principle equally legitimate" (Bickerton 2021, 3).

Although a thorough reading of Plato reveals his criticism of those who believe they have the answers to politics without having turned toward an examination of the Good, it is not easy to find a positive alternative teaching about how politics should be approached—especially one that would be usable in the modern political landscape. However, perhaps following the logic of *Technopopulism* can lead us to the following conclusion: if both technocracy and populism fall prey to the Platonic fallacy of failing to consider the Good, an alternative might be a sort of "regulated rivalry" that focuses on "specific values and interests within society," something that

Technopopulism identifies as lacking in both technocracy and populism. In order to avoid a political landscape in which consideration of the question of the Good is foreclosed by the attitude that disputation cannot be brooked, the sort of political activity in which actors with diverse viewpoints must solve real problems might prompt conversation to reopen—if not conversation about Plato's metaphysical idea of the Good, at least conversation about how a political community might best be served in specific situations.

The sort of "regulated rivalry" that must take place between those who compete to serve specific political interests would facilitate an emphasis on which outcomes are better than others, rather than merely debating which group has the best claim to power. In this way, the focus of political life would return to questions about the Good by asking about ends instead of means—although these questions would be about partial versions of the Good and not the Good itself (which, if we follow Plato's thought, is a subject matter for philosophy). Solving problems like how to distribute goods, provide access to services, or rebuild a community after a disaster would necessitate real thinking, if only in an oblique way, about the partial goods that these tasks have as their ends. The attempt to solve specific problems like this can and must lead to a consideration of the broad problem of what we want our society to look like—in other words, the Good at which politics aims. This would be by far preferable to a focus on choosing whom to appoint as the problem-solvers in this situation, and then sitting back and assuming that a single decision-making center composed of the "correct" politicians must produce the best outcomes.

Polycentricity might be a principle that, if adopted, will help catalyze this shift. Michael Polanyi, who first described polycentricity in *The Logic of Liberty*, began with the example of the scientific community, which he saw as "the body of a great and good society" (Polanyi 1951, 6). According to Polanyi, the members of the scientific community were characterized by two things: first, they were united in their dedication to the goal of discovering the truth. And second, they were able to make progress toward that goal inasmuch as science proceeds not like building a house, which requires a preexisting blueprint, but rather like a "polycellular organism," in which "the individual efforts of independent scientists" results in overall growth (ibid., 88). Polanyi argues that the scientific community, vis-a-vis the example of "a great and good society," works through many independent researchers all striving toward the same goal, but in such a way that many different views must exist simultaneously because that goal is not and by nature cannot be enforced by a single authority.

Polanyi applies the logic of his example of the scientific community to many different realms, including economics. He identifies "a big problem to be solved for a rational distribution of goods": a knowledge problem similar to the one identified by Hayek (ibid., 140). Polanyi holds that economic problems are polycentric problems that cannot be solved rigorously. Therefore, economic problems cannot be solved by a central authority but must be solved by a process similar to the one used by the scientific community; various independent actors must pursue the goal (in this case, something like economic prosperity) in such a way that the whole system is buoyed along toward the goal as if by an invisible hand, without the intervention of a central authority who directs these individual actors.

It is worth wondering whether the principle of polycentricity might be able to help us solve the political knowledge problem that can be deduced from Plato's *Republic* in a similar way that Polanyi suggests that it can solve the economic knowledge problem. Politics might be said to have a similar abstract goal (the Good) to that of science (truth), and like the goal of science, the goal of politics is not able to be worked out in advance and thereby administered by a single authority. Instead, political problems might be best solved by a multitude of centers of authority. In this polycentric way, the aim of the Good could still be pursued when solving political problems without it being presumed that the answer to the question of the Good is already known by some person or group (for instance, experts or "the people"). Furthermore, the polycentric emphasis on solving problems by incorporating input from a multitude of sources, including both political and nonpolitical organizations, can help avoid the antipluralism described in *What is Populism* and encourage intellectual humility. Being forced to contend with and select from opposing viewpoints assumes that any one decision-making center is unlikely to have all of the answers.

What this would mean in action would be a return to the ethos of self-government—not, perhaps, in the populist sense, but following the example of early America. Tocqueville described the early New England township system as the first stage of American political life. According to Tocqueville,

> In the township as everywhere, the people are the source of social powers, but nowhere do they exercise their power more immediately. The people in America are a master who has to be pleased up to the furthest limits of the possible. (Tocqueville 2000, 59)

Citizens of the township fill many public offices and take care of their own township's administrative affairs rather than relying on an administrative state. Although Tocqueville expressed many nuanced ideas about the advantages and disadvantages of early America, as well as about the possibility of its brand of self-governing democracy achieving longevity, at the time he visited America he was impressed with the way in which Americans resisted the tyranny of the majority through the absence of administrative centralization. He describes how

> Municipal bodies and the administrations of counties . . . form so many hidden shoals that delay or divide the flood of the popular will. Were the law oppressive, freedom would still find shelter in the manner in which the law was executed. (Tocqueville 2000, 250–251)

Thus, Tocqueville describes how the principles of self-governance and polycentricity in early America helped it to achieve its political success.

Of course, Tocqueville's early America cannot simply be recreated, but some thinkers like Vincent and Elinor Ostrom have used Tocqueville's insights into the advantages of polycentric political order to propose that a more polycentric approach be taken when solving various political problems today. Vincent Ostrom calls this "democratic administration," which he contrasts with Woodrow Wilson's famous theory of administration that looked to a single center of authority as the source of solutions (Ostrom 2008, Chapter 4). Instead, Ostrom suggests that Tocqueville recognized a polycentric alternative in which political administration is achieved through multiple self-governing segments of society. Such a system would have an advantage over Wilsonian bureaucratic administration when it comes to encouraging human wisdom and keeping the question of the Good open. Ostrom hoped that a system of democratic administration inspired by Tocqueville would recreate the conditions that inspired Tocqueville's remark: "every man is daily reminded of the need of meeting his fellow men, of hearing what they have to say, of exchanging ideas, and coming to an agreement as to the conduct of their common interests" (quoted in Ostrom 2008, 85). This corresponds to the "value heterogeneity," the irreducible variety in human viewpoints about the Good, which the Ostroms' writings "take for granted—without assuming that it can or, in most cases, should be aggregated away." The Ostroms took this principle of value heterogeneity and used it to re-envision "how a good political system looks":

> The goal is not to look for the best way to aggregate values into a single coherent system but instead to seek the best way in which heterogeneous, incommensurable, and incomparable values can coexist and if not enrich at least not undermine one another. (Aligica et al. 2019, 124)

In other words, a polycentric approach to political life would require differing opinions about the Good to come into dialogue. In another work, Vincent Ostrom wrote,

> If the conditions applicable to polycentric orders can be generalized to apply to all patterns of order in a society, we might then meet the conditions specified

> by Madison in essay 51 of *The Federalist* where he suggests that "this policy of supplying by opposite and rival interests, the defects of better motives, might be traced through *the whole system of human affairs, private as well as public.*" (original italics; Ostrom 2014, 45)

Those who conceived of the pattern of early American governance, including Madison, recognized the advantage of rivalry between interests. In Plato's language, we might call this rivalry between different partial understandings of the Good. The negotiation between these different understandings, which is necessitated by human life, can "supply the defects of better motives" by facilitating a closer examination of the Good—rather than leaving us with an unexamined, partial view of the Good that we mistake for a complete view—which is something we do when we presume that the ends of political life are already known and the primary question is which group should be given the power to pursue them.

This negotiation between competing opinions about the Good provides two advantages. First, we can come to the realization that our own views of the Good, like all views of the Good, are partial. We do not in fact know the Idea of the Good, which encompasses all knowledge in the world. We can recognize that the way we prefer to do things is not always the best way to do things, that we do not always know what is good for other people, and that others who disagree with us about what is good might actually possess some knowledge we lack. This pattern of coming to an awareness about our own ignorance through negotiating with those who disagree with us takes the same pattern as Plato's dialogues. In all of the dialogues, Plato presents interlocutors arguing for their own opinions, and the reader is made to understand the defects, advantages, and ultimately the partiality of the truth of those opinions. We might even say that Plato's dialogues present a literary version of an ideal political community: people with opposing views are able to engage with each other in a peaceful and productive way such that new truths are revealed, which the interlocutors had not previously seen. Second, the negotiations that take place between members of polycentric systems allow for opinions about the Good to not only be examined intellectually but also tested in the practical sphere. As Aylon R. Manor remarks, "practical orthodoxies—customs—pose a problem for progress if they are institutionalized in a way that prevents alternatives from being tested and explored" (Manor 2021, 362). It makes sense that "exploring" alternative solutions to political problems through multiple decision-making centers would produce better outcomes. The self-government which the early Americans practiced was an example of this kind of experimentation. Thus, George Washington wrote, "The establishment of our new Government seemed to be the last great experiment, for promoting human happiness, by reasonable compact, in civil Society" (Letter to Catharine Sawbridge Macaulay Graham, 1790).

It is not difficult to see how a lack of interest in self-governance can lead to a preference for monocentric political order over polycentric political order. Perhaps one of the major political problems America faces today is that many of its people would prefer to be told what the Good is, and have it enforced upon them by an authority, than to engage in the never-ending work of participating in self-governance and solving political problems in a way that reflects the complexity of the world. In their 2002 book *Stealth Democracy: Americans' Beliefs About How Government Should Work*, John Hibbing and Elizabeth Theiss-Morse found that a large portion of the American public finds politics distasteful. These Americans believe that political problems should be solved by "ensids"—empathetic, non-self-interested decision-makers—rather than participating in the political process themselves through self-governance (Hibbing 2002, 161). According to Hibbing and Theiss-Morse, Americans' preferred political process would be something that happens behind the scenes through the work of these benevolent ensids, who need not engage in the messy process of negotiating between competing opinions about what is Good because the common good of the polity is already manifest to them. Governing would be simply a matter of implementing obvious solutions. As the introduction of the book explains,

> We show that people want to distance themselves from government not because of a system defect but because many people are simply averse to political conflict and many others believe political conflict is unnecessary and an indication that something is wrong with governmental procedures. People believe that Americans all have the same basic goals, and they are consequently turned off by political debate and deal making that presuppose an absence of consensus. (ibid., 7)

This rule by ensids is about as far as we can get from the townships observed by Tocqueville, in which ordinary citizens self-governed by serving in political positions that were essential to the township's functioning and were compelled to negotiate between their differing viewpoints. Hibbing and Theiss-Morse's work indicates that in the extreme difference between the ethos of the sovereignty of the people and the current "stealth democracy," distaste for political participation is in part characterized by contemporary Americans' belief in consensus—that is, our disbelief in the fact that we (or our representative ensids) do not in fact possess knowledge of the Good, and that the question of the Good is still open, and therefore competing opinions about it must be considered as legitimate contenders in the political process. In fact, we can now see how a failure to acknowledge our ignorance about the Good, and our belief that someone with the right specialized knowledge could simply figure out all the best political solutions, results in an odd vision of what the political process should look like.

CONCLUSION

Although Plato has often been considered a proto-technocrat due to his apparent advocacy of rule by philosopher-king in the *Republic*, a closer examination of the knowledge that legitimates the philosopher-king's rule reveals a different picture. Plato's Socrates wryly suggests that the ruler of the ideal polity must possess knowledge of the Good, which turns out to be something that cannot simply be acquired. Rather, the knowledge of the Good which would constitute expertise in ruling is tantamount to knowledge of the deepest mysteries of metaphysics, epistemology, and ethics. After all, the Good is that which is responsible for the being of everything, the possibility of things being known, and all of man's motivations. Thus, Plato highlights how politics is unlike any other domain in which one can become an expert; whereas other fields can be mastered through technical knowledge of the partial domain with which they are concerned, politics concerns itself with all of human life, and thus with the Good in the most complete sense. To have the expertise that confers the right to rule would mean knowing the Good as such, and thus knowing everything: something impossible in a human lifetime. Socrates, who dedicated himself to the pursuit of this knowledge, claimed to have attained only knowledge of his own ignorance. We might conclude, then, that humble awareness of our limitations when it comes to political expertise is as much as we can hope to attain.

In practice, the world of contemporary politics might seem too far removed from Plato's world for his thought to bear on our political problems. However, the question of whether rule by experts would produce the best political outcomes is still relevant. The modern political world includes—or perhaps is plagued by—the debate between technocrats and populists. Plato can help us see that not only are the technocrats mistaken in their presumption that good politics is a matter of expertise in the manner of other *techne* but also that the entire debate between technocrats and populists over who should rule has forgotten that the question of the Good, which lies at the center of politics, must remain open. Advocates of both technocracy and populism focus on the means of politics—which rulers will achieve their desired outcomes—rather than its ends. In doing so, they foreclose the possibility of negotiation between competing views of the Good, which leads to forgetting the fact that every view of the Good, no matter whose, must be partial. Such logic is blinded by its lack of humility.

Applying Plato's wisdom to modern democracies would require an emphasis on properly investigating the ends at which politics aims. It would also mean a move away from the reasoning that leads to the conclusion that any single center of political power can simply discover what is best and implement it (and that therefore the task of citizens is to put the "right" people in power). Instead, citizens of democracies must take it upon themselves to engage in questioning the Good. This need not mean becoming philosophers as Plato describes them in the *Republic*. Rather, citizens can participate in governance while investigating the Good by solving political problems themselves. This can be achieved through structuring politics in a polycentric way such that political problems are worked on by multiple decision-making centers simultaneously. Polycentricity allows for more people to be involved in the solutions to political problems and requires that those with competing views of the best outcomes and how to achieve them must exchange ideas. Thereby, progress can be made through testing competing views and questioning what is truly best—which also leads away from the idea that anyone can have a complete understanding of the Good. The result would be a form of governance that exhibits Socrates' humble "human wisdom."

REFERENCES

Aligica, Paul Dragos, Peter J. Boettke, and Vlad Tarko. 2019. *Public Governance and the Classical-Liberal Perspective: Political Economy Foundations*. New York, NY: Oxford University Press.

Bai, Tongdong. 2020. *Against Political Equality: The Confucian Case*. Princeton, NJ: Princeton University Press.

Bickerton, Christopher J. and Carlo Invernizzi Accetti. 2021. *Technopopulism: The New Logic of Democratic Politics*. New York: Oxford University Press.

Brennan, Jason. 2016. *Against Democracy*. Princeton, NJ: Princeton University Press.

De Tocqueville, Alexis. 2000. *Democracy in America*. Translated by Harvey C. Mansfield and Delba Winthrop. Chicago: University of Chicago Press.

Dimock, Michael. 2020. "How Americans View Trust, Facts, and Democracy Today." Pew.org. February 19, 2020. https://www.pewtrusts.org/en/trust/archive/winter-2020/how-americans-view-trust-facts-and-democracy-today.

Friedman, Jeffrey. 2019. *Power Without Knowledge: A Critique of Technocracy*. Oxford: Oxford University Press.

Funk, Cary, Meg Hefferon, Brian Kennedy, and Courtney Johnson. 2019. "Trust and Mistrust in Americans' Views of Scientific Experts." Pew Research Center Science & Society. Pew Research Center Science & Society. August 2, 2019. https://www.pewresearch.org/science/2019/08/02/trust-and-mistrust-in-americans-views-of-scientific-experts/.

Hayek, Friedrich A. 2011. *The Fatal Conceit: The Errors of Socialism*. Chicago: University of Chicago Press.

Hibbing, John R. and Elizabeth Theiss-Morse. 2002. *Stealth Democracy: Americans' Beliefs About How Government Should Work*. Cambridge: Cambridge University Press.

Kennedy, Brian, Alec Tyson, and Cary Funk. 2022. "Americans' Trust in Scientists, Other Groups Declines." Pew Research Center Science & Society. February 15, 2022. https://www.pewresearch.org/science/2022/02/15/americans-trust-in-scientists-other-groups-declines/.

Koppl, Roger. 2018. *Expert Failure*. Cambridge: Cambridge University Press.

Manor, Aylon R. 2021. "Experiments in Living: Moral Polycentricity versus Epistemic Polycentricity." *Social Theory and Practice* 47 (2): 351–375.

Nichols, Tom. 2017. *The Death of Expertise: The Campaign against Established Knowledge and Why It Matters*. New York: Oxford University Press.

Ostrom, Vincent. 2008. *The Intellectual Crisis in American Public Administration (Third Edition)*. Tuscaloosa, AL: University of Alabama Press.

Ostrom, Vincent and Elinor. 2014. *Choice, Rules, and Collective Action: The Ostroms on the Study of Institutions and Governance*. Wivenhoe Park: ECPR Press.

Plato. 1980. "Apology." In *The Collected Dialogues of Plato*. Translated by Hugh Tredennick. Princeton, NJ: Princeton University Press.

Plato. 1991. *The Republic of Plato*. Translated by Allan Bloom. New York: Basic Books.

Polanyi, Michael. 1951. *The Logic of Liberty: Reflections and Rejoinders*. Chicago: University of Chicago Press.

Popper, Karl R. 2020. *The Open Society and Its Enemies*. Princeton, NJ: Princeton University Press.

Werner-Muller, Jan 2016. *What is Populism?* Philadelphia, PA: University of Pennsylvania Press.

Wilson, Woodrow. 1887. "The Study of Administration." *Political Science Quarterly* 2 (2): 197–222.

———. 1918. *The State: Elements of Historical and Practical Politics*. Boston, MA: DC Heath & Co., Publishers.

Chapter 6

James M. Buchanan and the Unromantic Rhetoric of Public Choice

Alexander W. Morales

James M. Buchanan's primary contribution to political thought was the concept of public choice, which applied economic reasoning to political activity and constituted a fundamental challenge to orthodox thinking about politics. Influenced by the theoretical work of Swedish economist Knut Wicksell, Buchanan criticized the prevailing assumption that governments were made up of "benevolent despots" who effortlessly made policy decisions based on what they determined to be socially optimal. As Buchanan himself argued, governments should not be conceived "as some supra-individual decision-making agency," but as a "complex of institutions through which individuals make collective decisions" (2000, 4). Above all, Buchanan upheld that the provisioning of public goods and services should ultimately be determined by voluntary agreements among members of a political community, a view he characterized as "politics as exchange" (Buchanan 1999, 2000a, 2000b). In this regard, Buchanan conceived public choice as an approach that would replace "romantic and illusory notions about the workings of governments and the behavior of persons who govern" with "a set of notions that embody skepticism about what governments can do and what governors will do" (1999, 46). For Buchanan, understanding political behavior from an economic vantage point required an awareness of how individuals actually participate in political processes and how institutions (i.e., the rules of the game) shape political action.

Buchanan's public choice perspective also challenged the professional hubris and scientific enthusiasm that he associated with the Samuelsonian and Keynesian revolutions in economics. As Peter Boettke and Alain Marciano argue, the innovations of Paul Samuelson and John Maynard Keynes encouraged many twentieth-century economists to adopt "a progressive policy science approach that saw economics as [a] tool of social control rather than as a framework for social understanding" (2015, 54). Buchanan, among many others, rejected this autocratic posture of modern economists and denounced the hyper-specialization of the economics profession. "I want economists to quit concerning themselves with allocation problems," Buchanan declared, because once economic problems are framed in such terms, "our whole study becomes one of applied maximization of a relatively computational sort" (Buchanan 1964, 33). "If there is really nothing more to economics that this," he added, "we [might] as well turn it all over to the applied mathematicians" (1964, 33). Ultimately, Buchanan was perturbed by the *follies* of modern economics, and for this reason he attempted to persuade his professional colleagues to

> exorcise the maximizing paradigm from its dominant place in our tool kit, that we quit defining our discipline, our "science," in terms of the scarcity constraint, that we change the very definition, indeed the very name of our "science," that we stop worrying so much about the allocation of resources and the efficiency thereof, and, in place of this whole set of ideas, that we commence concentrating on the origins, properties, and institutions of exchange, broadly considered. (Buchanan 2000b, 16)

In this way, Buchanan's new framework of public choice denounced the mathematical or managerial bent of his profession and promoted an alternative understanding of political processes, which he defined in terms of the voluntary agreements and social interactions among individuals within clearly defined institutional contexts. In doing so, Buchanan articulated a more modest role for political economists as assisting "individuals, as citizens who ultimately control their own social order, in their continuing search for those rules of the political game that will best serve their purposes" (2016, 58). The political economist, in other words, was presented as a humble guide toward social understanding rather than a benevolent bureaucrat bent on social control.

Overturning the hubris associated with mainstream economics led Buchanan to rethink the foundations of economic analysis, but he also used rhetoric to persuade his contemporaries to embrace a new conception of the economics profession. He transformed what political economists did, in other words, by redefining what it meant to study politics from an economic perspective. For instance, Buchanan argued throughout his career that his mission was to encourage readers to see the world "from different vantage points, through different windows" (2000, 3). In this way, Buchanan argued that public choice is "not a method" nor "a set of tools" but is instead "a perspective on politics" that reorients how political economists perceive their subject matter and their role as professional scholars (2000, 15). "The great majority of modern economists," he writes, "do not really think much about the process of government, and when they do, they adopt implicitly the same broad conceptions that the orthodox political scientist adopts" (2000, 13). By viewing "some aspects of our world, specifically our world of politics," through a public choice window, Buchanan argues that economists would be able to "model the realities rather than the romance of political institutions" (1979, 46). In so doing, Buchanan utilized specific rhetorical techniques to frame his public choice perspective as a realistic, pragmatic alternative to the romantic, illusory approaches commonly used by his contemporaries. This chapter thus examines how Buchanan rhetorically framed public choice as "an exciting and new field of theoretical inquiry" that merged the disciplines of politics and economics in ways that "promise to attract more and more young scholars in the decades ahead" (2000, 14).

Interdisciplinary scholars have thoroughly expounded the nuances and tensions of Buchanan's public choice approach to politics, but they have largely overlooked how he used persuasive language to transform how professional economists discussed their own discipline. To be sure, political economists have done an excellent job highlighting the importance of rhetoric for advancing economic ideas (Boettke 2012, 2021; McCloskey 1998; Ostrom 1997, 2008). Public choice economists, for instance, have shown a rhetorical sensitivity when investigating political entrepreneurship (Martin and Thomas 2013), interjurisdictional competition (Lemke 2016), the social costs of rent-seeking (Choi and Storr 2019), and how culture shapes economic processes (Cowen 1998; Lavoie and Chamlee-Wright 2000; Hirschman 2003). In fact, Stefanie Haeffele and Virgil Storr maintain that focusing on the rhetorical strategies of political actors "complements public choice economics" by explaining "why certain policies are deemed acceptable even when their costs outweigh their benefits" (2021, 2). Similarly, Buchanan cared deeply about how economic ideas were communicated and even described his own works as "essay[s] in persuasion" because they attempted to reorient how his contemporaries perceived both their professional responsibilities and their subject matter (1999, 29). It appears, therefore, that the objective of Buchanan's writing was to persuade his audience to reconsider how they understood the economic profession by changing how people discussed politics.

This chapter, thus, examines how Buchanan communicated his public choice perspective to an audience with diverse and conflicting predispositions. Through a rhetorical analysis of Buchanan's persuasive works—namely, selected passages from his Inaugural Lecture "Politics without Romance" (1973) and his Nobel Prize lecture "The Constitution of Economic Policy" (1987)—this chapter demonstrates how Buchanan appeals to his audience through an ethos that frames public choice economists as having three qualities: good sense (*phronesis*), good will (*eunoia*), and good moral character (*arete*). This analysis is significant because it reveals how Buchanan was able to challenge orthodox approaches to political and economic processes by framing public choice as a morally significant perspective that, when fully embraced, constrains the scope and autocratic proclivities of mainstream economists. What I describe as Buchanan's *unromantic rhetoric* thus denotes how he attempted to persuade his audiences to embrace his public choice perspective by demonstrating the virtues he associated with the mainline tradition of political economy.

This argument unfolds in three sections. First, I establish a framework for analyzing Buchanan's persuasive communication by reviewing the rhetoric of science literature. This literature review includes research on how prominent scientists have utilized rhetorical techniques to accommodate their ideas to public and professional audiences. Second, I explain the rhetorical concept of ethos and its significance within a tradition Peter Boettke characterizes as "mainline economics" (2012, xvii). Third, I analyze how Buchanan framed his public choice perspective as a morally virtuous alternative to mainstream understandings of political processes. In doing so, this chapter builds on two assumptions that have been previously expressed by public choice economists: first, rhetorical analysis does indeed complement public choice economics and, second, "the words we use [represent] the most fundamental part of human reality," as Vincent Ostrom puts it (1997, 8).

SCIENTIFIC PERSUASION: HOW SCIENTISTS MAKE KNOWLEDGE MEANINGFUL

As the core of humanist learning through at least the seventeenth century, the study of persuasion, what ancient Greeks named rhetoric, did not belong to a specific set of subjects but had universal implications for them all. Students of rhetoric were taught to craft persuasive arguments and learned critical concepts that would allow them to read texts in any subject with understanding (Crowley and Hawhee 1999). Even scientific subjects (e.g., astronomy and mathematics) were seen as spaces that required a rhetorical sensitivity since persuasion demanded an awareness of one's audience and the kinds of arguments that would win their favor. Economics is no different. In fact, Deirdre McCloskey argues that "what distinguishes good from bad economists . . . is additional sophistication about the rhetoric" used to advance economic ideas (1998, 5). Good economists, McCloskey adds, can understand and thoroughly explain the substance and style of scientific arguments. And yet, because of the present-day view of economic scientists, the fact that someone like Buchanan used rhetoric to advance his ideas may trouble those who, as Bruno Latour observed, consider "rhetoric [as] a fascinating albeit despised discipline"; as something that obstructs inquiry rather than promotes it (1987, 30). However, I argue that studying how prominent scientists communicate their ideas can continue to help scholars understand how rhetoric influences the development and public perception of scientific disciplines.

Most notably, rhetorical scholars over the past several decades have underscored how scientific and technical documents are amenable to rhetorical scrutiny (Campbell 1995; Fahnestock 2005; Harris 2018, 2020). "On the whole," Leah Ceccarelli writes, rhetoricians of science "have done an excellent job of showing that rhetorical analysis can provide novel and intriguing commentary on the prototypical scientific text and its place in history" (2001, 3). Without adopting the totalizing view that science is "merely rhetoric," Ceccarelli argues that "most of those who read this literature recognize that scientists are indeed advocates for their own theories" and that successful scientists are often those individuals "who can couch their findings in terms that are most persuasive to their peers" (2001, 3). As noted, Haeffele and Storr similarly argue that rhetoric is used by both political economists and public policy officials to "convey legitimacy, clarify intentions, and ultimately affect [a] speaker's popularity" (2021, 2). Savannah Downing likewise explores the limitations of specific rhetorical frameworks used by politicians and policymakers to convince public audiences about scientific issues related to reproductive justice (Downing 2023, 4–6). The insights garnered from this literature thus provides the necessary tools for understanding how Buchanan attempted to persuade his colleagues to embrace his public choice perspective.

In *Landmark Essays on Rhetoric of Science*, Randy Allen Harris traces how late-twentieth-century rhetoricians used rhetorical analysis to understand the persuasive aspects of groundbreaking scientific texts (Harris 2018, 2020). The phrase "Giants of Science" was used by Harris to denote research on the persuasive achievements of "individuals whose accomplishments have stamped their respective sciences in epoch-defining ways" (2018, 23). Such work—including research by John Angus Campbell and Alan Gross—investigates the interplay between the rhetorical choices of prominent scientists and their social milieus.

John Angus Campbell, for instance, demonstrates the value of rhetoric for investigating science in his pioneering work on Charles Darwin's *The Origin of Species* (Campbell 1970, 1975, 1986, 1987). More specifically, Campbell's work merges the speaker-centered, neo-Aristotelian perspective (i.e., rhetoric as an effective expression) with a conception of rhetoric as a social-level theory that, as Celeste Condit writes, "focuses on ideology, ethics, or various versions of place" (2019, 181). In other words, Campbell's analysis frames Darwin's creative use of language as a response to the social forces acting upon him. Above all, Campbell's work has shown that Darwin's

Origin of Species made the theory of evolution by natural selection palatable by satisfying the social expectations of his nineteenth-century audience. "To claim that Darwin was a rhetorician," Campbell argues, "is not to dismiss his science, but to draw attention to his accommodation of his message to the professional and lay audience whose support was necessary for its acceptance" (1987, 45). In this regard, Campbell analyzes Darwin's rhetoric by examining how he "marshaled his evidence, managed his ethos, and molded his argument" to align with "the scientific and religious expectations of the day" (Harris 2018, 22).

Campbell's work also reveals Darwin's ability to mask his rhetorical artistry and downplay the purely speculative aspects of his scientific observations. "Commonly overlooked," Campbell writes, "is that [Darwin] persuaded his peers and the wider community by using plain English words and plain English thoughts" (1987, 45). Darwin knew that members of the public would reject his ideas if they detected his use of rhetorical or persuasive techniques. For this reason, Campbell explains, "Darwin minimized his literary gifts [as well as] his formidable theoretical power" in order to temper or conceal certain aspects of his theory under the guise of plain language. "Darwin's dismissal of his own colorful language and deemphasizing of the hard, sustained theoretical work behind his theory" are thus understood as rhetorical choices that emerged in response to his social context and specific audience (1987, 47). Darwin's persuasive achievements, therefore, can be attributed to how he accommodated his revolutionary science with rhetoric that mirrored the social conventions and perspicuous style of Victorian culture.

Similarly, Alan Gross's examination of *Opticks* demonstrates how Isaac Newton communicated his optical theory in ways that aligned with the prevailing view of science and philosophy advanced in Rene Descartes's *Discourse on Method* (Gross 1988). Prior to Newton, scientific explanations of optics typically assumed, on Cartesian grounds, that reason, not experience, was epistemologically prior (Gaukroger 1980). Gross argues that, prior to *Opticks*, Newton's early attempts to challenge Cartesian logic failed precisely because he gave "epistemological priority to experiment over rational intuition," upending a central presupposition of Cartesian science (Gross 1988, 60). In other words, Newton's earlier scientific papers failed to overturn the Cartesian view because he plainly emphasized the stark differences between his theory and Descartes's. As Gross makes clear, Newton's revolutionary scientific ideas failed to resonate with his audience precisely because his rhetoric accentuated the fact that they *were* indeed revolutionary:

> Newton's explanation of light did not give a full account of its origin, an account that included the operation of its material cause. A startling claim, a new method, a different, more restrictive, style of explanation—seemingly,

> Newton needed to discharge a strong burden of proof. But in this early paper on light and color, in a rhetoric as transparent as that of Descartes, Newton did not discharge this burden; instead, he emphasized his conflict with traditional views and methods. (Gross 1988, 60)

On the contrary, Gross argues that *Opticks*, Newton's second persuasive attempt to challenge Cartesian science, was successful because he adopted a rhetoric that embraced a strict Euclidean form, included thorough descriptions of empirical experiments, and offered lay readers provocative speculations about the natural world. In this way, Newton made his ideas more persuasive by using language that connected his revolutionary scientific ideas with traditional assumptions about research methodology, thus masking his radical departure from Cartesian science through a perspicuous rhetorical style.

More specifically, Gross links the persuasive success of *Opticks* to Newton's use of arrangement, presence, and rhetorical questions. First, Gross demonstrates that the use of Euclidian form allowed Newton to "display the present as a deductive consequence of the past" (1988, 69). This differs from Newton's earlier papers that use narrative to dramatize the clash between the Cartesian theory of optics with his own empirical explanation. Second, *Opticks*'s use of meticulous and excessive detail created presence for Newton's experimental method, an observation that applies the argumentation theory of Perelman and Olbrechts-Tyteca (1969, 67–70). And third, the dissociation between science and speculation made possible by his use of rhetorical questions gave Newton permission to "speculate about mechanism so long as those speculations are not confused with science" (1988, 71). Newton's rhetoric thus masks a radical departure from Cartesian science by inventing a sense of coherence and continuity that does not actually exist.

Ultimately, Campbell and Gross effectively demonstrate how distinguished scientists gain acceptance of their ideas by tailoring their messages to broader public audiences. Similarly, Buchanan is also a scientific giant who accommodated his public choice perspective to an audience that was largely hostile to his ideas through the strategic use of rhetoric. In order to temper the hubris and overcome the prejudices of his contemporaries, Buchanan needed to marshal his own evidence, manage his own public persona, and mold his own arguments to the expectations of professional economists. In the next section, I situate Buchanan's rhetorical sensitivity within what Boettke characterizes as the mainline tradition of political economy in order to demonstrate the similarities between Buchanan's rhetorical practice and that of other prominent economic figures.

THE CHARACTER OF MAINLINE ECONOMICS

Public and professional audiences can find it difficult to judge the veracity of arguments based on their content alone. When faced with such difficulties, audiences often base their judgments on a speaker's character or *ethos*. As Aristotle noted 2,500 years ago, public speakers construct their own character by designing messages that bring an audience's perception of themselves into harmony with the purpose of their speech. He also tells us that speakers with strong characters are readily believed in moments of uncertainty when there is little else to go on. This is because, as Carolyn Miller explains, "we trust those in whom we sense goodwill (*eunoia*), those with moral qualities (*arete*), and those whose knowledge can be applied to our practical problems (*phronesis*)" (Miller 2003, 202). Contemporary research on ethos (especially in communication studies) remains indebted to Aristotle's conception of persuasion through character (Condit 2018, 2019; Condit and DeTora 2021; Pittman 2006; Wetzel 2014). Specifically, communication scholars regularly emphasize two interconnected aspects of Aristotle's ethos: first, the creative enactment of character through discourse and, second, the habituation of social norms and community values.

When scientists communicate their ideas, they often assume a fictional character that they believe will imbue them with credibility. "An established ethos is the most persuasive of scientific arguments," Deirdre McCloskey explains, "and scientists are therefore very busy establishing it" (1998, 7). Building from McCloskey's contention, Condit maintains that contemporary studies concerning scientific ethos have integrated an Aristotelian view of persuasion through character, with modern interpretations of ethos as a social-level concept (2019, 179). Her relational view of ethos, for instance, emphasizes how individuals persuade public audiences by appealing to certain characteristics that are highly revered by members of a community. As a result, Condit frames scientists (in this case, economic scientists) as creative individuals who continuously redefine their character or social position in society by aligning themselves with specific moral virtues that their audience already upholds (2019, 183).

Eric King Watts' exploration of Alain Locke's, *The New Negro*, similarly demonstrates how a community-based ethos comprised both the spirit of Harlem in the early-twentieth century and the distinctive, moral voice of Black intellectuals. As Watts explains, "[Harlem] was a dynamic forum for deliberations about the appropriate norms, premises, and practices of a distinct Black culture," which made "available to Black intellectuals the symbolic and material resources for the rhetorical invention and the articulation of a Black public voice" (2002, 19). And yet, constructing a community-oriented African American ethos proved difficult due to the "conflicting philosophies and conceptions of art" that exacerbated Harlem's rhetorical dilemma (ibid., 19). Watts' conception of ethos as the expression of community virtues thus informs his examination of Locke's rhetoric by attending to how he drew from the complexities of Black folk tradition, African artistry, and modern pragmatism to constitute an African American collective identity—an identity that nevertheless manifests itself differently among Black intellectuals living in Harlem during this period. Understanding the creative and social dimensions of ethos, therefore, requires scholars to closely read persuasive communication as both the construction of individual character and the embodiment of community virtues.

Political economists also communicate their ideas in ways that embody community virtues and reflect a specific attitude toward their profession. For example, Peter Boettke makes a distinction between mainline and mainstream economics by subtly attending to the attitudes associated with each tradition regarding the purpose of economic research. More specifically, Boettke describes mainline economics "as a set of positive propositions about social order that were held in common from Adam Smith onward" and mainstream economics as "a sociological concept related to what is currently fashionable among the scientific elite of the profession" (2012, xvii). Above all, Boettke argues that mainline economists extend Smith's holistic approach to studying human behavior as it occurs within the constraints of social life. Moreover, the ethical commitments of mainline economists, as Boettke contends, reflect Smith's creed:

> [That] the greatest improvement in the productive powers of labour, and the greater part of the skill, dexterity, and judgment with which it is any where directed, or applied, seem to have been the effects of the division of labour. As it is the power of exchanging that gives occasion to the division of labor, so to the extent of this division must always be limited by that power, or, in other words, by the extent of the market. (Smith 1981, 13)

Boettke's mainline designation thus recognizes Smith's exchange framework and the embrace of human fallibility in the scholarship of subsequent economists—namely, Friedrich Hayek, Ronald Coase, Vernon Smith, and Elinor Ostrom, among others. These economists typically adopt three propositions regarding the nature of human action and the role of institutions: first, individuals face cognitive and epistemic limits as they negotiate the social world; second, formal and informal institutions shape human activity; and third, social cooperation is possible without central direction (Boettke et al. 2016, 4).

Mainline economists also exhibit a shared rhetorical sensitivity when denouncing the shortcomings and oversights of their more mainstream contemporaries. As a result, many mainline economists attempt to rhetorically refashion the public identity of the economics profession by condemning the hubris of their colleagues while promoting Smith's exchange paradigm. Friedrich Hayek, for instance, frequently expressed his frustrations with the political and overly technical writing styles of *scientistic* economists. He repeatedly attempted to explain how certain concepts—such as liberalism and individualism—were causing confusion among scholars because they had "come to describe aggregations of quite heterogeneous principles" (2010, 48). It seemed odd, Hayek thought, that individuals who believed "contradictory and irreconcilable ideas" were seemingly united by words that they could not define (2010, 47). For this reason, Hayek understood that without understanding how economists were using rhetoric to advance their ideas, it would be extremely difficult, if not impossible, for them to understand each other's intellectual commitments and collectively agree on how to define (and ultimately solve) public problems. Thus, Hayek showed a concern for rhetoric by investigating how new forms of discourse shifted the economics profession away from Smith's exchange paradigm, which led to his famous condemnation of the pervasive "scientistic perspective" in post-WWII economics (Hayek 2007, 2010, 2011).

Similarly, Elinor Ostrom expressed her dissatisfaction with mainstream economists for using overly simplistic models of social behavior. In her 2009 Nobel Prize lecture, Ostrom argued that social science research had strayed quite far from Smith's exchange framework and, as a result, overlooked the complex relationships between social interactions and institutional arrangements. "The most important lesson for public policy analysis," Ostrom maintained, "is that humans have a more complex motivational structure and more capability to solve social dilemmas than posited in earlier rational choice theory" (2016, 237). Put differently, Ostrom's concern was that scholars had become unwilling to deal with humanity's complexity and attempted to avoid it by using scientific approaches that simplified human behavior in ways that made it appear controllable and easy to predict. What makes Ostrom an effective communicator (and, dare I say, a thoughtful rhetorician) is her ability to challenge one-dimensional, rational choice approaches without denouncing the role rationality plays in collective action. Ostrom's Nobel lecture thus encouraged her professional colleagues to embrace the complexities of social life by asking better questions and accepting that "a core goal of public policy should be to facilitate the development of institutions that bring out the best in humans" (2016, 237).

As noted, Buchanan is also associated with the mainline tradition because he too embraced Smith's exchange framework. But, as Boettke et al. point out, Buchanan's mainline designation is also reflected in how he "used his Nobel lecture to remind economists that individuals in politics . . . act purposively, pursue their own interests, and engage in exchange in order to secure the (political) goods and services for themselves and others" (2016, 13). In doing so, Buchanan's discourse embodied the communal virtues that are echoed in Wicksell's creed: "economists should cease proffering policy advice as if they were employed by a benevolent despot, and they should look to the structure within which political decisions are made" (ibid., 13). As such, Buchanan made two fundamental observations of commercial society and the political process that align with the ethos, or character, of mainline economists: first, that individuals are self-interested and, second, that complex social orders align individual interests with the general interest of a community. What makes Buchanan's discourse significant, as I will show in my analysis, is how he expresses these concerns by enacting the good sense, goodwill, and good moral character of public choice economists while simultaneously encouraging his colleagues to avoid the autocratic temptations that seem so pervasive among mainstream economists. As a result, I contend that Buchanan rhetorically constructs a new public identity of the economics profession that ultimately influences how economists, even those who disagree with Buchanan's conclusions, study politics.

BUCHANAN'S UNROMANTIC RHETORIC

This analysis focuses on two of Buchanan's most obvious efforts in persuasion—his 1979 Inaugural Lecture "Politics without Romance" hosted by the Institute for Advanced Study in Vienna, Austria and his 1986 Nobel Prize lecture "The Constitution of Economic Policy." As noted, Buchanan used both speaking occasions to explicate his ideas regarding public choice economics and constitutional political economy and to express his frustrations with mainstream economics. What makes these lectures rhetorically significant is how Buchanan frames the public choice economist as having three qualities: good sense, good will, and good moral character. He does this by communicating his technical ideas about economic and political processes in ways that contrast specific mainline virtues with the idealistic, autocratic temperament of his more mainstream colleagues. Buchanan's mission was thus to persuade his audience to reconsider the purpose and limitations of the economic scientist by realigning the objectives of public choice research with the broader mainline tradition of political economy. In doing so, Buchanan demonstrates how character appeals are an effective rhetorical maneuver even for scholars engaged in technical debates about philosophical ideas and scientific methodologies.

Overall, I describe Buchanan's rhetoric as *unromantic* for two primary reasons. First, Buchanan often frames his public choice perspective in opposition to the romantic assumptions made by many of his colleagues. He specifically characterizes these assumptions as "romantic and illusory" because they are suggestive of an idealized view of human behavior. Combating this idealistic orientation toward political action forced Buchanan to offer his audience with a reasonable and pragmatic alternative, an unromantic perspective that promoted an understanding of political action that was based on empirical observations of how individuals behave in clearly defined institutional contexts. In this way, Buchanan's rhetoric attempted to rebuild public trust toward political economists that had been gradually eroded by the arrogance and elitism that many associated with the broader profession.

Second, Buchanan's rhetoric is considered unromantic in the sense that it aims to embody the scientific, descriptive orientation that is characteristic of mainline economics. As Buchanan explains, "the *theory* of public choice . . . is or can be a wholly positive theory, wholly scientific and *werfrei* in the standard meanings of these terms" (1999, 47; emphasis original). The aim of public choice research, in other words, is to examine and accurately describe the rules and conditions that influence how political agents act. As such, Buchanan's purpose was "ultimately normative rather than antiseptically scientific . . . [This means that he] sought to make economic sense out of the relationship between the individual and the state before proceeding to advance policy nostrums" (Buchanan 2016, 44). In this regard, Buchanan's rhetoric is considered unromantic in the sense that he attempted to use language that was precise, transparent, and that accurately corresponded to his subject matter.

Ultimately, Buchanan's unromantic rhetoric challenged various assumptions about politics by constructing an ethos that exposed the hubris associated with mainstream economics while also overturning the idealistic assumption that individuals "participate in politics through some common search for the good, the true, and the beautiful" (2016, 50). This "classical prejudice," as Buchanan described it, motivated generations of political scientists to embrace fallacious, and frankly unscientific, views of reality (Buchanan 2016, 50). In contrast, Buchanan believed that all individuals, whether they were politicians or government bureaucrats, acted in their own self-interest as they do in other contexts. In this way, Buchanan was a stern political realist who believed that "existing constitutions, or structures of rules, [should] be the [primary] subject of critical scrutiny" (2016, 55). In addition, Buchanan's public choice perspective was based on the idea that "people can be persuaded, by the force of good arguments, that certain kinds of rules are better for them than others" (Brennan and Munger 2014, 339). And though he spent his career overturning the idealism of his colleagues by contributing new approaches to economic analysis, he welcomed any opportunity to persuade those in his profession to reconsider their assumptions about politics.

Buchanan first attempts to convey good sense (*phronesis*) at the beginning of both lectures by merging traditional economic insights with personal anecdotes about his professional experiences studying economic and political theories. In his Nobel lecture, Buchanan shares a short story about how he discovered Wicksell's work: "One of the most exciting intellectual moments of my career was my 1948 discovery of Wicksell's unknown and untranslated dissertation, *Finanztheoretische Untersuchungen* (1896), buried in the dusty stacks of Chicago's old Harper Library" (2016, 43–44). This "dramatic example of learning by serendipity" was only possible, Buchanan tells us, because of the "immediate post-dissertation leisure of an academic novice" (ibid., 44). Put differently, it was only when Buchanan had the freedom to step away from mainstream economic research that he was able to discover ideas that had been discarded and/or forgotten. By framing Wicksell's dissertation as a lost or neglected treasure that contained essential economic insights, Buchanan conveys his good sense by recognizing something that many of his predecessors had overlooked. Buchanan further states that reading Wicksell gave him "a tremendous surge of self-confidence" once he realized that Wicksell's concerns regarding economic research were "congenial with [his] own developing stream of critical consciousness." This insight ultimately inspired Buchanan to follow in Wicksell's footsteps and "challenge the still-dominant orthodoxy in public finance and welfare economics" (ibid., 44). Buchanan's personal anecdote thus subtly portrays him as having the good sense to utilize Wicksell's underutilized economic wisdom to criticize the errors and shortcomings of contemporary economic research.

Buchanan also demonstrates his good sense by chiding the poor judgments and faulty assumptions that are frequently made by his more mainstream colleagues. For example, he argues that the most significant error of twentieth-century economists occurs when "efficiency in the allocation of resources [is] defined independently of the processes through which individual choices are exercised" (ibid., 46). Since at least in the eighteenth century, scholars have understood that voluntary exchanges between citizens can only be studied scientifically if the institutional frameworks that facilitate these exchanges are clearly defined. And yet, Buchanan suggests that this Enlightenment wisdom was eventually forgotten once "the market" was understood functionally "as if something called "the economy" existed for the purpose of value maximization" (ibid., 46). As Buchanan further explains, "given this subtle shift toward a teleological interpretation of the economic process, it is not surprising that politics, or governmental process, was similarly interpreted" (ibid., 46). Political systems were thus viewed as having a *telos* or purpose that enabled policymakers and government bureaucrats to believe that their professional obligations were to directly improve public well-being by advancing policy that determined the outcomes of political activity. Political scientists must remember, Buchanan declares, that "there is no political counterpart to Adam Smith's invisible hand. It is not surprising, therefore, that the attempt by Wicksell and other continental European scholars to extend economic theory to the operation of the public sector remained undeveloped for so many years" (ibid., 46–47). Thus, Buchanan exposes the romantic assumptions that are characteristic of mainstream economists in order to present himself as possessing the good sense to embrace the traditional wisdom of the past in order to overcome the misapprehensions of the present.

Similarly, Buchanan's lecture "Politics without Romance" also frames public choice economists as having the good sense to integrate philosophical ideas into their research on the constitutional limits of modern bureaucracies. He begins this lecture by reminding his professional audience that "the theory of public choice is not without antecedents" (1999, 46). More specifically, he praises the contributions of numerous European Enlightenment thinkers for providing the guidance to study economic processes by comparing "social institutions as they might be expected [to actually] operate" (ibid., 47). Though Buchanan describes this Enlightenment wisdom as "simple and obvious," he acknowledges that such knowledge has been "lost to the informed consciousness of Western man" and has been replaced by the romantic assumption that "the polity" is guided by some mystical force toward the public good. On this point, Buchanan writes:

> The socialist mystique to the effect that the state, that politics, somehow works its way toward some transcendent "public good" is with us yet, in many guises, as we must surely acknowledge. And, even among those who reject such mystique, there are many who unceasingly search for the ideal that will resolve the dilemma of politics. (1999, 47)

Indeed, this passage showcases Buchanan's willingness to criticize the ethos or character of mainstream economists. By characterizing his profession as being blinded by "romantic fallacies" or "socialist mystiques," Buchanan gradually encourages his audience to recognize the good sense or practical reasoning required to dispel the illusions that continue to obstruct the judgment of so many professional economists. In doing so, he enacts *phronesis* by demonstrating the virtue of recognizing how specific Enlightenment philosophies continue to serve as the basis for the comparative evaluation of political institutions.

After solidifying the reasonableness and practical wisdom of public choice economists, Buchanan conveys goodwill (*eunoia*) by defining the purpose of public choice research as a quest for social understanding rather than as a means toward social control. In both lectures, Buchanan provides thorough definitions of economic theory and carefully explicates the limitations of his public choice approach to politics. In "Politics without Romance," for instance, he writes:

> [Economic theory] is a body of analysis that offers an understanding, an explanation, of the complex exchange process that we call "an economy." It is a body of analysis that allows us to relate the behavior of individual participants in the market activity . . . to the results that are attained for the whole community, results that are not within the purposes or the knowledge of the separate participants themselves. (2016, 47)

The purpose of public choice theory, as Buchanan envisions it, is to offer reasonable explanations regarding "the complex institutional interactions that go on within the political sector" (ibid., 48). In contrast, Buchanan chastises his more mathematically inclined colleagues for striving to predict political outcomes by modeling possible political behaviors. Buchanan's condemnation of the use of mathematical models for this purpose resembles Friedrich Hayek's characterization of many professional economists after the World War II (Buchanan 2016, 25–27). More specifically, Hayek accuses his profession of being too eager "to act on the belief that [economists] possess the knowledge and the power . . . to shape the processes of society entirely to our liking" (Buchanan 2016, 37). Similarly, Buchanan writes that embracing social understanding as the goal of economic theory "is disturbing to [those] political economists or philosophers" who uphold "the constructivist urge to assume a role as a social engineer" (2016, 57). In this regard, both Buchanan and Hayek frame the *constructivist* or *scientistic* proclivities of mainstream economists as representative of a malevolent ethos. The public choice economist, in contrast, conveys their trustworthiness by embracing the normative bent and methodological limitations of economic theory.

Moreover, Buchanan further establishes his goodwill toward his audience by reiterating that all economists can (and should) do is propose testable propositions based on the notion that individuals "seek to maximize their own utilities" without assuming what the results of political processes should be (1999, 49). The goal of public choice research, in other words, is not to discover new knowledge but to reconsider the frameworks scholars use to understand political behavior. Further demonstrating his aptitude for philosophy, Buchanan confesses that he often recalls Ecclesiastes' famous creed "that there is nothing new under the sun" when he sees his "younger colleagues . . . rediscovering almost every wheel that older economists have ever talked about" (ibid., 46). This kind of statement is an example of how Buchanan subtly reinforces his persona while simultaneously chiding the hubris of his colleagues for failing to "look at some aspects of our world, and specifically our world of politics, through a different window" (ibid., 46). The romance of Buchanan's colleagues ultimately blinds them from realizing the practical utility of the public choice perspective, and in overlooking this approach to politics, Buchanan contends that his more mainstream colleagues seem unwilling to accept that

> The romance is gone, perhaps never to be regained. The socialist paradise is lost. Politicians and bureaucrats are seen as ordinary persons much like the rest of us, and "politics" is viewed as a set of arrangements . . . in which many players with quite disparate objectives interact so as to generate a set of outcomes that may not be either internally consistent or efficient by any standards. (1999, 57)

In short, Buchanan conveys goodwill toward his audience by expressing his intention to simply understand political behavior by seriously considering the humanity of those who occupy social life. It is this concern for the individual that not only characterizes public choice theory, but it also conveys a sense of trustworthiness when this commitment is contrasted with the constructivist ambitions of the economic quasi-engineer (i.e., the economist bent on control via social and political design).

Finally, Buchanan frames public choice economists as possessing good moral character (*arete*) by articulating their intention to limit the power of modern government bureaucracies. It seems obvious to Buchanan that governments have largely failed "to deliver on their promises" (1999, 58). Observing these failures has made political experts and lay citizens realize the importance of constraining the reach and authority of specific government agencies. And yet, Buchanan explains that it is a mistake to assume "that electoral constraints [are alone] sufficient to hold the Leviathan-like proclivities of government in check." He further explains that "having come to command shares in national income that were undreamt of even in the most roseate of early democratic socialist predictions, modern governmental bureaucracies will not relinquish their relative positions in society without struggle" (ibid., 58). Nevertheless, Buchanan concludes his inaugural lecture by describing the actions of public choice economists as having spurred serious efforts to reduce the reach and oversight of federal and state agencies. Consider, for instance, the following passage:

> In America, 1978 was the year of Proposition 13, when the voters of California turned back, by a two-to-one margin, the growth of government spending and taxing. This event sent political shock waves throughout the Western world. The United States is now (1979) inundated with various proposals, at all levels of government, designed to limit the expansion of governmental powers. "Bridling

> the passions of the sovereign"—this eighteenth-century slogan has resurfaced to command political respectability. (Buchanan 1999, 58)

Buchanan tells this story for at least two reasons. First, this anecdote illustrates the influence public choice theory has had on anti-government movements. Second, it conveys the moral duty of public choice economists to not only shift attitudes about bureaucracies and politicians but also to re-examine and rebuild political institutions "so as to keep governments as well as citizens within the limits of tolerance" (ibid., 58). It is here that public choice and constitutional political economy become morally significant. Specifically, Buchanan tells his audience that it is not enough to merely criticize the hubris of mainstream economists and the shortcomings of governments. "Criticism alone," he writes, "can generate chaos, whether this be in the form of gradual breakdown or in the form of violent disruption." Public choice economists, therefore, are morally obligated to persuade the public "to understand the limits of change as well as the value" (ibid., 59). In other words, Buchanan presents his own moral character by demonstrating his willingness to embrace his civic and professional obligation to promote change in ways that keep society from "[drifting] toward anarchistic terror," otherwise known as "the jungle against which Hobbes warned us all" (ibid., 59). The public choice economist is thus presented as a harbinger of social change and as a guard against the dogmatism of certitude that is too often embraced by intellectual tyrants.

CONCLUSION

This chapter undertakes a rhetorical analysis of Buchanan's persuasive communication to understand how he constructs an ethos that frames public choice economists as having three qualities: good sense (*phronesis*), goodwill (*eunoia*), and good moral character (*arete*). This analysis reveals how Buchanan was able to challenge orthodox approaches to economic research by framing his public choice perspective as a virtuous and pragmatic alternative that tempers the scope and the hubris of mainstream economists. What I describe as Buchanan's *unromantic rhetoric* thus denotes how he attempted to persuade his audiences to embrace his public choice perspective by practicing the virtues he associated with the mainline tradition of political economy.

Despite his self-conscious preoccupation with persuasive communication, studies of Buchanan's philosophical and political corpus have paid little attention to how he made his ideas appealing to a large audience of interdisciplinary researchers. Likewise, scholars in political economy and communication studies have failed to consider how Buchanan's argumentation style influenced the production and reception of his ideas. This essay acknowledges the extensive research that has been conducted on Buchanan's concern for language, but it also recognizes that Buchanan's distinction as a communicator remains understudied. For this reason, the analysis offered in this chapter carefully reads Buchanan's most obvious efforts in persuasion to provide an explanation of the rhetorical techniques that Buchanan utilized when he communicated his public choice perspective to large public audiences.

Recognizing the rhetorical significance of Buchanan's public choice perspective has serious implications for understanding how political economists (as scientific communicators) publicly express their ideas to both technical and lay audiences. Reading Buchanan in context—that is, as responding to a transforming intellectual landscape within the social sciences, broadly defined—fosters an understanding of the social and historical forces that influenced his communication style. This approach also makes readers aware of the persuasive techniques that economists and policymakers use to make their technical explanations both meaningful and socially relevant. Indeed, Buchanan clearly understood the power of rhetoric when he wrote that "political economists try to stimulate open and lively discussion of how a free society should be organized and preserved" (1958, 5). With this ideal in mind, Buchanan showcases his own rhetorical sensitivity by promoting public choice as something much more than a mere perspective about economic and political inquiry. Instead, Buchanan articulated his public choice perspective as signifying a general attitude toward social life. As such, Buchanan brilliantly voiced his *unromantic vision* using a rhetoric that demonstrated his practical wisdom, noble purpose, and willingness to acknowledge the limits of his ideas.

REFERENCES

Boettke, Peter J. 2005. "Teaching Economics through Ayn Rand: How the Economy is like a Novel and How the Novel Can Teach Us About Economics." *The Journal of Ayn Rand Studies* 6 (2): 445–65.

———. 2012. *Living Economics: Yesterday, Today, and Tomorrow.* Oakland, CA: The Independent Institute.

———. 2021. *The Struggle for a Better World.* Arlington, VA: Mercatus Center at George Mason University.

Boettke, Peter J. and Alain Marciano. 2015. "The Past, Present and Future of Virginia Political Economy." *Public Choice* 163: 53–65.

Boettke, Peter J. and Solomon Stein, eds. 2018. *Buchanan's Tensions: Reexamining the Political Economy and Philosophy of James M. Buchanan.* Arlington, VA: Mercatus Center at George Mason University.

Boettke, Peter J., Bobbi Herzberg, and Brian Kogelmann, eds. 2020. *Exploring the Political Economy and Social Philosophy of Vincent and Elinor Ostrom.* Lanham, MD: Rowman and Littlefield.

Boettke, Peter J., Jayme Lemke, and Virgil Henry Storr, eds. 2018. *Exploring the Political Economy and Social Philosophy of F. A. Hayek.* Lanham, MD: Rowman and Littlefield.

Brennan, Geoffrey, and Michael Munger. 2014. "The Soul of James Buchanan?" *The Independent Review* 18 (3): 331–342.

Buchanan, James M. 1958. "The Thomas Jefferson Center for Studies in Political Economy." *The University of Virginia News Letter* XXXV (2): 5–8.

———. 1999. *The Collected Works of James M. Buchanan, Volume 1: The logical Foundations of Constitutional Liberty.* Indianapolis, IN: Liberty Fund.

———. 2000a. *The Collected Works of James M. Buchanan, Volume 7: The Limits of Liberty: Between Anarchy and Leviathan.* Indianapolis, IN: Liberty Fund.

———. 2000b. *The Collected Works of James M. Buchanan, Volume 13: Politics as Public Choice.* Indianapolis, IN: Liberty Fund.

———. 2016 [1986]. "The Constitution of Economic Policy." In *Mainline Economics: Six Nobel Lectures in the Tradition of Adam Smith,* edited by Peter Boettke, Stefanie Haeffele-Balch, and Virgil Henry Storr, 41–59. Arlington, VA: Mercatus Center at George Mason University.

Campbell, Charles P. 1995. "Ethos: Character and Ethics in Technical Writing." *IEEE Transactions on Professional Communication* 38 (3): 132–138.

Choi, Ginny Seung and Virgil Henry Storr. 2019. "A Culture of Rent Seeking." *Public Choice* 181 (1/2): 101–126.

Condit, Celeste M. 2018. "The Character of Scientists in the Nobel Prize Speeches." *Public Understanding of Science* 27 (1): 417–432.

———. 2019. "Public Health Experts, Expertise, and Ebola: A Relational Theory of Ethos." *Rhetoric and Public Affairs* 22 (2): 177–216.

Condit, Celeste, and Lisa DeTora. 2021. "Multiple Voices, Messy Truths: Rhetoricians on Ethos, Authors, and Authority." *Rhetoric of Health and Medicine* 4 (1): 92–110.

Cowen, Tyler. 1998. *In Praise of Commercial Culture.* Cambridge, MA: Harvard University Press.

Crowley, Sharon and Debra Hawhee. 1999. *Ancient Rhetorics for Contemporary Students.* Boston, MA: Allyn and Bacon.

Downing, Savannah Greer. 2023. "Toward Reproductive Justice Rhetorics of Care: State Senator Jen Jordan's Dissent of Georgia's Heartbeat Bill." *Quarterly Journal of Speech* 109 (4): 376–399.

Fahnestock, Jeanne. 2005. "Rhetoric of Science: Enriching the Discipline." *Technical Communication Quarterly* 14 (3): 277–286.

Haeffele, Stefanie and Virgil Henry Storr. "Rhetoric as a Way of Limiting the Range of Acceptable Policy Positions." *Journal of Private Enterprise* 36 (1): 1–16.

Hayek, Friedrich A. 2007 [1944]. *The Road to Serfdom: Texts and Documents.* Edited by Bruce Caldwell. Chicago, IL: University of Chicago Press.

———. 2010. *Studies on the Abuse and Decline of Reason: Texts and Documents.* Edited by Bruce Caldwell. Chicago, IL: University of Chicago Press.

———. 2011 [1960]. *The Constitution of Liberty*. Chicago, IL: University of Chicago Press.

———. 2016 [1974]. "The Pretense of Knowledge." In *Mainline Economics: Six Nobel Lectures in the Tradition of Adam Smith*, edited by Peter J. Boettke, Stefanie Haeffele-Balch, and Virgil Henry Storr, 25–39. Arlington, VA: Mercatus Center at George Mason University.

Hirschman, Albert O. 2003. *The Passion and the Interests.* Princeton, NJ: Princeton University Press.

Lavoie, Don, and Emily Chamlee-Wright. 2000. *Culture and Enterprise: The Development, Representation, and Morality of Business.* New York: Routledge.

Lemke, Jayme S. 2016. "Interjurisdictional Competition and the Married Women's Property Acts." *Public Choice* 166 (3): 291–313.

Martin, Adam and Diana Thomas. 2013. "Two Tier Political Entrepreneurship and the Congressional Committee System." *Public Choice* 154 (1): 21–37.

McCloskey, Deirdre N. 1998. *The Rhetoric of Economics.* Madison, WI: University of Wisconsin Press.

Ostrom, Vincent. 1997. *The Meaning of Democracy and the Vulnerability of Democracies: A Response to Tocqueville's Challenge.* Ann Arbor, MI: University of Michigan Press.

———. 2008. *The Intellectual Crisis in American Public Administration.* Foreword by Barbara Allen. Tuscaloosa, AL: University of Alabama Press.

Perelman, Chaïm and Lucie Olbrechts-Tyteca. 1969. *The New Rhetoric: A Treatise on Argumentation.* Trans. John Wolkinson and Purcell Weaver. Notre Dame: University of Notre Dame Press.

Watts, Eric King. 2002. "African American Ethos and Hermeneutical Rhetoric: An Exploration of Alain Locke's the New Negro." *Quarterly Journal of Speech* 88 (1): 19–32.

Part II

APPLICATIONS

Chapter 7

Aura and the Aesthetics of Constitutional Creation

Knowledge and Representation in the Drafting of the Constitution of the Empire of Japan

Todd Maslyk

In 1853, so the common narrative goes, the arrival of the "Black Ships" under the command of Commodore Matthew Perry of the United States off the coast of Kanagawa precipitated a sequence of events that would see Japan open to the world after two and a half centuries of national closure. Faced with the prospect of imminent colonization by Western countries in the wake of the "opening," the Japanese embarked upon an extensive project of national modernization and westernization.[1] The shogunal government scrambled to manage intrusion by Western states and began sending officials and students abroad to study the modern world. These programs took place against a background of domestic political instability that the Shogunate ultimately found itself incapable of handling. In 1868, imperialist activists returned the emperor to power in the so-called "Meiji Restoration." Having defeated the forces of the Shogunate in a brief civil war lasting from 1868 to 1869, the imperialist faction implemented a transformative agenda. The eponymous Meiji Emperor went from being a ceremonial figurehead cloistered in Kyoto to being the central figure of a new regime based in the erstwhile shogunal capital of Edo—now renamed Tokyo (Schwebell 1970; Keene 2002; Jansen 2002; Swale 2009).

By the early 1880s, that transformative agenda had gradually come to focus on the necessity of a new constitutional charter for the Japanese state (Takii 2019). The decision to introduce a written constitution culminated in the promulgation of the 1889 Constitution of the Empire of Japan. This

"Meiji Constitution"—so named for the emperor who presented it as a gift to his people—was the fundamental expression of the political order operative in Japan until its abrogation by a new constitution in the wake of World War II. The process of reformational constitutional creation that lay at the core of the Meiji Restoration, as well as its attendant economic, social, and political developments, have become central examples in influential works on the theory of social transformation (e.g., Moore 1966; Skocpol 2015).

At the same time, the creation of the Meiji Constitution offers a significant historical example of the successful implementation of a new institutional arrangement in the context of goals such as the acceleration of economic growth and the attainment of international recognition. At the same time, the decades since the conclusion of the World War II have seen the publication of a steady stream of scholarly work on the relationship between Germany and Japan as constituted by the connection of legal influence. Past scholarship on this process, in particular work focused on the drafting of the Constitution of the Empire of Japan of 1889 (the so-called "Meiji Constitution"), has largely hewed to examinations parallel to the above narrative. Starting with the opening of Japanese archives in the wake of World War II (Ando 2000), scholars in Germany, Japan, and beyond have gone searching for sources to document the creation of the Meiji Constitution and to track its influence on Japanese society and modes of thought. In this chapter, I take this work as a foundation for considering the process of reforming the constitution of Japan from a semicodified, abstract constellation of conventions for the distribution of power into a constitutional charter legible to Western diplomats as "modern" in character. I view this process of constitutional reformation, codification, and promulgation as a paradigmatic case (Ermakoff 2014) of the creation of a constitution under real historical conditions—and more narrowly, I view this as a case that brings into high relief the interaction between endogenous and exogenous conditions affecting the process of constitution creation.

Because of the way that it encompasses this range of interacting forces, the historical development of the Meiji Constitution and its associated legal regime offers us a window onto the issue of how likely new institutional arrangements are to take hold or not—what Boettke, Coyne, and Leeson have referred to as an institution's "stickiness" (Boettke, Coyne, and Leeson 2008), specifically, the success of institutions that are imposed by local elites. Moreover, the drafting of the Meiji Constitution also reflects the tensions that can develop in a constitution-creating community amidst pressures coming from within the community and claims being made by forces that will not be party to the new political order. Such tensions arose in the case of Meiji Japan because Japanese leaders, such as Itō Hirobumi, were not only responding to calls for a constitutional charter from within Japan, but also having to contend with demands from Western powers on the political forms that would be necessary for the renegotiation of unequal treaties signed by the shogun. In order to address those demands, the Japanese ministers opted to bring in Western legal experts—including predominantly German scholars in the constitutional sphere—as aides in the drafting of a constitutional charter and legal code (Takii 2014). Those documents were to be written along the lines of the most up-to-date Western legal scholarship. This situation reflects the recurring impulse in development scenarios to bring in outside experts—a decision that automatically raises questions about how such experts can possibly know how to structure institutions that match local conditions.

In this chapter, I undertake an examination of the creation of the Meiji Constitution that balances two main components arising out of these considerations. The first component is an examination of how the Meiji Constitution emerged as an expression of a rearranged political order amidst a context that was keenly aware of preexisting constitutional structures. The second component is the consideration of the role of aesthetics in this legal process. At root, when we are asking questions about the knowledge that is necessary to shape a political order to fit with preexisting cultural conditions—that is, to evaluate the potential for an institution to stick—we are already engaged in asking questions concerning representations and forms. The necessary intrusion of political form into any consideration of how the processes that generate political orders operate means that those considerations automatically carry with them an unavoidable aesthetic component. Moreover, given the explicit recognition of the Meiji Constitution as a tool for signaling Japan's status as deserving peer status in treaty negotiations with Western states (cf. e.g., Hozumi 1904), the nature of the constitution as a part of a communicative process again raises the need to handle its aesthetic character.[2]

Working from this perspective, I take Meiji-era Japan as a case of the process of constitutional creation under conditions requiring the balancing of internal and external forces in constitutional decision-making. That balancing necessarily entails consideration of the position of the object under contention—whether it be a constitutional document or a legal code—because of its position as the focus of negotiation. In order to use the Meiji Constitution as a site for understanding institutional development and its connection to the aesthetic, I first develop a theoretical lens that builds on the work of scholars of the Virginia and Bloomington Schools of Political Economy by joining the work of scholars in those traditions with the aesthetic theories of German critical scholar Walter Benjamin. I then shift from developing a general theoretical apparatus to a historical survey of the process that resulted in the promulgation of the Meiji Constitution. I use that survey as a case to illustrate the linkages undergirding my theoretical lens: I show in particular how that framework can inform our reading of Japan's experience dealing with the expression of constitutional rearrangement in an exogenous form. Finally, I return to considerations of how we can apply the insights from the case study to a broader understanding of constitutional transformation and institutional rearrangement.

THEORETICAL APPARATUS AND CONSIDERATION OF EXISTING SCHOLARSHIP

My theoretical approach combines the work of scholars in the traditions of the Virginia and Bloomington Schools with the work of the early twentieth-century theorist Walter Benjamin. This combined approach balances consideration of the drivers of individual action that goes into constitutional decision-making with a critical attention to form. I see both perspectives as ultimately agreeing on the notion that we, as individuals, are acting against a background of cultural influences that shape our approach to moments of decision. Ultimately, the decisions that are made by individuals in such moments loop back to make up the suprapersonal cultural force fields that shape the next round of individual decisions. I develop this framework with an eye to linking an understanding of how institutions can successfully "stick" to their contexts with an investigation of how those institutions produce impressions based on their formal properties.

I begin by noting that the very existence of constitutional systems—the fact of observable arrangements of power in a particular society. Of fundamental concern here is the fact that even though they may remain fixed over long stretches of time, such constitutional systems are not purely static. Any given political order and its component institutions are subject to change. An understanding of the changeability of any institution that is not somehow metaphysically fixed requires an examination of—at least—exactly *what* is changing, *who* is involved in changing it, and *how* those changes mesh with any existing cultural background. In the case of a constitution, this means that we must recognize that the very term "constitution" has a doubled meaning: it can refer to the form of political order that is an immanent characteristic of all organized social groups, or it can point to some specific written document—a constitutional charter—that is meant to express that order. A rough contrast along these lines can be drawn between the British "unwritten" constitution as a representative of the former, while the latter is exemplified by the Constitution of the United States. The British version is a collection of traditions and rules, and it describes the operations of power in British society, while the American Constitution is a literal document. At the same time, however, the possession of a charter does not mean that the United States lacks an uncodified constitution—rather, the charter is a concrete formulation of that order and forms a point of defining orientation for its interpretation and application.

Both types of constitutions can be changed, but with different levels of observability. The immanent constitution is an emergent order and changes in step with the understanding of the sovereign. In a society rooted in popular sovereignty, this means changing as the subject population and its views change. Consequently, changes to this form of the constitution from within the society can be difficult to notice, requiring a certain ability to take an outsider's viewpoint on one's own way of life. Under such conditions, culture acts as the sort of unifying medium that brings together the artisanal capacities of individuals to maintain the constitutional order, or alter it in response to changing conditions (Ostrom 1997). It is much easier to notice, even from an internal position, when a constitutional charter changes. This will usually involve some formal process that is outlined in the charter itself, requiring the action of the sovereign entity to declare an alteration. This difference in the ease with which alterations to the two types of constitutions can be observed will take on further significance in connection with Benjamin's aesthetic theory below, but first let us finish the line of thought on how the changes work out in form. Alterations to constitutional charters will necessarily be presented as correcting movements toward the state of the immanent constitution. In the event of such an alteration, the sovereign announces a need to bring the charter in line with its understanding of the "actual" constitution; if the sovereign has bound itself by the charter's form, then so long as no such external change is forthcoming, then no alteration to the immanent constitution would be recognized as having occurred, either.[3] This act of binding also lies at the core of the notion that a constitutional government is essentially a limited government (cf. e.g., McIlwain 1947), with any institutional change facing the need to overcome the preceding institutional form according to contextual conditions—conditions that include the sovereign saying whether or not they are bound by self-imposed rules.

This model of change clarifies two of the elements outlined above in my generic framework for examining institutional change: in the case of constitutional transformation, the object in transition is the constitution itself, whether in the form of an imminent constitution or of a physical charter, and the agent of change is the sovereign. These two interact against a contextual background, which itself acts on the path taken by the transformation. Boettke, Coyne, and Leeson have examined the typology of these interactions in their study of institutional stickiness, categorizing the way that an institution's mode of introduction relates to the success of the institution. They categorize institutions into three broad categories: "foreign-introduced exogenous (FEX) institutions, indigenously-introduced exogenous institutions (IEX), and indigenously introduced endogenous (IEN) institutions" (Boettke, Coyne, and Leeson 2008, 334–335).

In this schema, foreign versus indigenous concerns whether the institutions are designed by outsiders or insiders to the context. The contrast between exogenous and endogenous concerns the mode of introduction, with exogenous institutions being designed and imposed, while endogenous institutions emerge spontaneously without a formal process of design. Given the nature of the Meiji Constitution as a document designed and imposed by the Japanese political elite with the aid of foreign advisors, it is clear that it is an IEX-type institution.

For this reason, my framework directly addresses scenarios of indigenous imposition. In Boettke, Coyne, and Leeson's analysis, the key factor in an institution's staying power is the degree to which it is embedded in the *mētis* of a community. Characterized as "local knowledge resulting from practical experience" (Boettke, Coyne, and Leeson 2008, 338), *mētis* acts as the glue that attaches an institution to a population. If the institution arises spontaneously out of the individual actions of the members of the population, then it will naturally be securely embedded in the *mētis*, while a foreign-designed and -imposed institution is likely to go adrift because of a mismatch with local practices. In between these two scenarios lie IEX institutions such as the Meiji Constitution. Because their designers are indigenous, IEX institutions are likely to more closely link to the *mētis*, and thus have a higher chance of sticking to the populace.

Closer examination of the record of this category of institutions raises the following issue: is close linkage to the *mētis* a unitary matter, or can it be analyzed in component elements. Moreover, if the relationship can be broken down, what is the balance among those components? This issue arises in part out of the apparent disjuncture between the nature of the Meiji Constitution and its record of success in history. The Meiji Constitution represented a new political order on several levels. Not only did it explicitly import European legal norms—to the point that a side-by-side comparison of its provisions with contemporary German constitutions shows direct mirroring in the drafting process (Suzuki 1941a, 1941b, 1942)—but it also consolidated a fundamental shift in the arrangement of power within Japan. The most notable element of continuity between Japan's preceding immanent constitution and the concrete provisions of the 1889 charter—the sovereignty of the Emperor in fact as well as in name—was itself only two decades distant from overthrowing centuries of shogunal control, and yet despite this disjuncture, it proved a remarkably durable institutional foundation. The Meiji Constitution regime endured, its founding document formally unamended, until it was toppled from without at the end of World War II.

The Meiji Constitution is a paradigmatic example of an IEX institution; one that seems at first glance like an exhibit of an institution quite removed from its historical context, yet it proved quite sticky. Rather than hypothesizing that Japan experienced an outlier of success in this historical instance, I take this as an opportunity to analyze how the success of the Meiji Constitution may in fact represent a way in which a closeness to the *mētis* can be concealed by the overt form of an institution. By examining this instance, I aim to work toward a more granular understanding of both the potentially confusing success of the Meiji Constitution as well as the way in which IEX institutions function more generally. I take inspiration in this approach from the perspective that the construction of both understanding and causal chains for generic circumstances ultimately rests on the examination of particulars in the form of case studies (Steinmetz 2004).

This relationship between local knowledge and form arises out of the entanglement of two conditions: (1) that the constitution is being produced in a context that possesses preexisting constitutional structures and (2) that the agents involved in creating the constitution are not only concerned with conditions internal to their community but are also simultaneously reacting to external forces. In the case of Meiji, we can see these conditions embodied in the incentive for the constitutional drafters to construct an institution that would both stick to local, historically contingent conditions, as well as effectively signal to forces abroad that Japan was worthy of recognition as a peer civilization.

Thus, in order to understand the success of the Meiji Constitution, I hypothesize that a key point of analysis is its formal nature as related to the apparent distance between the Japanese *mētis* and the European legal structures to be utilized. This analysis of form is, I think, best characterized as an examination of the aesthetic character of the constitution and its context. The process of decision-making regarding the form of the constitutional order that proceeds from those needs is inherently aesthetic in character. This character arises on account of the way the process is rooted in reflection on the formal properties of the choices available (Nonaka and Takeuchi 1995, 37).

The actors are concerned with not only making decisions in line with abstract principles but also with making decisions that will fit with a specific vision. That vision is not only internal to the actor but also external in that it is to be projected as a signal toward other parties and that external signaling was a core part of the constitutional promulgation process in the Meiji case. These elements point to the fact that the constitution itself will possess a deeply embedded aesthetic element over and above the way in which it already takes on particular forms to convey the law.

In approaching the question of the interaction of the process of constitutional reformation with the notion of a constitution possessing an aesthetic character, I turn to the use of Walter Benjamin's essay on "The Work of Art in the Age of Its Mechanical Reproducibility" (Benjamin 1989, 2007). Benjamin's theme in this essay is to examine how, even though reproduction of works of art is an ancient undertaking, the advent of mechanized reproductive technologies such as lithography can influence our encounter with *objets d'art*. Specifically, Benjamin argues that the distinguishing characteristic of an original piece of art located at a particular point in time and space is the possession of "aura." This aura, which derives from the work's unique nature and its specific context, is an aspect of the work that is, Benjamin argues, outside of the technical sphere that can be handled by means of reproduction. For this reason, even though it has become possible to copy the physical form of a given work of art through such means as lithography, it remains impossible to impart to the copy the aura of the original (Benjamin 2007, 220–221). This remains the case even if, as becomes relevant for the case study undertaken in this chapter, the reproduced item ultimately does appear to take on an aura of its own.

Let us now take Benjamin's conceptual discussion and port it into the legal sphere: I propose that we can take Benjamin's analysis of the decline of the "aura" of a work of art and apply it essentially wholesale to "works of law" in cases represented paradigmatically by the legal knowledge exchange that Japan performed in the late nineteenth century. Benjamin opens his essay with the observation that "[i]n principle a work of art has always been reproducible" (Benjamin 2007, 218). Indeed, over and above the mere fact that a trained artist in a given medium would be able to copy an artwork with some degree of fidelity, reproduction of representative masterworks has been a core mode of training throughout history—as well as one of the main means by which artists' studios of the Renaissance and beyond have managed their workloads (Cole 1983).

The inherently reproducible nature of art that undergirds Benjamin's study is also observable in the case of the law, or at the very least in its positive expression in the world. Any lawmaking agent can look at a neighboring law-possessing entity and produce a copy of the laws perceived as possessed by the neighbor. In the case of a neighbor that has codified laws, the process of copying could be done more or less directly, making allowances for the contingency of linguistic and conceptual translation. Even in the event that the neighbor is not in possession of explicitly codified laws, the lawmaking agent is capable of observing the affairs of its neighbor and determining if it perceives there to "be something" along the lines of a fact of the social sciences that the agent might wish to codify explicitly for its own use (cf. Hayek 2014, 78ff).

This underlying reproducibility is illustrated in many historical legal systems through mechanisms such as, for example, the reception of Roman Law by European states. Beyond this though, I further contend that the legal sphere also reflects the evolutionary transition that Benjamin discusses in the artwork essay. Whereas certain types of artisanal products had been producible in mass quantities starting in the ancient era, the early modern period saw the appearance of technologies such as movable type printing, lithography, sound recording, and film that enabled the mechanical reproduction of works beyond the two traditionally available modes of stamping and molding (Benjamin 2007, 218–219). In the case of the law, the same technological advancements that enabled the formation of an industry for the mechanical reproduction of artworks have simultaneously smoothed the path to the adoption of foreign legal forms—a process that has been theorized as the creation of a "Legal Transplant" (Watson 1993).

In Benjamin's model, the process of mechanical reproduction generally proceeds by taking some original artifact and then transferring a recording or copy of that artifact to a new location. An example would be the recording of a landscape in a photograph followed by copying that photograph in each one of a myriad of newspapers. By contrast, although the law is subject to mechanical reproduction in the sense that copies of legal documents can be reproduced *en masse* by technological means, I primarily identify the mechanical nature of the reproduction of law in the case of Meiji Japan with the mentality of modular transferability that can be observed in the process.

This approach to the linkage between law and aura meshes naturally with the understanding of a connection between institutional success and closeness to *mētis*. The aura of an object and the *mētis* of an environment are corollaries in this approach, although not direct analogs. Both are the result of a natural process of generation in a particular context, but the aura has a much more definite connection to questions of perception.

It must be noted that as a point of differentiation that this approach breaks new ground relative to most of the scholarship that brings aesthetic considerations into contact with the study of the law. Well-developed work on the intersection of law and literature, positive and negative (e.g., White 1973; Weisberg 1992; Posner 2009), has predominantly focused on the representation of the law in literary narratives as a means of getting at a deeper understanding of the nature of the law. In this respect, the focus of much of that work hews closely to more traditional analyses of literary scenes and by extension judicial performances such as the course of trials.

Literary sources are also frequently used as source texts for the explication of the historical legal culture of a work's time and place (Bell and Vecchiato 2021). My approach emphasizes the aesthetics arising out of a specific processual characteristic of the existence of a law in context. Other approaches consider the operation of aesthetic concepts internal to legal activities, as is the case with Daniel Damler's monograph on the use of sensory analogies in legal thought (Damler 2016). By "internal" I denote the fact that such an analysis takes as its object the form of analogies that are being used instrumentally by legal thinkers in order to formulate laws or cogitate about them.

Rather than the aforementioned types of contemplation, my goal herein is to advance the development of a theoretical understanding of the relationships between the form of a (constitutional) law, the actors drafting the law in that form, and the exogenous and endogenous factors conditioning the behavior of those actors in regard to the goal of producing a successful institutional form.

These perspectives combine to form the analytical lens that I turn on the case of the Meiji Constitution in the next section. To briefly summarize the structure of the lens developed thus far, I build on an understanding of institutional uptake as being linked to how closely the institution fits with the local conditions by linking that framework with a critical attention to aesthetic form and attendant signaling behavior. In my case study, I examine how the indigenous group of Japanese constitutional actors—the Meiji oligarchs—worked to match the form of the constitution to the simultaneous demands of attaining successful uptake by the Japanese people and attaining recognition from Western observers. To do so, I turn my attention to the activities of a liminal group: the foreign legal advisors hired by the oligarchs. These Western legal scholars were external in their viewpoint, but under the direction of the indigenous powers, and they thereby provide a means of examining the process of constitutional formation from multiple directions at once.[4]

THE CASE OF THE MEIJI CONSTITUTION OF 1889

Let us now turn to the specifics of the case of the Meiji Constitution. As described in the introduction, following the consolidation of imperial power in the 1870s, the Japanese government under the leadership of figures such as Itō Hirobumi continued, and indeed expanded, the program of modernizing development that had begun under the Tokugawa Shogunate. Those efforts continued under the seemingly ever-looming threat of direct colonization by Western powers, but they were also conducted with an eye to ameliorating other impositions on Japan's sovereignty.

In particular, the government sought to alter the conditions of the "unequal treaties" forced upon the Shogunate by a range of countries, starting with the United States and running through Denmark and the Kingdom of Hawai'i (Kayaoğlu 2010, 67). This situation led the government to go beyond policies aimed at economic and military development sufficient to defend its territorial integrity: the government also focused on authoring and implementing a new legal system, which was itself to be founded on a new constitution (Samuels 1994; Ando 2000). This new system would be crafted using Western legal and constitutional theories, under the guidance of foreign experts. With the help of these legal experts, the Meiji oligarchs planned to promulgate a western-style constitution that would provide not only an institutional scaffold for further economic development, but also a means of signaling Japan's status as a civilized country. This latter component was a necessary ingredient in Japan's efforts to renegotiate the unequal treaties to which it had been subjected since the "opening" of the country (Hozumi 1904; Takii 2007, 2014).

The advisors in question, known generally as the *O-yatoi Gaikokujin*—that is, the "honorable hired foreigners"—were drawn from around the world to aid the development of everything from metallurgical and forestry industries, to police and postal systems, to the drafting of the imperial constitution and its attendant law codes (Burks 1985; Pedlar 1990; Meißner 2018). The list of legal advisors included figures from France, the United Kingdom, and America, but the team working on the drafting of the new imperial constitution was dominated by Germans (Pedlar 1990, 184–190; Röhl 2005).

These advisors were hired for their expertise in modern European legal forms. Their job was to take that knowledge and apply it to the production of charters and legal codes for Japan. These documents would in turn be used not only for driving socioeconomic transformation but also as centerpieces of a campaign aimed at rectifying the inequalities in Japan's treaty status. Such rectification was necessary because, to legal observers of the mid-nineteenth century, Japan was a country not fully equal to Western powers in terms of its standing in international law. This differential was in turn the basis for demands for extraterritoriality in the so-called "unequal treaties" signed by Japan.

Extraterritoriality operated on the principle of subjecting non-Japanese nationals to the courts of their home countries for actions performed in Japan, removing them from the jurisdiction of the Japanese government and thus explicitly intruding upon Japan's sovereignty. This imposition was not based in some notion that Japan was lawless, rather it arose from the view that Japan was possessed of laws that were defective relative to those operating in the West. Japan's status as simultaneously fundamentally different and yet possessing a capacity for recognizable legal activity can be illustrated by the selection of Japan as a hyperbolic case in *The Federalist Papers*.

In Federalist 82, Alexander Hamilton discusses the consequences for the jurisdiction of state courts in the event of the erection of a federal judiciary. Amidst this discussion, Hamilton defends against accusations that such a federal system would appropriate the domains of the state courts by arguing that no such prerogative would be lost outside of certain appeal rights. In the course of this defense, Hamilton states that

> The judiciary power of every government looks beyond its own local or municipal laws, and in civil cases lays hold of all subjects of litigation between parties within its jurisdiction, though the causes of dispute are relative to the laws of

the most distant part of the globe. *Those of Japan*, not less than of New York, may furnish the objects of legal discussion to our courts. (Hamilton, Jay, and Madison 2001, emphasis added)

This statement that courts in a Western jurisdiction were capable, and indeed in some cases would presumably be obliged, to take cognizance of the laws of Japan illustrates the long history behind the belief in the potential for legal alignment. This perception of potential alignment is the root of Japanese efforts to acquire a westernized constitutional charter and then signal that acquisition. If there had been an insuperable gap in the perception of Japan, even if only in the short run, then no potential renegotiation of such perceptions would have been in the cards as a factor in the process of constitutional reformation.

We can thus consider the nature of those signals by conceiving of the constitution as a means for attaining interstate recognition. Contra interpretations of state success in attaining diplomatic ends as resting on the power-projection capacities of the state in question, Jonah Stuart Brundage (Stuart Brundage 2018) has emphasized the importance of state actors attaining legibility in the eyes of their interlocutors—before it is possible for a state to wield power in diplomatic interactions, it must be recognized as being a state capable of holding such power. The acquisition of a western-style constitution on the part of Japan was, I argue, the precondition for the military and economic power accumulated by the modernizing Japanese state to be recognized. In fact, we can observe that the possession of the constitution was not only necessary but also sufficient to affect the start of renegotiations.

Applying Mill's method of difference (Mill 1950, 214ff) to the cases of Japan prepromulgation and postpromulgation (i.e., Japan at time points where its macropolitical circumstances differ only in whether or not the world was aware of Japan's possession of a western-style constitutional charter), we can see that the shift corresponds with the successful opening of treaty renegotiation. This step led to the conclusion of the first renegotiated treaties, with the United States and United Kingdom, in 1894—in advance of other military and economic signals of Japan's successful modernization, such as the acquisition of colonies (Taiwan in 1895 after defeating China in the First Sino-Japanese War), recognition as a peer nation through a western alliance (conclusion of the Anglo-Japanese Alliance, 1902), or defeat of a recognized global power (victory in the Russo-Japanese War, 1905).

The Japanese government faced a conundrum as a result: how to thread between generating the sort of Western-style legal tools necessary to show credible commitment to reform and to attain treaty renegotiation, and working to have a system that would fit with their local context. Put slightly differently, there was a need to transition the legal regime from the traditional, organically grown constitutional order of which Japan was possessed, to a Western-style constitution. Further, that transition would need to be communicated in a way that grafted the innovations onto the existing social stock if the nascent imperial regime was to consolidate itself fully.

Both barriers can be seen in relation to the problem of commitment in institutional restructuring. In a reconstruction scenario, this problem runs in the direction of an outside reconstructing power toward the populace of the country being reconstructed (Coyne and Boettke 2009); the reconstructor must demonstrate a credible commitment to the process of institutional construction and reform, else the populace will distrust the process and the reform will fail. The case at hand runs in both directions: the Empire of Japan was operating under external pressure from the threat of further violations of its sovereignty, but it was also driving its own process of constitutional reformation.

More than just committing to its own populace that changes would be favorable and understandable, in order to attain the goal of renegotiation, Japan had to demonstrate a credible commitment to Western modes of governance such that it would overcome the perception from the early days of the opening process that "[i]t would have been positively criminal for the Foreign [viz. Western] Powers to have placed their nationals at the mercy of the ignorant, untrained, brutal Japanese judges" (Pedlar 1990, 186). The status recognition by Western powers thus arose from the recognition of credible commitment to Western law; the nature of that credible commitment in the study at hand was the promulgation of a constitutional charter and associated law codes that fit with contemporary, Western legal forms. But going too far in that direction would run the risk, when viewed from our observational position, of severely damaging the new institution's ability to "stick" to the social structures in place. The question then becomes what exactly the Japanese were interested in producing as the object of demonstration toward the West—that is, what was the operative constitutional form selected by the oligarchs and their advisor-employees?

The differentiation of the notion of a constitution as either "all rules which directly or indirectly affect the distribution or the exercise of the sovereign power in the state" (Dicey 1960, 24) or as a concrete document that codifies and reifies those principles of distribution takes on additional significance when we analyze the transactional and aesthetic dimensions of a process of constitutional reformation. While both notions of a constitution can certainly possess an aesthetic dimension, since both have some core sense of form—either form of power distribution or form in style and concrete existence—it is certainly easier to contemplate this character when dealing with a case involving a circumscribed charter. At the same time, of course, there exists an interchange of content between these two forms, and it is not obvious how some elements end up expressed in one form versus the other (Elkins 2019). In the case at hand, we can leverage linguistic evidence to analyze how this separation of forms played out and consequently how both constitutional concepts intertwined with the range of audiences for the reformation process and its products.

To perform this analysis, we can turn to an overview of the intellectual landscape in which the Japanese leaders and their employees were working in the late nineteenth century. On the Japanese side, although access by Europeans was heavily restricted in the two and a half centuries prior to the arrival of Commodore Perry, that access was not cut off in its entirety. The Dutch were permitted to maintain a trading presence at their manufactory on the island of Dejima at Nagasaki (Friday 2012). While the Dutch presence was for the purpose of trade, the Japanese also took advantage of this line of contact to the Western world to acquire knowledge of various subjects, birthing the field of *Rangaku*, or Dutch Studies, under which the Japanese subsumed the study of all western-sourced knowledge.

This process of knowledge importation through Dutch-language materials continued after the opening, but by the early 1870s, other European languages such as English, French, and German had almost wholly supplanted Dutch as the major Western languages in use in Japanese society. This changeover is visible in the careers of some of the individual Japanese involved in the modernization process of the Meiji era; many began traditional studies of the Chinese classics alongside education in Western topics using Dutch as children in the 1850s and 1860s, only to transition to the use of another language such as German (Rimer 1975, 20).[5] This replacement had a significant effect on the development of the Japanese language, with new loan words being sourced from English and German.

The Japanese also began coining new words to capture the meaning of the terminology that they were adopting from abroad. Of particular interest in our case is the legal terminology that the Japanese developed as part of the modernization program. The modern term for "constitution" in Japanese is "kenpō," which the modernizers adopted from their historical tradition (Ashibe 1992, Vol. 1, 2f). Yet whereas both the English "constitution" and the German "Verfassung" have a doubled meaning along the lines of what we have examined earlier in this chapter—referring not only to a society's basic law charter but also to the structure and organization of that society as a whole by analogy to physical constitution—the Japanese "kenpō" is used only in regard to the former, documentary notion. This delimitation is illustrated by the attachment of the term to the most notable of Japan's historical constitutional documents—the so-called "Seventeen Article Constitution of Prince Shōtoku." Although that seventh-century document does bear indications of the general form of the Japanese state, it is more concerned with the instantiation of Buddhist and Confucian moral principles (De Bary, Gluck, and Tiedemann 2005, Vol. 1).

In the case of the German-language scholarship that formed the tradition used by advisors, this ambiguity was occasionally mitigated through the use of the word "Verfassungsgesetz" to refer to the concrete realization of the concept (cf. e.g., Schmitt 2017, 11–20; Badura 1973). This separation helps us to realize that, on the one hand, the Japanese modernization effort was being precise about the production of a charter that could be used in an exemplary fashion. Such a charter had the potential to be used apodictically in the demonstration of Japan's acquisition of western legal order: by virtue of being written in a style legible as modern to Western diplomats, the document backstopped an argument that might not correspond to all elements of the constitutional functions in operation (Elkins 2019, 178).

Yet the Meiji oligarchs were not only concerned with the acquisition of a modern "kenpō" but also with the way such a change would affect the transformation of the structure of the nation—they evinced awareness of exactly the sort of dynamic elements that could result from the interaction of an imposed institution with preexisting structures. So, for instance, in the early stages of the modernization process, one Nakamura Masao discussed "Changing the Character of the People" in the *Meiroku Zasshi*, a prominent organ for the westernizing elite; in a speech given in 1875, he stated that the political structures created by a new legal system would "contribute to a renewal of the public mind . . . [and] change attitudes" (Braisted 1976, 373). There were also those who took a stance aimed at modernizing without westernizing, gaining the advantages of economic modernity without sacrificing a uniquely Japanese way of being (Swale 2000). The charter, then, takes center stage in the externally oriented negotiations, while it also takes a representative role, expressing the change in the totality of power relations that would shape the evolution of society internally.

Connected to this tension between formal dynamism and structural status is the fact that one dominant school of legal thought in both Germany and Japan during this period was committed to the notion that a nation's laws were the outgrowths of just the sort of indigenous national character, or *Volksgeist,* that the oligarchs were interested in preserving (Dumoulin, Stolte, and Schiffer 1939; Wittkau 1994; Beiser 2011; Wachutka 2013; Dilcher 2017; Schröder 2020). The Meiji oligarchs and their German expert employees were engaged in a project predicated on the idea that a constitution and ancillary statutes can be shaped according to imported forms and norms. Moreover, the attitude toward laws as an expression of a *Volksgeist* had enough staying power to take the stage in later decades as a justification used by Nazi ideologues for the affinity of Germany and Japan as military allies—the two having similar state forms was taken as a reflection of the two countries having compatible national spirits (Koellreutter 1941).

Most prominent among the German experts active in the constitutional drafting process was Hermann Roesler, the longest-serving of the German legal advisors (Becker 2001; Menkhaus 2017). Roesler produced a complete draft proposal for the Meiji Constitution based primarily on German models. Roesler's draft reflects a modular mentality; he was working in accordance with general theories of constitutional normativity, such as internal consistency, while also taking inspiration from the usage of provisions in the German Imperial Constitution of 1871 as well as the individual constitutions of the federated states of which the Wilhelmine *Reich* was comprised (Siemes 1968).

This mode of mechanical transference, of making an essentially direct transfer of a constitutional provision from one context to another rather than allowing for organic institutional evolution, was recognized by contemporary commentators, and generally applauded as the primary means by which the Japanese had succeeded in producing a constitution that was recognizably modern in style (*Constitution with Speeches* 1889; Wilson 1969). Such a modular approach takes advantage of the separation of constitutional functionality from the form of a constitutional charter to produce a facsimile of constitutional models. The consequence of this mechanical reproduction, however, is that thc constitution that is generated as output will be felt to be lacking in aura.

Parallel with how a lack of aura in the case of the work of art lends a sense of inauthenticity, the lack of aura in the case of mechanical constitutional transference helps to explain the lack of a sensation of connection that can arise with such imposed institutions. We can observe this sensation of lack even on the part of external observers by reading Roesler's own comments on his draft constitutional proposal. In working on the position of the emperor in the constitution, Roesler ran into conflict with his employers over their demand that the constitution itself explicitly recognize the divinity of the imperial house, which Roesler viewed as in logical conflict with articles providing for the freedom of religion in accordance with contemporary liberal ideals (Siemes 1968; Thomas 2019). That is to say, the local elites knew that there was a significant historical institution—the imperial throne—which they were dependent on for legitimacy in addition to their ideological commitment to imperialism. But there was an apparent conflict between the incorporation of that content and the formal expressions needed to be perceived as committed to western legal style.

At the same time though, Roesler was attached to the idea that a constitution should express national character, stating that his draft captured the "natural constitution" of the Japanese. The fact that Roesler felt the need to voice a conscious attempt to incorporate the particulars of this "natural constitution" into the charter is indicative of the fact that the mechanical transfer of constitutional norms into a new scenario is unable to copy over the aura of an original. Moreover, the expressed tensions between the concept of what embodies the unique character intended for the constitution and the imported norms only heighten this contrast.

Viewed from an external perspective, the unique aura of the constitution, which cannot be reproduced by mechanical means, is ultimately of no interest though. It is in fact the mechanically reproducible normative form that is of interest—the Japanese did not have to produce a Westernized legal regime that embodied their context in order to satisfy the prerequisites for renegotiation, they only needed to acquire a westernized legal regime full stop. The closeness to historical context was relevant primarily in that, on the one hand, it aligned with the conservative tendencies of the oligarchs regarding the Japanese spirit, and on the other hand, that we would tend to view such closeness to the *mētis* as increasing the institution's chances of survival.

The conveyance of this Western form is visible both in the Japanese government's rhetoric surrounding the "modern" theoretical structure of the constitution (*Constitution with Speeches* 1889) and in the Western stylings of the court ceremonial that accompanied the promulgation ceremonies in April 1889 (Kokaze 2011; Antoni and Antoni 2017). In contemplating the messaging about the "Western" and "modern" form of the Meiji Constitution, I note that this was not merely a matter of epiphenomenal appearance along the lines of the Japanese product needing to mirror, say, the German Imperial Constitution of 1871 or the American Constitution, in having a written structure consisting of clauses. If this were the case, then we would have to discount the possibility of Japan's pursuing a British-style unwritten constitution grounded in common law—which they did in fact consider.[6] Rather, the "style" that needed to be pursued and conveyed was one more intimately related to the content that undergirds the protective state as described by Buchanan (Buchanan 1999b); interpreted contemporarily as the requirement for formal provisions regarding certain rights that were then regarded as belonging to the content of a civilized constitution.

Aside from hailing foreign powers, the Japanese regime also needed to incorporate awareness of the constitution into the domestic popular mentality. Because the constitution was imposed by the elites rather than growing naturally, in order to ingrain the new institution into practice, some mode of propagation was necessary. To this end, the government promoted the promulgation ceremony through selected newspaper reports and a massive program of woodblock prints circulated to the general populace (Keene 2002; Lavenberg 2021).

In considering the nature of the Meiji Constitution as an object and its associated aesthetic presentation, the centrality of the emperor to the document itself becomes a significant anchoring point when considering the messaging to the domestic public. In that decision, we can see how the historical context of the Japanese immanent constitution, which had traditionally regarded sovereignty as residing with the emperor even when he was not the de facto ruling power, was instrumentalized for the purpose of smoothing the transition to a formally different regime in the shape of the western-style charter that was the Meiji Constitution of 1889.

The constitution was formulated as being a gift from the emperor to his people, a claim expressed in both the emperor's speech from the throne at the promulgation ceremonies and in the preamble to the constitution itself (*Constitution with Speeches* 1889). The latter further emphasizes the fact that rights to sovereign initiative reside in the imperial person, stating that

> [t]he rights of sovereignty of the State, We [the emperor] have inherited from Our Ancestors, and We shall bequeath them to Our descendants. Neither We nor they shall in future fail to wield them, in accordance with the provisions of the Constitution hereby granted. (Röhl 2005, 60)

I argue that in both the efforts to persuade Western states and to communicate the stature of the new constitution to the people, regime actors were implicitly aware of the aural considerations attached to their machinations.

In handling the exogenous factor of demands for certain formal characteristics in the constitutional order, the oligarchs resorted to a mechanical process that inherently wipes away aura to produce a blank (approximate) copy. At the same time, they worked to reimbue some sense of contextual specificity in accordance with a nativist, imperialist ideology by directing experts like Roesler to include certain provisions in the charter and by executing a campaign to shape the perception of the constitutional document as a gift from the divine emperor. Indeed, the creation of the imperial family in its modern institutional form is directly traceable to the promulgation ceremonies and subsequent efforts on the part of the government to promote the imperial cult (Fujitani 1996). In this way, the Japanese oligarchy of the late nineteenth century navigated the tension between their desire to have a western-style legal charter and their ideologically driven need to maintain "natural" native institutions in a way that legitimized the new regime. These efforts to consciously infuse a specific aural aspect into the constitution were performed predominantly through the use of quintessentially mass-produced media such as newspapers and woodblock prints.

CONCLUSION

In this chapter, I have examined the structure of the process of constitutional creation with an eye to expanding our understanding of how exogenous shocks impact that process and what lessons we can learn through attention to the formal character of a constitution when examining institutional development. By reference to the case of the drafting and promulgation of the 1889 Constitution of the Empire of Japan, we have seen how questions around the survivability of an imposed institution can be illuminated by the consideration of a sort of "aesthetics of legality" in the case of legal institutions. Such institutions, in taking a modular, mechanical approach to the crafting of institutions by reference to external structures, will tend to produce institutions that are empty of aura. This lack is akin to, but differentiated from, the content-oriented issue of the distance of the institution from indigenous practice that tends to occur with imposed institutions.

In trying to formulate an IEX institution, institutional innovators would reasonably aim to maximize the stickiness of the institution by attempting to closely follow the *mētis* of their nations. But in some circumstances, such as that of Meiji Japan, external factors can limit the extent to which that nearness is formally obtainable. Consequently, the issue of the form of the institution—in Japan's case its constitutional charter and legal codes—becomes significant for navigating the reception of the institution by different audiences. In the case of Meiji Japan, the Western stylings of the charter, such as its formal adherence to contemporary European legal theories, were emphasized to the external audience, while its institutional innovativeness in terms of economic and social reform was submerged beneath a symbolic emphasis on its adherence to traditional notions of imperial sovereignty.

Beyond this analysis, further investigation is possible. Although the case study presented in this chapter looked at an instance in which the misalignment between form and content for internal and external audiences was one that weighted externally oriented form and internally oriented content as primary, the reverse is also possible—when a regime innovates in a way that looks formally like what has previously been practiced in a society, but in reality introduces a significant break from preexisting structures. Overall, such further examination would continue to contribute to the goal of this chapter, namely the creation of a more granular theory of the way that institutions and legal structures innately express their aesthetic character, and of how the examination of that character can illuminate the ways in which institutions of various types are ultimately communicated to and throughout societies.

NOTES

1. While access to Japan was limited between roughly 1600 and 1850, the extent of that limitation varied by country. It is important to note that Japan was not hermetically sealed off from the outside world during this period—and a perspective that considers the closure to have been total apart from access for the Dutch through Nagasaki generalizes unjustifiably from the European experience (Hellyer 2002). In this study, my general lack of discussion of Japan's relationships with its local environment is not a function of a lack of such relationships before and after the 1850s, but rather of the fact that Japan's leaders did not regard neighbors such as China as powers capable of levying demands on the Japanese state as to how it should structure its constitution.

2. The power of such constitutional signals has been generally recognized, but it is necessary to simply run off into a flight of fancy over the potential embedded in within them. James Buchanan recognized as much in his observation that "shock waves" reverberated throughout the Western world as a result of California's 1978 ratification of Proposition 13 (Buchanan 1999a, 58). The aesthetic aspect of the constitutional, indeed the institutional, transformation process is one more element of the emergent phenomenon of social order that needs dispassionate consideration in the service of building our way toward durable institutions of our own.

3. It is, of course, possible that an individual sovereign could "lie" by doing such things as giving guarantees of rights in the charter that are not enforced; it is also possible that a group could so bind itself that it is unable to express an actually occurring change in its immanent constitution through successful alteration of the charter, in which case they would have to act (when formally called to adjudicate in the legal sphere at least) as if no such change had come to pass.

4. In terms of linking this distinction of internal and external with the framing of IEX and other institutional forms, the western advisors are external insofar as they have no built-up lived experience of the Japanese context—most of them had no Japanese language skills, even after years of residence—but they are liminal, between an external and internal position, in that they were under the direction of the oligarchs, who were themselves culturally invested insiders. In this framing, the general Japanese populace is the generative site of native context while any observer from the West, such as a U.S. diplomat, would be a purely external party.

5. This example is based on the life of Mori Ōgai. After completing studies in medicine in Japan, Mori was sent to Germany by the Imperial Japanese Army to conduct further academic work before ultimately returning to a career as an army medical officer and prominent literary author. Mori's linguistic arc is typical of the men of his generation, starting with some amount of *Rangaku* work in Dutch before transitioning to one or several of English, German, and French as main secondary languages. All three of the latter group were used extensively by those working in the field of law, a field that divided itself into factions along lines of adherence to the language and legal model of particular countries (Michaelis 1922; Hara 1977; Burks 1985).

6. On which note, a pragmatic factor in the selection of Germany as model over and above the perceived cultural similarity (Takii 2014) and Germany's reputation for being at the cutting edge of legal science (Gale 1982) was likely the fact that the

transplantation of a legal system rooted in codes along the lines of civil law was simply more feasible than trying to organically grow a common law system alongside of training a generation of judges to implement and manufacture it (Watson 1993).

REFERENCES

Ando, Junko. 2000. *Die Entstehung der Meiji-Verfassung: Zur Rolle des deutschen Konstitutionalismus im modernen japanischen Staatswesen, Monographien aus dem Deutschen Institut für Japanstudien der Philipp Franz von Siebold Stiftung*. München: Iudicium Verlag.

Antoni, Klaus, and Yvonne Antoni. 2017. "Inventing a State Ceremony: Ottmar von Mohl, Jinmu-tennō and the Proclamation of the Meiji Constitution on February 11th 1889." *Beiträge des Arbeitskreises Japanische Religionen* 11.

Ashibe, Nobuyoshi 芦部信喜. 1992. *Kenpōgaku* 憲法学 [Constitutional Law]. 3 vols. Tōkyō: Yūhikaku.

Badura, Peter. 1973. "Verfassung und Verfassungsgesetz." In *Festschrift für Ulrich Scheuner zum 70. Geburtstag* edited by Horst Ehmke et al., 19–39. Berlin: Duncker & Humblot.

Becker, Bert. 2001. "Der Staatsrechtler Hermann Roesler als Regierungsberater in Japan." In *Mecklenburger im Ausland: historische Skizze zum Leben und Wirken von Mecklenburgern in ihrer Heimat und in der Ferne*, edited by Martin Guntau, 92–98. Bremen: Temmen.

Beiser, Frederick C. 2011. *The German Historicist Tradition*. Oxford: Oxford University Press.

Bell, Matthew, and Daniele Vecchiato. 2021. "Legal Cultures in the Age of Goethe: An Introduction." *Law & Literature* 34 (2): 165–170.

Benjamin, Walter. 1989. *Das Kunstwerk im Zeitalter seiner technischen Reproduzierbarkeit*. Reclam.

———. 2007. *Illuminations : Essays and Reflections*. New York, NY: Schocken Books.

Boettke, Peter J., Christopher J. Coyne, and Peter T. Leeson. 2008. "Institutional Stickiness and the New Development Economics." *American Journal of Economics and Sociology* 67 (2): 331–358.

Braisted, William Reynolds, ed. 1976. *Meiroku Zasshi: Journal of the Japanese Enlightenment*. Cambridge, MA: Harvard University Press.

Buchanan, James M. 1999a. *The Collected Works of James M. Buchanan, Volume 1: The Logical Foundations of Constitutional Liberty*. Indianapolis, IN: Liberty Fund.

———. 1999b. *The Collected Works of James M. Buchanan, Volume 3: The Calculus of Consent: Logical Foundations of Constitutional Democracy*. Indianapolis, IN: Liberty Fund.

Burks, Ardath W., ed. 1985. *The Modernizers: Overseas Students, Foreign Employees, and Meiji Japan*. Boulder, CO: Westview Press.

Cole, Bruce. 1983. *The Renaissance Artist at Work: From Pisano to Titian*. New York, NY: Harper & Row.

The Constitution of the Empire of Japan with the Speeches Addressed to Students of Political Science in the Johns Hopkins University: Baltimore, April 17, 1889. 1889. Baltimore, MD: Publication Agency of the Johns Hopkins University.

Coyne, Christopher J., and Peter J. Boettke. 2009. "The Problem of Credible Commitment in Reconstruction." *Journal of Institutional Economics* 5 (1): 1–23.

Damler, Daniel. 2016. *Rechtsästhetik: Sinnliche Analogien im juristischen Denken*. Berlin: Duncker & Humblot.

De Bary, Wm. Theodore, Carol Gluck, and Arthur E. Tiedemann, eds. 2005. *Sources of Japanese Tradition*. 2 ed. 2 vols. Vol. 2: 1600 to 2000. New York, NY: Columbia University Press.

Dicey, Albert Venn. 1960. *Introduction to the Study of the Law of the Constitution*. London: MacMillan.

Dilcher, Gerhard. 2017. *Die Germanisten und die Historische Rechtsschule: Bürgerliche Wissenschaft zwischen Romantik, Realismus und Rationalisierung, Studien zur europäischen Rechtsgeschichte*. Frankfurt am Main: Vittorio Klostermann.

Dumoulin, Heinrich, H. Stolte, and W. Schiffer. 1939. "Die Entwicklung der Kokugaku. Dargestellt in ihren Hauptvertretern." *Monumenta Nipponica* 2 (1): 140–164.

Elkins, Zachary. 2019. "Constitutional Transition." In *The Oxford Handbook of Public Choice*, edited by Roger D. Congleton et al. Oxford: Oxford University Press.

Ermakoff, Ivan. 2014. "Exceptional Cases: Epistemic Contributions and Normative Expectations." *European Journal of Sociology* 55 (2): 223–243.

Friday, Karl F., ed. 2012. *Japan Emerging: Premodern History to 1850*. New York, NY: Routledge.

Fujitani, Takashi. 1996. *Splendid Monarchy: Power and Pageantry in Modern Japan*. Berkeley, CA: University of California Press.

Gale, Susan Gaylord. 1982. "A Very German Legal Science: Savigny and the Historical School." *Stanford Journal of International Law* 18 (1), 123–146.

Hamilton, Alexander, John Jay, and James Madison. 2001. *The Federalist: The Gideon Edition*. Indianapolis, IN: Liberty Fund.

Hara, Yoshio. 1977. "From Westernization to Japanization: The Replacement of Foreign Teachers by Japanese Who Studied Abroad." *The Developing Economies* 15 (4): 440–461.

Hayek, Friedrich A. 2014. *The Collected Works of F.A. Hayek, Volume XV : The Market and Other Orders*. Edited by Bruce Caldwell. Chicago, IL: University of Chicago Press.

Hellyer, Robert. 2002. "Historical and Contemporary Perspectives on the Sakoku Theme in Japanese Foreign Relations: 1600–2000." *Social Science Japan Journal* 5 (2): 255–259.

Hozumi, Nobushige. 1904. *The New Japanese Civil Code, as Material for the Study of Comparative Jurisprudence: A Paper Read at the International Congress of Arts and Science, at the Universal Exposition, Saint Louis 1904*. Tokyo: Tokyo Printing Company.

Jansen, Marius B. 2002. *The Making of Modern Japan*. Cambridge, MA: Harvard University Press.

Kayaoğlu, Turan. 2010. *Legal Imperialism: Sovereignty and Extraterritoriality in Japan, the Ottoman Empire, and China*. Cambridge: Cambridge University Press.

Keene, Donald. 2002. *Emperor of Japan: Meiji and His World, 1852–1912*. New York, NY: Columbia University Press.

Koellreutter, Otto. 1941. *Der heutige Staatsaufbau Japans*. Berlin: Junker und Dünnhaupt.

Kokaze, Hidemasa 小風秀雅. 2011. "The Political Space of Meiji 22 (1889): The Promulgation of the Constitution and the Birth of the Nation." *Japan Review: Journal of the International Research Center for Japan Studies* 23: 119–141.

Lavenberg, Irwin. 2021. "The Lavenberg Collection of Japanese Prints." myjapanesehanga.com

McIlwain, Charles H. 1947. *Constitutionalism: Ancient and Modern*. Ithaca, NY: Cornell University Press.

Meißner, Kristin 2018. *Strategische Experten: die imperialpolitische Rolle von ausländischen Beratern in Meiji-Japan (1868–1912)*. Frankfurt am Main: Campus Verlag.

Menkhaus, Heinrich. 2017. "Images of Japan Held by German Legal Experts in the Meiji Period." In *Mutual Perceptions and Images in Japanese-German Relations, 1860–2010*, edited by Sven Saaler et al., 180–191. Leiden: Brill.

Michaelis, Georg. 1922. *Für Staat und Volk, eine Lebensgeschichte*. Berlin: Furche-Verlag.

Mill, John Stuart. 1950. *John Stuart Mill's Philosophy of Scientific Method*. New York, NY: Hafner Publishing Co.

Moore, Barrington. 1966. *Social Origins of Dictatorship and Democracy: Lord and Peasant in the Making of the Modern World*. Boston, MA: Beacon Press.

Nonaka, Ikujiro, and Hirotaka Takeuchi. 1995. *The Knowledge-Creating Company: How Japanese Companies Create the Dynamics of Innovation*. Oxford: Oxford University Press.

Ostrom, Vincent. 1997. *The Meaning of Democracy and the Vulnerability of Democracies: A Response to Tocqueville's Challenge*. Ann Arbor, MI: University of Michigan Press.

Pedlar, Neil. 1990. *The Imported Pioneers: Westerners Who Helped Build Modern Japan*. Kent: Japan Library, Ltd.

Posner, Richard A. 2009. *Law and Literature*. Third ed. Cambridge, MA: Harvard University Press.

Rimer, J. Thomas. 1975. *Mori Ōgai, Twayne's World Leaders Series*. Boston, MA: Twayne Publishers.

Röhl, Wilhelm, ed. 2005. *History of Law in Japan Since 1868, Handbuch der Orientalistik*. Leiden: Brill.

Samuels, Richard J. 1994. *"Rich Nation, Strong Army" National Security and the Technological Transformation of Japan*. Edited by Peter J. Katzenstein, *Cornell Studies in Political Economy*. Ithaca, NY: Cornell University Press.

Schmitt, Carl. 2017. *Verfassungslehre*. Berlin: Duncker & Humblot. Original edition, 1928.

Schröder, Jan. 2020. *Recht als Wissenschaft: Geschichte der juristischen Methode in der Neuzeit (1500–1990)*. 3., überarbeitete und wesentlich erweiterte ed. 2 vols. Munich: C.H. Beck.

Schwebell, Gertrude C., ed. 1970. *Die Geburt des modernen Japan in Augenzeugenberichten*. Düsseldorf: Karl Rauch Verlag.

Siemes, Johannes. 1968. *Hermann Roesler and the Making of the Meiji State; with his Commentaries on the Meiji Constitution, Monumenta Nipponica Monographs*. Tokyo: Sophia University Press.

Skocpol, Theda. 2015. *States and Social Revolutions: A Comparative Analysis of France, Russia, and China, Canto Classics*. Cambridge: Cambridge University Press. Original edition, 1979.

Stuart Brundage, Jonah. 2018. "The Social Sources of Geopolitical Power: French and British Diplomacy and the Politics of Interstate Recognition, 1689 to 1789." *American Sociological Review* 83 (6): 1254–1280.

Suzuki, Yasuzō. 1941a. "Hermann Roesler und die japanische Verfassung (Einleitung und Kap. I)." *Monumenta Nipponica* 4 (1): 53–87.

———. 1941b. "Hermann Roesler und die Japanische Verfassung (Kap. II-III)." *Monumenta Nipponica* 4 (2): 428–453.

———. 1942. "Hermann Roesler und die Japanische Verfassung (Kap. IV und Anhang)." *Monumenta Nipponica* 5 (2): 347–400.

Swale, Alistair D. 2000. *The Political Thought of Mori Arinori: A Study in Meiji Conservatism*. Richmond: Japan Library.

———. 2009. *The Meiji Restoration: Monarchism, Mass Communication and Conservative Revolution*. New York, NY: Palgrave Macmillan.

Takii, Kazuhiro. 2007. *The Meiji Constitution: The Japanese Experience of the West and the Shaping of the Modern State*. Translated by David Noble. Tokyo: International House of Japan.

———. 2014. *Itō Hirobumi: Japan's First Prime Minister and Father of the Meiji Constitution*. Translated by Takechi Manabu. London: Taylor & Francis.

———. 2019. "Itô Hirobumi und der japanische Konstitutionalismus. Ein kurzes Porträt eines Verfassungsdenkers." In *Rechtstransfer in der Geschichte: Internationale Festschrift für Wilhelm Brauneder zum 75. Geburtstag*, edited by Gábor Hamza et al., 395–406. Berlin: Peter Lang.

Thomas, Jolyon. 2019. *Faking Liberties: Religious Freedom in American-Occupied Japan*. Chicago, IL: University of Chicago Press.

Wachutka, Michael. 2013. *Kokugaku in Meiji-Period Japan: The Modern Transformation of "National Learning" and the Formation of Scholarly Societies*. Boston, MA: Global Oriental.

Watson, Alan. 1993. *Legal Transplants: An Approach to Comparative Law*. Athens, GA: University of Georgia Press.

Weisberg, Richard H. 1992. *Poethics: And Other Strategies of Law and Literature*. New York, NY: Columbia University Press.

White, James B. 1973. *The Legal Imagination: Studies in the Nature of Legal Thought and Expression*. Boston: Little, Brown and Company.

Wilson, Woodrow. 1969. *The Papers of Woodrow Wilson, Volume 6: 1888–1890*. Princeton, NJ: Princeton University Press.

Wittkau, Annette. 1994. *Historismus: zur Geschichte des Begriffs und des Problems*. 2. durchges. Aufl. ed. Göttingen: Vandenhoeck und Ruprecht.

Chapter 8

Masquerading Democracies

What Protest Actions Can Inform Us About the True State of the Regime?

Sargis Karavardanyan

In many self-proclaimed democracies, the prevalence of protests varies markedly. What underlies these discrepancies? Scholars posit that pervasive and recurrent protests can elucidate two distinct facets of a society: (1) a prevalent disenchantment with the governance quality or (2) the existence of robust institutions that facilitate self-expression and are tolerant of societal mobilization in the pursuit of individual rights and change. This chapter seeks to illuminate the factors that underpin variations in protest frequency across democratic nations. This research contends that while democracies inherently claim to possess robust institutional checks meant to curtail corruption, there are instances where these structures are masquerades. When these facades crumble, societal forbearance for corruption wanes, leading to intensified protest movements, an outcome explored herein.

In the context of this study, the term "masquerading" refers to countries that outwardly present characteristics and structures of established democracies, but internally exhibit tendencies of unstable or even autocratic regimes. The facade might manifest through various channels such as controlled media, electoral processes that are not entirely free or fair, or suppression of opposition. The crux of this study is to identify and understand the incongruence between the perceived democratic veneer and the actual state of governance, especially as revealed through protest actions. Thus, when referring to "masquerading democracies," the emphasis is on nations that portray themselves as fully-fledged democracies, while certain underlying attributes might suggest otherwise.

A vast majority of prior research has delved into the institutional and political determinants of regime collapse and democratic backsliding (Hollyer et al. 2018). However, few have ventured to investigate the patterns of collective action, particularly protests, specifically within democratic states. This chapter seeks to bridge this gap in the literature, positing that many democracies merely wear the facade of such systems, and witness elevated levels of protest compared to nations with more robust institutional underpinnings.

To comprehensively address this hypothesis, this study relies on panel data analysis with year and country-fixed effects on protest activities from eighty-three democracies between the years 1995 and 2014. The main outcome of interest in this study is protest per-capita.[1] The main independent variable of interest is regime corruption, which is employed in the quantitative models to predict any potential changes in per capita protest incidents in each country in a specific point in time. Additionally, GDP per capita, unemployment rate, and party formation barriers index are included, along with country and year-fixed effects, to control for unobserved characteristics driving trends in protest activities. While the size of a protest can be a crucial determinant of its impact and its potential to instigate policy or regime change, it is imperative to note the constraints of the present dataset: the data do not include the size of each protest, potentially masking variations in the scale of protests.

In this chapter, the inclusion of the party formation barriers index is a deliberate attempt to assess the intricacies of political inclusivity and representation in democratic societies. Elevated barriers to party formation often imply a constrained environment for formal political participation, a condition that could magnify public discontent by manifesting heightened protest activities or discourage participation depending on whether the society truly operates on democratic premises or masquerades as one. In this essay, I expect that where party formation barriers increase, protest participation will decrease, since many of the democracies that advocate for their institutions are only disguising as such. The predominant focus on corruption is premised on its ramifications on governance, institutional trust, and its potential to erode foundational democratic principles. Whereas barriers to party formation delineate the political arena, corruption permeates through various societal layers, affecting not just political processes but also economic and social interactions. While both elements distinctly influence the democratic fabric, corruption is a more overarching gauge of governance efficacy across diverse democratic settings.

The panel data model's results demonstrate a nuanced yet statistically significant relationship in our sample of eighty-three democratic nations: as regime corruption intensifies, there is a modest positive escalation in per-capita protest activities. This trend aligns with our primary hypothesis, positing a surge in protest activities beyond original levels concurrent with rising regime corruption in democracies. This correlation persists even when accounting for previously mentioned confounding variables. Addressing the question of the authenticity of democracies, the visualizations in figures 8.3, 8.4, and 8.5, comparing between original and predicted per capita protests, indicate a pattern of higher protest levels in the model's predictions for most sampled nations. These results suggest that, while well-functioning democracies foster social cooperation, those marred by chronic corruption witness increased societal pushback in the form of protests.

The organization of this chapter unfolds as follows: The ensuing section discusses existing literature, including theories on democracies, institutional volatility, political corruption, democratic protests, and the interplay between democracy and corruption. The third section discusses this chapter's hypothesis, bridging concepts highlighted in the literature review, discussing the data sources, and detailing the rationale underpinning the empirical models. The fourth section presents the results of the empirical models and discusses their implications, taking note of constraints, and laying down avenues for prospective research to further refine and expand upon both the theoretical and empirical framework. The final section summarizes the findings and discusses further implications.

EXISTING THEORIES AND CONCEPT

The notion of protest movements has been conceptualized in scholarly circles in various ways. For some, it underscores an effort toward positive societal and political change (Bosi et al. 2016). Distinguished scholars like Della Porta (2020) and Almeida (2018), on the other hand, posit that protest movements epitomize the vitality and operational efficacy of a democracy. The enigma surrounding the prevalence of protests even within the most robust democracies has intrigued and occupied academic discourse for numerous decades (Meyer 2004). Within this section, a comprehensive examination of theoretical positions on this issue is undertaken, and an attempt is made to bridge the established view of the determinants of protests with the nuanced interplay of regime corruption, examining its pivotal role in catalyzing public mobilizations.

Democracies and Institutional Instabilities

Differences within political regimes, particularly within democracies, emanate from variances in their public, economic, social, and military institutions. These disparities are further rooted in historical determinants encompassing cultural values, religious and ethnic norms, and a mixture of formal and informal practices (Weede 1996). A plethora of democratic governmental forms exist, such as representative, electoral, dominant-party, parliamentary, presidential, and nonpartisan systems, to name a few (Bjørnskov and Rode 2020). While a detailed exposition on each type is beyond the scope of this chapter, these democratic regimes can be divided into "full" and "flawed" categories. As delineated in the 2022 Democracy Index report by *The Economist*, only 14.4 percent of nations achieve the status of full democracies. In contrast, flawed democracies represent 28.7 percent (Economist Intelligence Unit 2022). This proportion of flawed democracies even surpasses the global tally of hybrid regimes, which stands at 21.6 percent.

In *Autocracy*, Gordon Tullock delves into the intricate dynamics of autocratic governance, underscoring the implications of an unchecked concentration of power for corruption. He posits that the absence of checks and balances in autocratic settings often leads to pervasive corruption and rent-seeking behaviors, as the ruling elite maneuver to extract economic and political advantages. Central to Tullock's argument is the idea that autocratic leaders, much like market participants, behave as rational actors, making decisions motivated by the desire for personal gain. Though primarily analyzing autocratic regimes, Tullock's insights on corruption are useful in the study of protests in self-proclaimed democracies. When ostensibly democratic institutions mirror unchecked power structures, it lays the foundation for corruption, aligning with the conditions for widespread public dissent. In such settings, where democratic representation is eroded by pervasive corruption, citizens may perceive protest as a rational response to these governance failures.

Gordon Tullock's theory of revolution offers a profound reconceptualization of the factors driving collective actions, positioning them within a framework of rational choice and economic incentives. Central to Tullock's thesis is the *paradox of revolution*, which encapsulates the collective action problem inherent in uprisings: while it may be beneficial for a populace to protest collectively, individual actors must weigh the personal costs and risks of participation. This calculus of self-interest, rooted in economic incentives, aligns with this chapter's focus on the role of regime corruption in influencing protest activities in democracies. If individuals in purportedly democratic nations perceive heightened regime corruption as increasing their potential personal gains from protests—be it in the form of improved governance, increased transparency, or other tangible or intangible benefits—they might be more inclined to participate in collective action. Tullock's perspective thus offers an intricate layer to the analysis, suggesting that an increase in per capita protest activities, as a function of escalating regime corruption, could be driven by individuals' rational calculations of potential benefits versus costs.

A core vulnerability of democracies manifests in their skewed public administration, which often consolidates power within a select elite, fostering regime corruption (Rock 2009). Vincent Ostrom's insights into democratic power dynamics underscore this fragility (Ostrom 1997, 47–48). Power in democracy necessitates unwavering accountability; it must remain nonarbitrary, and the accruing benefits should not be monopolized by a privileged few. Deviations from these tenets can trigger institutional instability, amplifying social unrest due to corruption-induced imbalances in resource allocation.

Institutional structure critically influences the trajectory of collective actions, orchestrating a vast array of human endeavors (Bjørnskov and Rode 2020). The robustness and efficacy of these institutional frameworks, however, differ markedly among nations purporting democratic ideals. In nations like Mexico and Namibia, societal-state confrontations have historically facilitated iterative institutional refinement, as exchanges refine each side's demands, reshaping state capacities to assuage the conflict. Yet, an examination of their histories reveals that despite such interactions, sustained public dissidence persists, suggesting unresolved tensions.

Academics have pinpointed many challenges that cripple effective problem-solving in fragile democracies, spurring waves of protest movements. These include (1) a deficit in social frameworks that foster cooperative incentives, (2) an eroding trust in government entities, (3) a bureaucratic ascendency overshadowing democratic governance, and (4) an enfeebled system of checks and balances both within government and public spheres (Della Porta 2020; Arce and Rice 2019; Klein and Regan 2018; Dudouet 2013). An important aspect of regime corruption in democracies is its clandestine nature in administrative sectors, primarily because bureaucrats report to political actors who operate below the head of state. This web of decentralized principal-agent dynamics in some democratic governments exposes societies to the perils of regulatory capture by a select elite, nurturing an environment rife with corruption.

The Logic of Political Corruption

This chapter delves into a specific facet of corruption, often called *regime corruption* but more broadly known as *political corruption*. Political corruption, as various scholars have suggested, encapsulates a gamut of malpractices, be it bribery, nepotism, misappropriation, or the intricate dynamics of rent distribution, all primarily orchestrated by governing agents to further personal interests (Saha and Sen 2021; Rose-Ackerman and Paflika 2016; Jetter et al. 2015; Philp 1997).

Joseph Nye characterized corruption as behavior that diverges "from the formal duties of a public role for private gain" (Nye 1989, 966). Augmenting this perspective, James Scott posited a more layered understanding, melding both constitutional and societal optics, he underscored that our perception of corruption is not merely tied to legal contraventions, but also hinges on broader societal interpretations. This argument stems from the premise that, in many instances, especially within autocratic regimes, citizens may endure injustices without any official transgressions by the governing body or its agents (Scott 1972, 5). Thus, while the letter of the law remains inviolate, the spirit of governance may be deeply tainted.

Gardiner (1989) underscores a nuanced dimension to Scott's argument, positing that individuals' perceptions of corruption are significantly molded by the cultural underpinnings of their local communities. These localized understandings can, at times, starkly deviate from the perspectives endorsed by central authorities.

John Gardiner (1989) delineates corruption through two lenses: legalistic and public opinion. He notes that solely relying on legal standards can sometimes overlook broader societal ethics. He posits, "if an official's act is prohibited by laws . . . it is corrupt; if it's not prohibited, it is not corrupt even if it is abusive or unethical" (1989, 29). Drawing from Scott's work, Gardiner warns against equating legality with morality. He illustrates this with two examples: one from Nazi Germany, where an inspector's illegal yet morally justified act saves a Jewish family, and the other from the 1950s to 1960s U.S. urban renewal programs, where legal decisions marginalized underprivileged communities. Gardiner's analysis challenges strict legal definitions, underscoring the need for ethical considerations.

Lending credence to this argument, Mark Philp (1997) underscores a potential rift between collective public perceptions of corruption and the real-world actions such as public and legal accountability, rule of law, and investigation of bureaucratic conduct taken to minimize corruption. Such a disconnect can be detrimental, as it might inadvertently foster a milieu wherein corruption is tacitly normalized. This normalization emerges when the populace's ability to discern a clear set of ethical public norms or an overarching public interest becomes blurred, leading to what Philp describes as the "entrenchment of a corrupt culture" (Philp 1997).

Implications of Corruption on Protests

The pervasiveness and persistence of governmental corruption play a pivotal role in precipitating antigovernment protests. Central to this is Susan Rose-Ackerman's argument that corruption is not confined to the government but permeates the wider societal fabric. She suggests that "The relationships between government agents and citizens coexist within a unified political system; thus, anyone, whether inside or outside the government, could partake in or be affected by various facets of corruption" (1978, 4). This perspective extends culpability beyond just government officials to all who benefit indirectly through corrupt affiliations. Consequently, protests are more likely to surface in societies where a significant portion of the citizenry lacks ties to corruption in the government, underscoring a perception that corruption is a problem internal to the government.

Protests often emerge as a reflexive response when government corruption becomes widespread (Tansey, Koehler, and Schmotz 2017). If the benefits of a corrupt system are not distributed broadly, those excluded are more inclined to voice their dissent. Gardiner (1989) underscores the importance of political processes in shaping public perceptions of corruption. A vital facet of legitimate politics is equitable policy formulation and implementation: if specific groups feel marginalized or overlooked, societal trust in the government diminishes. Moreover, when there is a clear disconnect between public perception of corruption and official stances on corruption, trust erodes further. Public sentiment isn't static: it intensifies amidst scandals involving state officials, particularly when such scandals become recurrent. Over time, as corruption scandals become routine, public disillusionment deepens, cultivating a perception of pervasive dishonesty within a society.

Novak (2021) provides an important framework for understanding the social impact of social movements, interpreting social movement activities and their eventual outcomes through the lens of liberal political economy, she underscores the essence of dynamic collective choices that thrive within a gamut of economic, political, and social milieus. Novak sheds light on how social movements, despite the repressive environments they often emerge in, catalyze collective endeavors that challenge the established power structure. Through a series of historical and contemporary case studies, she delineates how advancements in human liberty are intrinsically shaped by the persistent struggles of social activists seeking acknowledgment and respect for their concerns.

Protests and Democracies

Even in robust democracies, protests can arise (Arce and Rice 2019). Every society has diverse groups, each with unique experiences under the regime's policies and regulations (Bergstrand 2014). When a regime's operations are tainted by corruption, societal repercussions ensue. Research highlights that deep-seated regime corruption can result in economic downturns, limited political accountability, flawed legal systems, and shaky institutions safeguarding individual rights (Rock 2009; Aidt et al. 2008; Warren 2004). Collectively, these factors shape individuals' perceptions of, and satisfaction with, the political landscape.

The *economic grievances* hypothesis posits that stagnant economic growth, often stemming from regime corruption, intensifies individual frustrations over financial resources (Portos 2021). Such frustrations can catalyze collective actions like street protests (Solt 2015). While authoritarian regimes traditionally counter these grievance-driven challenges with force, recent times have seen such coercive responses even in self-proclaimed democracies, with notable instances in countries such as Canada, France, the United Kingdom, and the United States.

The resource mobilization theory posits that in a society rife with grievances, the means—financial and otherwise—to participate in organized actions are crucial for mobilization efficacy (Jenkins 1983). Closely related is the political opportunity theory, which suggests that the resources harnessed by individuals for protests can amplify their chances of effecting positive socio-political change (Meyer 2004).

Many self-claimed democracies often fail to fully protect human rights. Research highlights countries like the Democratic Republic of Congo, Ivory Coast, India, and Zimbabwe, showing their weak institutions often neglect the rights of minorities, workers, and marginalized groups in areas such as liberty, religious freedom, expression, and self-determination (Hathaway 2007). Regimes employ various tactics to repress potential threats, including corruption, bribery, military, and police interventions during uprisings and electoral fraud (Dudouet 2013; Davenport 2007; Dragu and Lupu 2018; Escriba-Folch 2013; Earl and Soule 2006).

Coexistence of Corruption and Democracy

Corruption and democracy, while often positioned as opposing forces, can indeed coexist, and the relationship between the two is more nuanced than a simple binary of presence and absence (Rock 2009; Warren 2004). Democracy is characterized by a system where elected representatives make decisions on behalf of the people, with checks and balances in place to prevent the abuse of power (Mair 2002). Corruption is the abuse of entrusted power for private gain (Rose-Ackerman 1978). Theoretically, a fully functional democracy should limit opportunities for corruption due to its inherent system of checks and balances, transparency mechanisms, and accountable governance (Jetter et al. 2015).

However, in practice, many democracies, both nascent and mature, have experienced varying levels of corruption. The Jacksonian era of the United States offers a compelling example: while the period witnessed an expansion of suffrage rights to a larger segment of the white male population, making the system more democratic in terms of political participation, it also saw the rise of the "spoils system" where political allies and supporters were awarded public offices (Ratcliffe 2000). This system inherently allowed for more patronage and potential corruption (Remini 1998).

It is essential to differentiate between *democratization* as a process and *democracy* as an ideal type. While the democratization process can indeed open up spaces for corruption (as power structures are in flux, and institutional checks might be weak or evolving), a mature, ideal-type democracy would, in theory, have robust mechanisms to deter corruption (Ostrom 1971). However, the reality is that no democracy is perfect, and lapses can occur where corrupt practices creep in. Thus, while corruption is not consistent with the ideal principles of democracy, it can, and often does, emerge within democratic settings (Rock 2009). The challenge for democratic systems is to continually evolve and refine their checks and balances to mitigate and reduce these corrupt practices.

MAIN ARGUMENTS

This section constructs a theoretical framework and hypothesis, drawing from seminal works in collective action, public choice, and the political economy of social conflict (Gause 2022; Klein and Regan 2018; Wagner 2016; Coyne and Boettke 2009; Coyne 2006; de Mesquita et al. 2005; Olson 1971). The study's impetus stems from two main motivations. First, there is a gap in the literature that fails to properly account for the relationship between regime corruption and protest activities in democracies with different levels of institutional strength and accountability for the exploitation of power in public office. A possible reason for this oversight might be that the scholarly community has understudied the possibility that even democratic nations can harbor enough discontent to spark widespread societal protests against corruption. Put differently, the nexus between regime corruption and democracies leading to protests has been overlooked by previous research.

Dissatisfaction with governments often stems from recurrent instances of regime corruption, even in nations with seemingly robust democratic institutions. Such instances, surprisingly overlooked by many experts and scholars, lead to public complacency. In democratic settings, this pervasive corruption becomes both elusive to detect and challenging to address, as many assume their democratic systems are immune. However, when such faux democracies fail to cloak their systemic corruption, societal awareness and unrest inevitably grow.

Various indicators, such as surging unemployment, economic downturns, and political suppression, signal regime instability and fuel public resentment. As Rock (2007) highlights, new democracies, particularly those with low per capita GDP, are especially vulnerable to corruption. However, contrary to prevailing assumptions, empirical analysis from 1986 to 2016 indicates several autocratic nations experienced robust economic growth amidst widespread corruption, challenging long-held beliefs (Saha and Sen 2021). This "East-Asian paradox" reveals that while countries in this region witnessed significant economic advancements and evolving political institutions, the prosperity did not necessarily translate to political satisfaction. Despite their economic successes, numerous autocracies experienced extensive protest movements (Weede 2004).

The second driving force behind this study is to understand why certain democratic nations, whether genuine democracies or self-proclaimed, witness protest movements while others remain quiet. Specifically, how does regime corruption influence these patterns? The dearth of research on this topic warrants a deeper investigation into the complexities surrounding social upheaval in democratic settings, especially with respect to regime corruption. The intricacies of how corruption affects protest movements are as diverse as the root causes of corruption itself. A clearer perspective emerges when comparing features of corruption across democratic and nondemocratic systems. Established arguments posit that corruption in democracies stems from institutional failures to uphold inclusivity and safeguard individual and collective rights (Della Porta and Vannucci 1999; Rose-Ackerman 1999).

Corruption manifests differently in democracies than in autocracies, affecting the fabric of society and governance in each case in unique ways. In democracies, corruption—such as bribery, nepotism, extortion, abuse of discretion, electoral fraud, and theft—directly erodes the principles of collective decision-making. It not only breaches norms but also diverts resources intended for the broader public to a privileged elite, thereby reinforcing disparities between the governed and those in power. Over time, this leads to a decline in public trust toward bureaucrats, political elites, and governmental representatives, potentially inhibiting timely institutional reforms toward genuine regime shifts (Solt 2015). However, the democratic framework offers mechanisms for accountability, allowing citizens to react vigilantly to episodes of corruption. They possess the power to pursue change through formal political means, such as voting, thus providing a direct avenue for addressing and potentially rectifying systemic corruption.

In contrast, autocracies often lack these mechanisms for accountability and change. The presence of corruption in such regimes—encompassing similar acts of bribery, nepotism, extortion, and abuse of discretion—serves to dissuade citizens from seeking institutional change. Given the centralized control of power and the absence of meaningful voting outlets, citizens find it challenging to pursue change through formal political means. This environment fosters a sense of helplessness and apathy among the populace, as corruption becomes entrenched as the status quo. Consequently, public trust in the government wanes significantly, with little hope for timely institutional reforms or genuine regime shifts (Tansey et al. 2017). The lack of a democratic outlet for discontent in autocracies starkly contrasts with the responsive and corrective measures available in democracies, highlighting the fundamental differences in how each system confronts and is affected by corruption.

While corruption is this chapter's focal point, party formation barriers elucidate how political dissidence manifests in democracies. These barriers can stifle formal political engagement, often steering dissatisfaction toward informal protests. Elevated barriers may also curtail new political entities addressing corruption, amplifying regime corruption and potential unrest. Thus, integrating party formation barriers offers a comprehensive understanding, juxtaposing corruption with the systemic factors affecting democratic reactions.

When examining the impact of escalating corruption exclusively within democratic nations, I posit that corruption will amplify the prevalence of protests. This surge emerges in environments where democratic institutions have fostered a culture with minimal tolerance for corrupt practices. Given this, I propose the following hypothesis: *Ceteris paribus*, the democratic countries with high levels of regime corruption will witness more protests than democratic countries where the corruption is low.

In essence, I seek to measure the influence of the institutional backdrop inherent in diverse democratic societies to discern the genuine state of their democratic health, as evidenced by the frequency of social uprisings. Thus, I aim to empirically substantiate the following inquiry: What do varying levels of protests reveal about a nation's true democratic health over time, especially in light of changing corruption indices? This query is underpinned by the theoretical conundrum proposing that, while heightened protest activity may indicate pervasive disillusionment with the governing body, it could equally signify a society's liberty in voicing dissent and exercising the right to assembly. Unraveling this enigma through empirical backing is the focal point of this chapter.

DATA AND EMPIRICAL APPROACH

High protest frequencies in democracies, whether genuine or merely self-proclaimed, can sometimes be strategic narratives crafted by the ruling class to project an image of regime stability (Dalton et al. 2010). Such posturing aims to demonstrate to international observers that the nation encourages civic freedoms and discourse. This is particularly salient when these observers include influential economic stakeholders (Grauvogel et al. 2017). However, persistent protest activity often serves as an alarming indicator, suggesting that the state's relationship with its citizens might be marred by sociopolitical injustices and potential human rights violations (Hathaway 2007).

Systemic regime corruption can obscure the genuine democratic status of any self-identifying democratic nation. The data on protests, spanning from 1995 to 2014, is extracted from the Integrated Crises Early Warning System (ICEWS) (Boschee et al. 2015).

The democratic countries in this sample are identified by using the Polity V scores from the Varieties of Democracy version ten dataset developed by Coppedge et al. (2020). The Polity V scores originate from the Systemic Peace Project, originally collected and published by Jaggers and Gurr (1995). Coppedge et al. compose a combined version of the polity scores, which "is computed by subtracting the autocracy score from the democracy scores. The resulting unified POLITY scale ranges from +10 (strongly democratic) to –10 (strongly autocratic)" (Coppedge et al. 2020, 355). I filter the democratic countries from the autocratic ones in this sample by isolating any items that have scores of 6 and above, consistent with the categorization of regime types by the Polity Project. Those categorization groups are "autocracies" (–10 to –6), "anocracies" (–5 to +5 and three special values: –66, –7, and –88), and "democracies" (+6 to +10). After applying the filtering procedure to extract democracies from other categories, I obtain a dataset of 1,401 observations which consists of eighty-three countries spanning the years 1995 to 2014, with missing years for specific cases. To avoid spurious within-country relationships in the empirical models, I omit countries that have less than ten years of data.

The main dependent variable used to test the proposed hypothesis is the total number of protests in a given country in a specific year. Initially, from the comprehensive set of conflict activities in ICEWS, I extract only protest incidents by computing annual aggregates for each country and year available in the dataset. Violent activities and riots are excluded from the final calculations. Next, I construct a unique measure from the initial aggregated count, *protest per capita,* for each country and year. This measure is a weighted variable that estimates the ratio between raw protest counts and the population of each country in a specific year. Unlike previous studies that have relied on the count of protests (Klein and Regan 2018), I formulate this weighted measure to avoid coverage bias that can arise from differences in country size, media transparency, and freedom of the press within some regimes but not others. For instance, a country like the Democratic Republic of Congo could have more actual incidents of protest than are reported in the media compared to a country such as France. This difference can be a function of some country-specific characteristics such as the history of protest participation, oppression against protesters, electoral manipulation, and the number of protest participants. The weighted protest count per capita variable enables us to avoid concerns of reporting bias and fix any disproportions that will yield spurious relationships across countries in the observed sample. I normalize the protest per capita (henceforth, NPPC) to range between 0 and 1 for ease of interpretation with other similar other explanatory variables included in the empirical models.

The main independent variable used to examine the proposed hypothesis is the regime corruption index from V-Dem ten dataset. This variable is continuously scaled and ranges between 0 and 1 where 0 indicates lowest level of corruption and 1 denotes the highest level of corruption. Relying on the formulated hypothesis, I expect that as regime corruption scores increase within each country, the protests per capita levels will also increase. To tease out the influence of an unstable economy on protest activities in each country in a specific year, I include gross domestic product (GDP) per capita (current $US) and unemployment rates extracted from the World Bank database (WB 2022). Lower levels of unemployment correlate not only with poverty and economic underdevelopment but also institutional instability, corruption, and democratic backsliding in many countries (Bjørnskov and Rode 2020; Aidt et al. 2008). Lastly, I incorporate another control variable, *party barriers*, which is normalized to range between 0 and 1 where the value of 0 indicates that political parties are not allowed to be formed and the value of 1 suggests that there are no substantial restrictions to party formations.[2]

In this study, there are intrinsic limitations tied to the measures and data utilized. A central concern is the reliance on perceived corruption data sourced from experts, who often derive their insights from media outlets like newspapers. This overlap presents a potential issue where corruption could inadvertently be represented in both the independent and dependent variables, thereby complicating causal inference. Media-based perceptions may introduce biases, conflating reported incidents with actual prevalence. Future research should endeavor to triangulate data sources or adopt methodologies that can circumvent these inherent challenges.

Prior to discussing the empirical models and their results, figure 8.1 shows some general trends in annual averages of regime corruption and NPPC. We may notice that for most years as the regime corruption in the democratic countries increases there are similar increases in protest activities per capita. Some exceptions are the years 2002, 2005, 2009, 2011, and 2012. The trajectories depicted in this figure do not account for unobserved factors such as market size and economic performance which are proxied with GDP per capita and unemployment rate in this study, or for party barriers which illustrate the true level of civic freedoms associated with forming new political parties.

In figure 8.2, we notice that as regime corruption increases in some Scandinavian countries in the sample, such as Sweden, Denmark, and Norway, the magnitude of NPPC also increases, yet not as much as in other countries such as Latvia, Greece, Serbia, Cyprus, and Montenegro. Surprising cases are Japan, Brazil, Ghana, and Burundi, where,upon increases of regime corruption

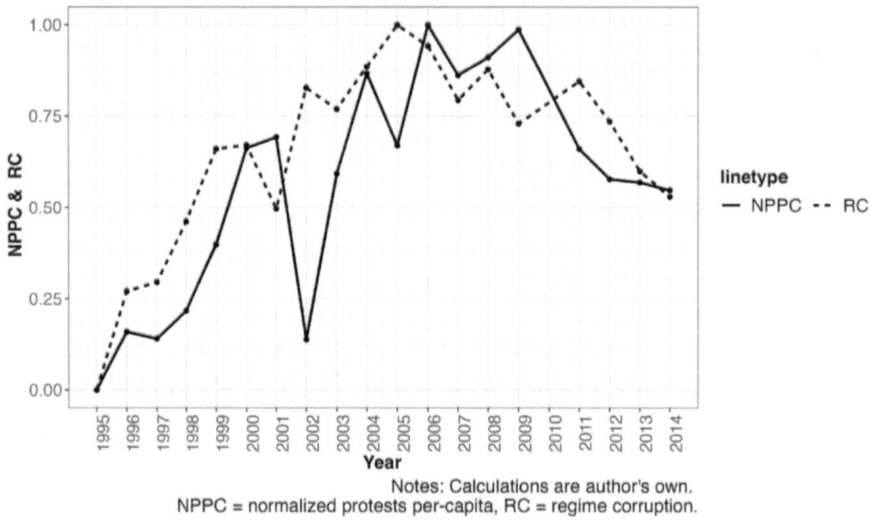

Figure 8.1 Average Protests Per Capita and Regime Corruption by Year. *Source*: Created by author.

index, there are lower levels of NPPC than in most other countries in the sample. Other historically prominent democratic countries such as the United Kingdom, United States, Belgium, Canada, France, and Spain appear at the average range in the cross section between regime corruption and NPPC.

Given the time series and cross-sectional structure of the dataset used in this study I employ a panel fixed-effects model. Several authors have argued that the fixed-effects model provides greater depth for analyzing differences in groups when relying on the assumption that their means are not a result of a random sampling of the population (Hsiao 2022; Malikane and Chitambara 2017; Schafer and Ramsey 2003). The fixed-effects estimator allows some freedom of variance between observed and unobserved variables, as this model can, to a certain degree, control for time-invariant variables and their effects (Allison 2009). The values of the variables in this model are fixed, meaning that it includes a separate intercept for both cross sections and time periods (Raffalovich and Chung 2014). The fixed-effects estimator controls for time-invariant variables by adding a dummy variable to the model. The coefficients of the dummy values will distribute fixed effects to the regression of the variables.[3] The panel fixed-effects empirical model looks as follows:

$$Ln(NPPC) = \beta_1 Ln(RC) + \beta_2 Ln(Unemployment) + \beta_3 Ln(GDP\ pc) + \beta_4 Ln(Party\,barriers) + \alpha_i + \delta_t + \varepsilon_{it} \tag{8.1}$$

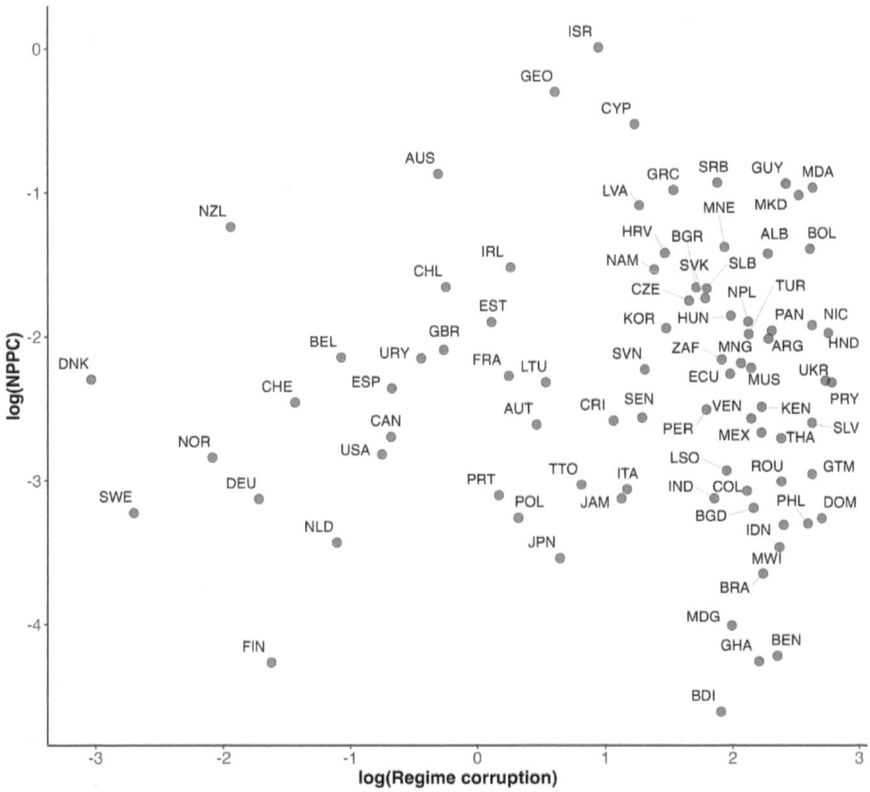

Figure 8.2 Average NPPC vs. Regime Corruption by Country. *Source*: Created by author.

where β_1, β_2, β_3, and β_4 are estimated coefficients for regime corruption, unemployment, GDP per capita, and party barriers, respectively. Additionally, α_i and δ_t are the parameters for country and year fixed effects, respectively, and ε_{it} is the error term. The country and year fixed-effects models are estimated separately in the empirical models. All variables are logarithmically transformed from their original measurements for ease of interpretation of results, which make the model a log-log. On a more technical note, with log-log models, the expectation is that for every percent change in the β_i coefficients, there will be a certain percentage change in the dependent variable of interest, NPPC. It is important to caution the reader that this study is not attempting to establish absolute causality between the variables of interest, as there may be multiple other factors shaping the true impact of regime corruption on protests that empirically were not possible to account for in numerically measured variables.

Table 8.1 Correlation of Main Variables

	A	*B*	*C*	*D*	*E*
A. NPPC	1	–0.01	–0.03	0.2	–0.1
B. RC	–0.01	1	–0.7	–0.1	–0.4
C. GDP per capita	–0.03	–0.7	1	–0.2	0.3
D. Unemployment	0.2	–0.1	–0.2	1	0.01
E. Party barriers	–0.1	–0.4	0.3	0.01	1

Source: Created by author.

Reflecting on key theories discussed earlier such as the *resource mobilization* and *economic grievances* hypotheses, I include unemployment rates to account for the level of grievances with the regime in each country in a specific year, and the GDP per capita to account for the extent of possible resources available to society for civic engagement (Bergstrand 2014; Dalton 2010). Following the suggestions from existing studies, I expect to obtain a positive coefficient for both unemployment rates and GDP per capita as these theories suggest that when grievances increase, the society is more likely to retaliate against the regime on the streets (Solt 2015). Similarly, having access to economic resources also tends to increase protest participation as people have better opportunities to dedicate time and efforts to engage in protests (Gause 2022). Additionally, I expect that the sign on the *party barriers* coefficient would be negative as stronger restrictions on political party formations imply that the regime has low tolerance toward issue representation among various underrepresented groups (Escribà-Folch 2013).

Table 8.1 shows the correlation between the main variables used in empirical models. We notice that NPPC is negatively correlated with regime corruption, GDP per capita and party barriers variables, while positively correlated with unemployment. This indicates that as there are lower levels of protests in the democratic countries when regime corruption, GDP per capita, and party barriers increase, yet slightly more protests per capita occur when unemployment rises. There is a negative correlation between unemployment and regime corruption, as well as unemployment and GDP per capita in the sample of eighty-three democratic countries. Lastly, a strong negative correlation exists between regime corruption and GDP per capita which suggests that in the democratic countries analyzed in this study, when regime corruption increases the market size measured in GDP per capita output decreases.

RESULTS AND DISCUSSION

Table 8.2 displays the results of the panel data analysis with both country and year fixed effects, which were utilized to restrict any unobservable influences

Table 8.2 Results of Panel Fixed-Effects Models

	Dependent variable: average NPPC			
Variables	*Model 1*	*Model 2*	*Model 3*	*Model 4*
Regime corruption	0.10***	0.013**	0.075**	0.05***
	(0.036)	(0.006)	(0.037)	(0.009)
Unemployment			0.026	0.104***
			(0.020)	(0.013)
GDP per-capita			0.081***	0.054***
			(0.015)	(0.010)
Party barriers			–0.239***	–0.097***
			(0.053)	(0.033)
Observations	1,401	1,401	1,401	1,401
Fixed Effects	Country	Year	Country	Year
R2	0.003	0.003	0.036	0.10
F-Statistic	4.149**	04.591**	12.183***	25.708***

Source: Created by author.
* Significance at 0.10 level ** Significance at 0.05 level *** Significance at 0.01 level

on NPPC that were due to geographically and temporally invariant factors. The result in model 1, with country fixed effects and regime corruption as the only independent variable, shows that as expected, a 1 percent increase in RC led to 0.10 percent increase in NPPC. In other words, in line with the hypothesized causal direction, holding country-specific unobserved characteristics constant across units generates statistically significant positive effect on NPPC in the sample of democratic countries. In model 2, with year fixed effects, we also discover a positive and small but statistically significant effect, with a 0.013% increase for each 1 percent increase in RC.

In addition to country fixed effects, model 3 includes control variables such as unemployment rate, GDP per capita, and party barriers. The results indicate that in line with the main hypothesis, after accounting for unique features of countries, the regime corruption still produces a statistically significant positive effect on NPPC. However, the size of this impact is relatively smaller than the result in model 1, as model 3 shows that there is a 0.075 percent increase in the NPPC for every 1 percent increase in RC. The predicted coefficient for unemployment rate in this model is not statistically significant, whereas the ones estimated for GDP per capita and party barriers are statistically significant. The coefficient on GDP per capita suggests that the NPPC increases by 0.081 percent for every percent increase in its measurement. By contrast, the coefficient on party barriers has a negative effect on NPPC based on its estimated coefficients. This result indicates that as the barriers to political party formation become stricter, there are fewer per capita protest movements occurring in the sample of democratic countries.

In model 4 with year fixed effects, we find some statistically significant results for the regime corruption on NPPC: for every 1 percent increase in

RC, there is a 0.05 percent increase in the NPPC outcome variable. However, unlike in the model 3, in this model, we discover that as unemployment rate increases by 1 percent there are 0.104 percent more per-capita protests occurring in the democratic countries observed in the main sample. The predicted coefficients of GDP per capita have a statistically significant effect on NPPC, increasing it by 0.05 percent. In model 4 we establish statistically significant negative impact of the party barriers variable on NPPC. Only the results of predicted coefficients in model 4 provide some degree of empirical support for the main hypothesis and related expectations regarding the control variables. In summary, the results demonstrate that while regime corruption, unemployment, and GDP per-capita increase the incidents of protests per capita, the restrictions on party formations have the opposite effect.

The trajectories of predicted versus original NPPC levels across years are illustrated in figure 8.3. One interesting trend in this figure is the variation of directionality between the original values of NPPC and its predicted levels with only RC (model 1 in table 8.2) and RC plus other controls (model 3 in table 8.2). The predicted model with only RC as the independent variable reveals that the correlation between its values and the original levels of NPPC move in opposite directions between the years 1999 and 2003 after which there is some upward trending linkage for the years 2003 to 2008, followed by a decay in the estimated levels until the year 2014. Another noteworthy variation is that, although both predicted values with only RC and the ones with additional controls intersect at various years between 1997 and 2004, once the control variables are implemented, there is a significant decay in predicted NPPC levels for the line RC plus other controls. This difference

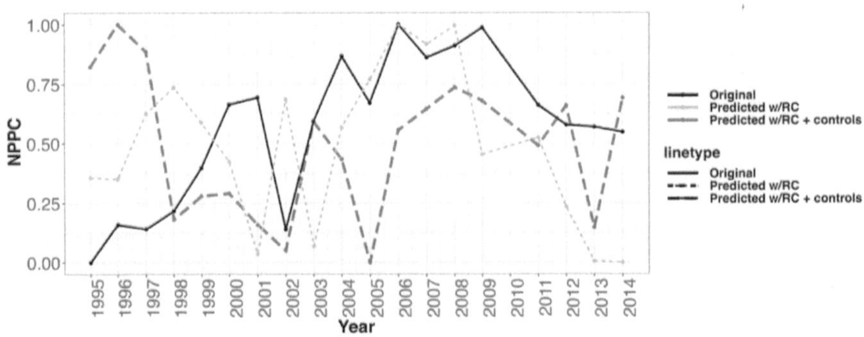

Notes: Calculations are author's own. NPPC = normalized protests per-capita, RC = regime corruption.

Figure 8.3 Original vs. Predicted Normalized Protests Per Capita by Year. *Source*: Created by author.

between original and predicted levels of NPPC suggests that the control variables are essential determinants of per capita protests in the sample of democratic countries as they shift the original trends in the protests across years.

Lastly, figures 8.4 through 8.7 show average levels of original and predicted NPPC models based on year-fixed effects across all countries in the main sample. First, we may notice that except for Cyprus, Georgia, and Israel, all other countries obtain higher levels of predicted NPPC with both RC as the only independent variable and with RC plus other controls. In all other countries, there are significantly higher predicted NPPC levels once accounting for GDP per capita, unemployment rate, and party formation barriers. Both original and predicted levels of NPPC allow a better understanding of the differences in protest activities between various democracies. For example,

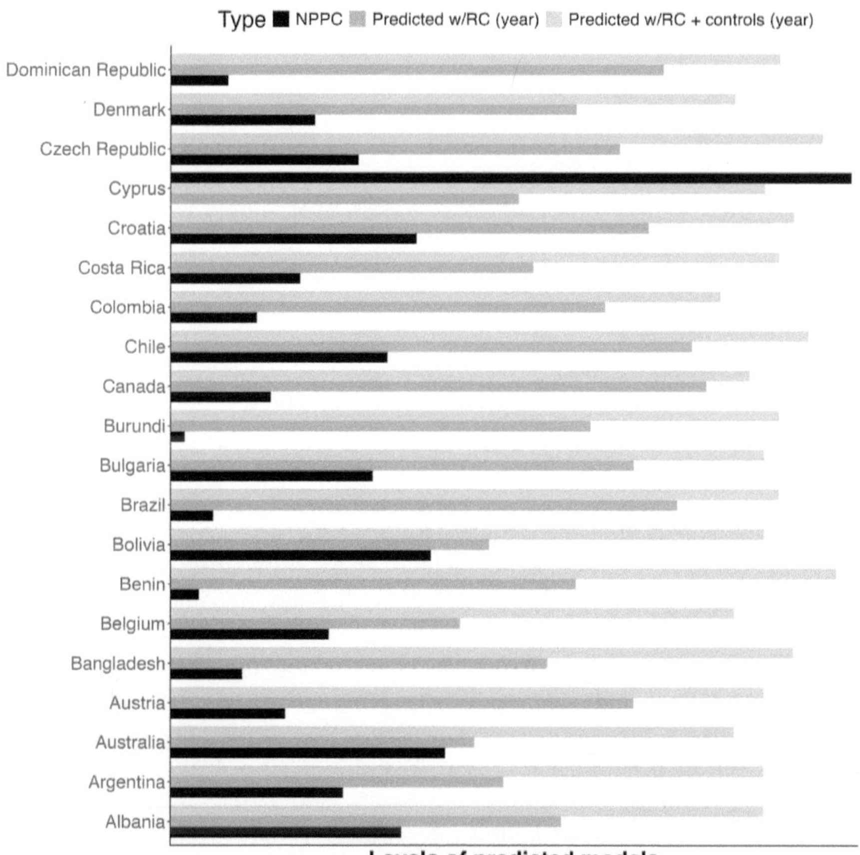

Figure 8.4 Original vs. Predicted NPPC by Country. *Source*: Created by author.

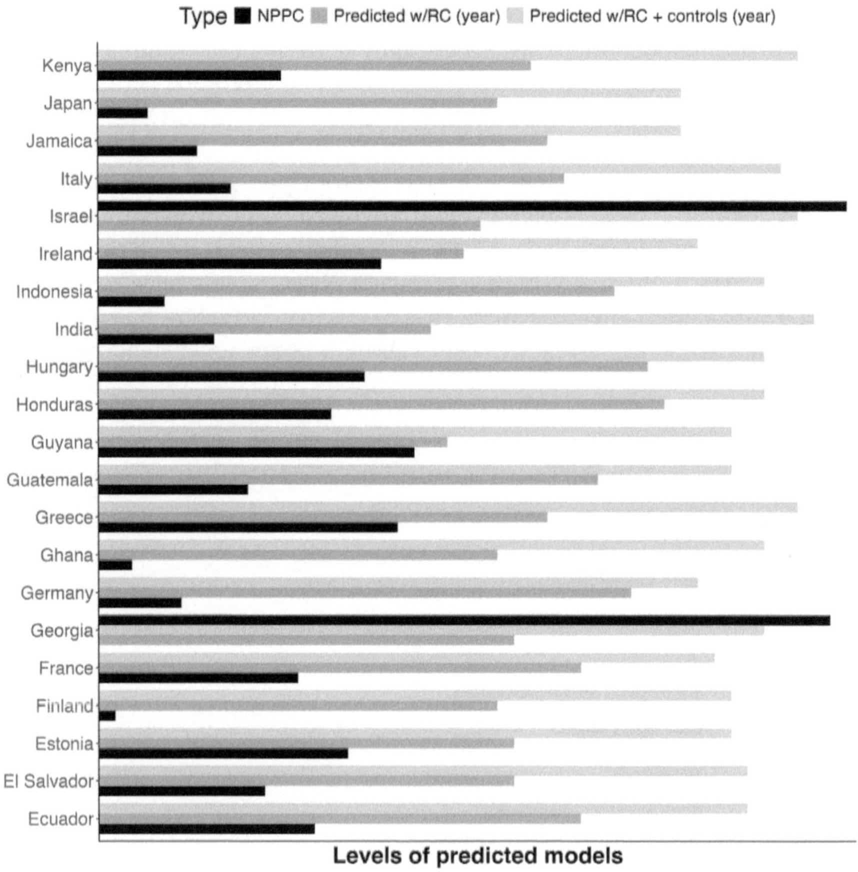

Figure 8.5 Original vs. Predicted NPPC by Country (continued). *Source*: Created by author.

democracies such as the United States, Netherlands, and Belgium have lower levels of original NPPC than democracies such as Bolivia, Bulgaria, Ecuador, Estonia, Guyana, Latvia, Moldova, and New Zealand, to name a few.

The country-specific differences in predicted levels of NPPC, with only RC as a control and with year-fixed effects, reveal that the estimated extent of per capita protests is high for countries that originally had substantial collective action activity. For instance, regime corruption seems to increase protest incidents from their original levels in Australia, Benin, Bolivia, Honduras, Montenegro, Namibia, Slovakia, South Korea, and Turkey after controlling for year-fixed effects. After adding the control variables to the year-fixed effects, we observe the predicted levels of protest activity increase even further in those countries. Nevertheless, we also notice that the difference in estimated per-capita levels does not differ drastically across countries based on the results of the model with RC and additional controls. Countries such as Czech Republic, North Macedonia, Portugal, Romania, and Slovenia all have relatively higher average predicted per capita protests than other countries in the sample.

What new insights can these results provide? There are several inferences that can be drawn from the regression outcomes that examined the impact of regime corruption on per capita protests, focusing only on eighty-three democratic countries from 1995 to 2014. First, although not to the same extent as in autocracies and other forms of repressive regimes, democratic countries remain responsive to escalating corruption within their socio-political systems. The results revealed that there is about a 12 percent increase in the annual rate of normalized per capita protest levels in each state for every percent increase in regime corruption. Even after controlling for country-specific

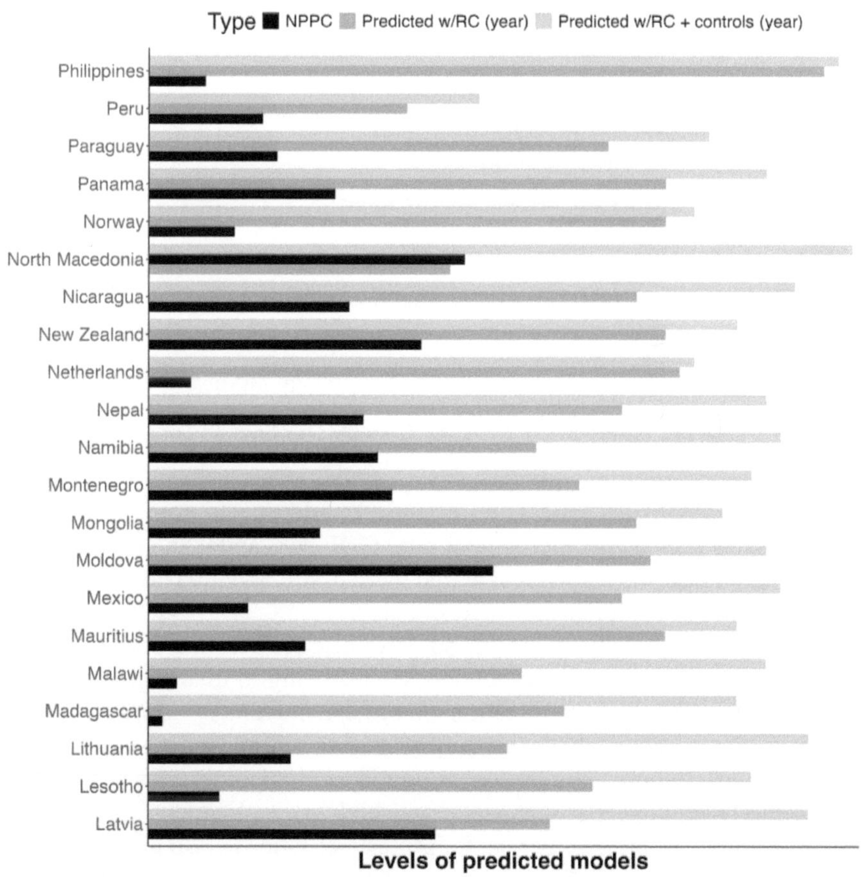

Figure 8.6 Original vs. Predicted NPPC by Country (continued). *Source*: Created by author.

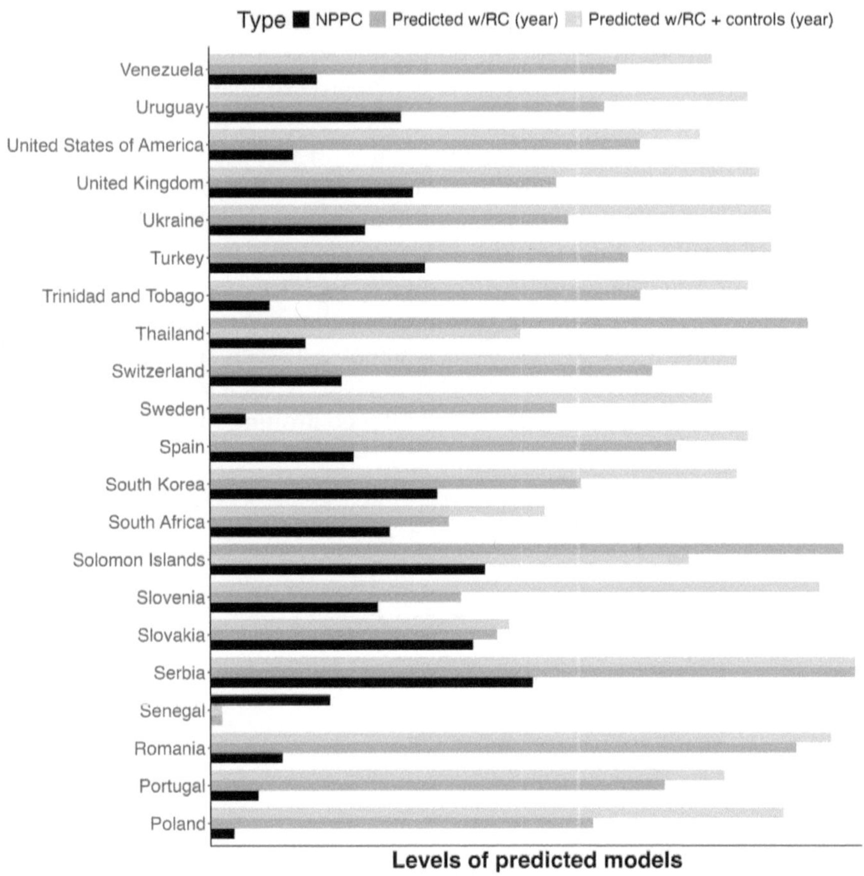

Figure 8 7 Original vs. Predicted NPPC by Country (continued). *Source*: Created by author.

invariant characteristics with fixed effects, in addition to some alternating characteristics such as unemployment rate, GDP per capita, and party formation barriers index, the results reveal that there is still about 9 percent increase in normalized per capita protest levels.

Second, the outcomes of this empirical exercise suggest that despite market improvements that enhance the economic well-being in many institutionally stable democracies, the examination of protest movements shows that the society in democracies challenge corrupt regimes. This study showed that, consistent with the *resource mobilization* theory, in democracies with growing regime corruption, party barriers, and high unemployment, as GDP per capita increases, the rate of per capita protest activities is also amplified.

Third, as shown by different variants of the *economic grievances* theory, financial conditions can mobilize or paralyze society's ability to raise awareness about dissatisfaction with the regime. After controlling for the unemployment rate as a proxy for poor economic performance, this study shows that only after accounting for time-invariant factors with year-fixed effects do we find some statistically significant positive impact from the unemployment rate variable on the per capita protest rates. Economic conditions can politicize issues pertaining to social welfare, depending on the type of political propaganda initiated by the regime. Some prior studies found that corrupt, autocratic regimes more so than democratic ones tend to hide the true economic performance of the society through false propaganda (Hollyer et al. 2015).

Fourth, we establish that the effect of regime corruption on per capita protests in selected democratic countries is not evenly distributed across years. The significant fluctuations in estimated NPPC levels after controlling for different country characteristics attest to the existence of other unobserved factors. However, this study highlighted the importance of economic challenges in investigating the relationship between corruption and protests in democracies. The reason is that long-run protest engagements can be costly in terms of imposing heavy economic burdens on those participating. Democratic countries are not less prone to regime corruption than autocratic or institutionally unstable governments. As argued by this study and shown with a small sample of data used in empirical models, this particularly applies to countries with income and employment insecurity, low GDP per capita, and barriers to forming new political parties.

LIMITATIONS AND FUTURE RESEARCH

The potential avenues for expanding upon the current research framework, given the inherent limitations in the data and the methodological approach used, are manifold. First, the present analysis is constrained by its reliance on a singular source for documenting protest activities. Subsequent investigations or parallel inquiries could juxtapose various metrics of protests with other manifestations of collective action, thereby refining the analysis. Second, pertinent to the primary dependent variable—per capita protests—this study abstains from delineating among diverse protest typologies. Ensuing research endeavors could provide granularity by differentiating among collective action variants, such as violent versus nonviolent, antiregime versus pro-regime, and economic versus social. Such differentiation could illuminate the impacts of corruption in bureaucratic, governmental, commercial, and political elements of society on protest rates.

Third, this chapter's scope is somewhat circumscribed by its singular focus on regime corruption. Future scholarship might explore corruption typologies, aiming to discern their respective impacts on collective behavior. Fourth, while this chapter focuses on the macro interplay between corruption and protests in democratic settings, subsequent analyses could pivot to the micro-ramifications of the propounded framework. Such an orientation would shed light on individual-level responses to corruption, proclivities toward protest participation, trust in governmental institutions, and factors influencing satisfaction with governance. Repositories like Afrobarometer, Latinobarometer, World Values Survey, and European Social Survey stand as potentially useful reservoirs of data capturing individual sentiments across a spectrum of socio-political and economic paradigms.

Fifth, a recognized constraint is the reliance on perceived corruption data primarily sourced from expert opinions, which may be influenced by media coverage, potentially introducing a bias. This overlap between media-based corruption perception and actual reported events poses a challenge in discerning genuine patterns in the data. Specifically, it is difficult to ascertain whether shifts in expert opinions reflect actual changes in corruption levels or are simply reactions to media coverage, which can sometimes misrepresent reality due to factors like sensationalism or selective reporting. The current analysis does not fully delve into this problem, and consequently, there could be redundancy between independent and dependent variables. Future studies would benefit from diversifying the sources of corruption perception, aiming to capture a more nuanced and uncontaminated perspective of corruption that's free from media influence.

CONCLUSION

Existing scholarship on protest determinants lacks a comprehensive theoretical framework that explains variations in protest levels across democracies. Prior research, rooted in the social movements literature, has underscored factors such as financial resources, trust in governance, economic grievances, and institutional (in)stabilities as key drivers behind societal protest escalation (Portos 2021; Malikane and Chitambara 2017; Solt 2015; Earle and Soule 2006; Meyer 2004; McAdam et al. 2003; Jenkins 1983). This chapter introduces a framework that interweaves these elements, spotlighting the pervasive and disruptive influence of regime corruption in democracies. Such corruption fosters public administration inconsistencies, disproportionately benefiting select groups at the expense of broader societal inclusion.

This chapter illuminates the blurred lines distinguishing genuine democratic institutions from mere facades of democracy. It posits that surges in regime corruption within democratic nations correlate with heightened annual per capita protest events. The underlying goal is to decipher the authenticity of democratic labels when juxtaposing actual per capita protests against projections, accounting for regime corruption and other state-specific determinants.

The empirical examination of this hypothesis employed panel data from eighty-three countries, identified as democratic at different junctures by the Polity V project. The findings underscored a consistent trend: in the face of increasing regime corruption, protest events per capita rise—even after controlling for salient economic and political variables.

These findings present a challenge to prevailing conceptions of democratic stability and resilience. Historically, democracies have been heralded as bastions of stability and order, characterized by a relative immunity to societal tumult. Yet, this research unveils a more intricate tapestry of responses within democracies, suggesting that even they aren't insulated from the repercussions of deep-seated corruption.

In a world increasingly gravitating toward democratization, the upswing in protest activities in purported democratic nations is symptomatic of problems in their sociopolitical fabric. It accentuates the notion that corruption can catalyze public disillusionment and galvanize collective action. Thus, it is not merely the existence of democratic institutions but their integrity and functionality that determine societal responses. Furthermore, by juxtaposing observed per capita protests rates against projected rates—adjusted for regime corruption and other nuances—this study furnishes a stark realization: many democracies, rather than being paragons of equity and representation, may be grappling with systemic discrepancies and disenfranchisement.

This study offers an imperative for both scholars and policymakers. For the former, it beckons to a reevaluation of how we delineate and comprehend democracies, urging a departure from monolithic categorizations to more granular, behavior-centric assessments. For the latter, it underscores the need for holistic governance reforms, ensuring that democratization isn't just about institutional facades, but genuinely resonates with the ideals of justice, transparency, and inclusive representation. In sum, this research transcends its empirical bounds, offering critical insights into the complexities of democratic dynamics in the modern era and emphasizing the urgency of preserving the sanctity of democratic ethos.

NOTES

1. This variable is normalized between 0 and 1 before running the regression models.

2. The original measurement of this variable was a five point scale with zero: Parties are not allowed; (1) It is impossible, or virtually impossible, for parties not

affiliated with the government to form (legally); (2) there are significant obstacles (e.g., leaders face high levels of regular political harassment by authorities); (3) there are modest barriers (e.g., party leaders face occasional political harassment by authorities); (4) there are no substantial barriers.

3. Since the fixed effects discard the between-group variation and focus more on within-group variation, one can expect high standard errors when implementing this estimator in panel data analyses. According to Allison (2009), when the within-group/individual variation is less than the between-variation, the standard error of the coefficients of fixed-effect models may become too large to be considered for drawing inferences.

REFERENCES

Aidt, Toke, Jayasri Dutta, and Vania Sena. 2008. "Governance Regimes, Corruption and Growth: Theory and Evidence." *Journal of Comparative Economics* 36 (2): 195–222.

Almeida, Paul D. 2018. "The Role of Threat in Collective Action." In *The Wiley Blackwell Companion to Social Movements*, second edition, edited by David A. Snow, Sarah A. Soule, Hanspeter Kriesi, and Holly J. McCammon, 43–62. Hoboken, NJ: John Wiley & Sons.

Allison, Paul D. 2009. *Fixed Effects Regression Models*. Thousand Oaks, CA: SAGE Publications.

Arce, Moisés, and Roberta Rice. 2019. *Protest and Democracy*. Calgary: University of Calgary Press.

Bergstrand, Kelly. 2014. "The Mobilizing Power of Grievances: Applying Loss Aversion and Omission Bias to Social Movements." *Mobilization: An International Quarterly* 19 (2): 123–142.

Bjørnskov, Christian, and Martin Rode. 2020. "Regime Types and Regime Change: A New Dataset on Democracy, Coups, and Political Institutions." *The Review of International Organizations* 15: 531–551.

Boschee, Elizabeth, Jenniver Lautenschlager, Sean O'Brien, Steve Shellman, James Starz, and Michael Ward. 2015. "ICEWS Coded Event Data." Harvard Dataverse, V37.

Bosi, Lorenzo, Marco Giugni, and Katrin Uba, eds. 2016. *The Consequences of Social Movements*. Cambridge: Cambridge University Press.

Coppedge, Michael, John Gerring, Carl Henrik Knutsen, Staffan I. Lindberg, Jan Teorell, David Altman, et al. 2020. "V-Dem Dataset v10." Varieties of Democracy (V-Dem) Project. University of Gothenburg, V-Dem Institute. https://v-dem.net/data/dataset-archive/

Coyne, Christopher J. 2006. "Reconstructing Weak and Failed States: Foreign Intervention and the Nirvana Fallacy." *Foreign Policy Analysis* 2 (4): 343–360.

Coyne, Christopher J., and Peter J. Boettke. 2009. "The Problem of Credible Commitment in Reconstruction." *Journal of Institutional Economics* 5 (1): 1–23.

Dalton, Russell, Alix Van Sickle, and Steven Weldon. 2010. "The Individual–Institutional Nexus of Protest Behaviour." *British Journal of Political Science* 40 (1): 51–73.

Davenport, Christian. 2007. "State Repression and Political Order." *Annual Review of Political Science* 10: 1–23.

De Mesquita, Bruce Bueno, Alastair Smith, Randolph M. Siverson, and James D. Morrow. 2005. *The Logic of Political Survival*. Cambridge, MA: MIT Press.

Della Porta, Donatella. 2020. *How Social Movements Can Save Democracy: Democratic Innovations from Below*. Hoboken, NJ: John Wiley & Sons.

Della Porta, Donatella, and Alberto Vannucci. 1999. *Corrupt Exchanges: Actors, Resources, and Mechanisms of Political Corruption*. Piscataway, NJ: Transaction Publishers.

Dragu, Tiberiu, and Yonatan Lupu. 2018. "Collective Action and Constraints on Repression at the Endgame." *Comparative Political Studies* 51 (8): 1042–1073.

Dudouet, Véronique. 2013. "Dynamics and Factors of Transition from Armed Struggle to Nonviolent Resistance." *Journal of Peace Research* 50 (3): 401–413.

Earl, Jennifer, and Sarah Soule. 2006. "Seeing Blue: A Police-Centered Explanation of Protest Policing." *Mobilization: An International Quarterly* 11 (2): 145–164.

Economist Intelligence Unit. 2022. *Democracy Index 2022*. New York: The Economist Intelligence Unit Limited.

Escribà-Folch, Abel. 2013. "Repression, Political Threats, and Survival Under Autocracy." *International Political Science Review* 34 (5): 543–560.

Gardiner, John. 1989. "Defining Corruption." In *Political Corruption: A Handbook*, edited by Arnold J. Heidenheimer, Michael Johnston, and Victor T. Le Vine, 963–965. New York: Routledge.

Gause, LaGina. 2022. "Revealing Issue Salience via Costly Protest: How Legislative Behavior Following Protest Advantages Low-Resource Groups." *British Journal of Political Science* 52 (1): 259–279.

Grauvogel, Julia, Amanda A. Licht, and Christian Von Soest. 2017. "Sanctions and Signals: How International Sanction Threats Trigger Domestic Protest in Targeted Regimes." *International Studies Quarterly* 61 (1): 86–97.

Hathaway, Oona A. 2007. "Why Do Countries Commit to Human Rights Treaties?" *Journal of Conflict Resolution* 51 (4): 588–621.

Hollyer, James R., B. Peter Rosendorff, and James R. Vreeland. 2018. *Information, Democracy, and Autocracy*. Cambridge: Cambridge University Press.

Hsiao, Cheng. 2022. *Analysis of Panel Data*. No. 64. Cambridge: Cambridge University Press.

Jaggers, Keith, and Ted Robert Gurr. 1995. "Tracking Democracy's Third Wave with the Polity III Data." *Journal of Peace Research* 32 (4): 469–482.

Jenkins, J. Craig. 1983. "Resource Mobilization Theory and the Study of Social Movements." *Annual Review of Sociology* 9 (1): 527–553.

Jetter, Michael, Alejandra Montoya Agudelo, and Andrés Ramírez Hassan. 2015. "The Effect of Democracy on Corruption: Income is Key." *World Development* 74: 286–304.

Klein, Graig R., and Patrick M. Regan. 2018. "Dynamics of Political Protests." *International Organization* 72 (2): 485–521.

Mair, Peter. 2002. "Populist Democracy vs Party Democracy." In *Democracies and the Populist Challenge*, edited by Yves Meny and Yves Surel, 81–98. London: Palgrave Macmillan UK.

Malikane, Christopher, and Prosper Chitambara. 2017. "Foreign Direct Investment, Democracy and Economic Growth in Southern Africa." *African Development Review* 29 (1): 92–102.

McAdam, Doug, Sidney Tarrow, and Charles Tilly. 2003. "Dynamics of Contention." *Social Movement Studies* 2 (1): 99–102.

Meyer, David S. 2004. "Protest and Political Opportunities." *Annual Review of Sociology* 30: 125–145.

Novak, Mikayla. 2021. *Freedom in Contention: Social Movements and Liberal Political Economy*. Lanham, MD: Rowman & Littlefield.

Nye, Joseph S. 1989. "Political Corruption: A Cost Benefit Analysis." In *Political Corruption: A Handbook*, edited by Arnold J. Heidenheimer, Michael Johnston, and Victor T. Le Vine, 963–965. New York: Routledge.

Olson, Mancur. 1971. *The Logic of Collective Action: Public Goods and the Theory of Groups, with a New Preface and Appendix*. Vol. 124. Cambridge, MA: Harvard University Press.

Ostrom, Vincent. 1997. *The Meaning of Democracy and the Vulnerability of Democracies: A Response to Tocqueville's Challenge*. Ann Arbor, MI: University of Michigan Press.

Philp, Mark. 1997. "Defining Political Corruption." *Political Studies* 45 (3): 436–462.

Portos, Martín. 2021. *Grievances and Public Protests: Political Mobilisation in Spain in the Age of Austerity*. Cham: Palgrave Macmillan.

Raffalovich, Lawrence E., and Rakkoo Chung. 2014. "Models for Pooled Time-Series Cross-Section Data." *International Journal of Conflict and Violence (IJCV)* 8 (2): 209–221.

Ratcliffe, Donald John. 2000. *The Politics of Long Division: The Birth of the Second Party System in Ohio, 1818–1828*. Columbus, OH: Ohio State University Press.

Remini, Robert V. 1998. *Andrew Jackson: The Course of American Democracy, 1833–1845*. Vol. 3. Baltimore, MD: JHU Press.

Rock, Michael T. 2009. "Corruption and Democracy." *The Journal of Development Studies* 45 (1): 55–75.

Rose-Ackerman, Susan. 1978. *Corruption: A Study in Political Economy*. New York: Academic Press.

Rose-Ackerman, Susan, and Bonnie J. Palifka. 2016. *Corruption and Government: Causes, Consequences, and Reform*. Cambridge: Cambridge University Press.

Saha, Shrabani, and Kunal Sen. 2021. "The Corruption–Growth Relationship: Does the Political Regime Matter?" *Journal of Institutional Economics* 17 (2): 243–266.

Schafer, Daniel W., and Fred L. Ramsey. 2003. "Teaching the Craft of Data Analysis." *Journal of Statistics Education* 11 (1). https://doi.org/10.1080/10691898.2003.11910692

Scott, James C. 1972. *Comparative Political Corruption*. Englewood Cliffs, NJ: Prentice Hall.

Solt, Frederick. 2015. "Economic Inequality and Nonviolent Protest." *Social Science Quarterly* 96 (5): 1314–1327.

Tansey, Oisín, Kevin Koehler, and Alexander Schmotz. 2017. "Ties to the Rest: Autocratic Linkages and Regime Survival." *Comparative Political Studies* 50 (9): 1221–1254.

Tullock, Gordon. 1971. "The Paradox of Revolution." *Public Choice* 11 (1): 89–99.

———. 2012. *Autocracy*. New York: Springer Science & Business Media.

Wagner, Richard E. 2016. *Politics as a Peculiar Business: Insights from a Theory of Entangled Political Economy*. Cheltenham: Edward Elgar Publishing.

Warren, Mark E. 2004. "What Does Corruption Mean in a Democracy?" *American Journal of Political Science* 48 (2): 328–343.

Weede, Erich. 1996. "Political Regime Type and Variation in Economic Growth Rates." *Constitutional Political Economy* 7: 167–176.

The World Bank (WB). 2022. *World Development Indicators*. Washington, DC: The World Bank (producer and distributor). Accessed December 12, 2022. http://data.worldbank.org/data-catalog/world-development-indicators.

Chapter 9

Re-examining Commerce's Impact on Peace and Conflicts

Paa-Kwesi Heto

War makes our perennial quest for a better world daunting. It interrupts and disrupts human progress, setting us back sometimes years if not centuries. However, students of Classical Liberalism, past and contemporary, argue that liberal political and economic institutions can prevent wars, create conditions for peaceful coexistence, and curtail individual, societal, and governmental predatory tendencies. Contemporary scholars, such as Gartzke (2005) and L. J. Graham (2023), consider commerce, especially economic interdependence, the most robust causal variable identified by the Classical Liberals. Proponents of the "trade leads to peace" argument have identified many causal paths through which trade tames conflict and creates the conditions for peaceful coexistence. Dominant explanations focus on how commerce changes our incentives (see Norman 1910; Rosecrance 1986; Gartzke, Li, and Boehmer 2001) and transforms our morals, making us develop habits of peacefulness and less prejudiced attitudes (see Montesquieu 2018; Storr and Choi 2019; Coyne, Romero, and Storr 2022). Other explanations focus on the direct role of entrepreneurs in bringing about positive peace (Coyne, Romero, and Storr 2023).

Nevertheless, the persistence of wars despite decades of liberalization in various parts of the world has given critics of Classical Liberalism a reason to cast doubt on many of the mechanisms that Classical Liberal theories identify as necessary and sufficient conditions for perpetual peace. Critics, especially Realist scholars like Walt (2022) and Mearsheimer (2018), have consistently argued that Classical Liberal policies increase the levels of conflict in international politics rather than reduce or eliminate them. In this chapter, I ask: How does commerce tame war and create peace? Under what conditions do international trade's influence matter, and when does it not?

My main argument is that these questions arise because students of international security and political economy have overlooked essential connections between commerce, peace, and armed conflict. If we lack a proper understanding of commerce's contribution to peace and cooperation between nation-states, we will keep making strategic mistakes that put humanity on a path of war rather than peace. Besides, policies predicated on inaccurate associations between trade and peace could create more problems than they solve. Put simply, a nuanced understanding of why some countries have been less prone to start wars than others is vital to humanity's ability to realize sustainable peace and enjoy the benefits of peaceful coexistence. Such knowledge is necessary because we must guard against complacency, which can cause us to sleepwalk into avoidable armed conflicts, especially great power wars.

DISTINGUISHING COMMUNAL VIOLENCE FROM STATE-CENTRIC WARS

Before continuing, let me explain the rationale for examining commerce's impact on peace and armed conflict at the communal and state levels. There are two reasons why this distinction is necessary—wars have an equifinality problem, and the nature of communal wars differs from state-centric wars.

The Equifinality Problem

Wars have an equifinality problem: they are the result of many causes and occur in many forms. For instance, Miller (2015) concluded after extensive discussions with renowned international relations scholars at the Harvard University workshop on the centenary anniversary of World War I in 2014, that not a single factor caused the war. Even bilateral wars like Russia's war on Ukraine do not have single or straightforward explanations. In his speech justifying the invasion on February 24, 2022, the President of Russia, Vladimir Putin, gave five main reasons for starting the war—his disdain for the United States' quest for world domination, NATO expansion, an increase in the number of hostile anti-Russian actors under the complete control of the Americans, ethnic cleansing in the Donbas, and a lack of alternative means for protecting the Russian state from terrorists and hostile state actors in Kyiv (Putin 2022). Aside from the five primary reasons, Putin listed many other grievances, making it challenging to decipher the war's exact cause(s). Similarly, a committee set up to study the causes of Kenya's inter and intra-communal conflicts in 2005 identified about twenty root causes (Government of Kenya 2014).

Given the equifinality problem, discussing the causes of war without oversimplification and omission is challenging. Thus, we would benefit from studying commerce's impact at different levels of analysis. However, we must also be wary of the problem associated with fragmentation, which is the inability to comprehend the overall picture. A two-level approach offers us the benefit of disaggregation without losing focus on the context. If the two-level analysis is done right, we will realize that one of the advantages of commerce is that it is the most effective and efficient tool for dealing with an equifinality problem, like war.[1] It is a multipurpose instrument that is adaptable to a great variety of circumstances and allows for the provision of bottom-up and top-down solutions to violent conflicts.

Difference between Communal and State-Centric Wars

The two-level approach allows for a better understanding of commerce's impact on conflict. As already discussed above, armed or unarmed conflict has many causes, but all causes are not the same: some are more organic and widespread, while others are not. For example, the nature of state-involved wars (state-centric wars) differs from intra/inter-communal armed conflicts. State-centric wars, intra/inter-state, do not simply explode. A legitimate authority must issue a legitimate command before a country's armed forces can deploy or fight in a war. In democracies, political representatives sometimes must deliberate for days or weeks before declaring war on another state.

Carl von Clausewitz, a renowned Prussian military theorist, argues, "Politics, moreover, is the womb in which war develops—where its outlines already exist in their hidden rudimentary form, like the characteristics of living creatures in their embryos involving states" (Clausewitz 1989, 30). Clausewitz means that a state's decision to settle a clash between major interests with bloodshed and not diplomacy is political. Given the political nature of such wars, they cannot be an accident: political actors have a role in deciding whether they happen or not.

If we agree with Clausewitz that wars are political, it is worth pondering how commerce convinces or forces political actors to choose a path of peace instead of war. In other words, how does trade reach into the womb of politics to prevent it from birthing war or, at least, delay the war-birthing process? Except for Erik Gartzke's 2005 economic freedom paper (I will discuss Gartzke's argument later), this is a challenge for existing explanations. They are adept at specifying scope conditions but overlook how and why those conditions become politically salient.

In this chapter, I focus on some of the overlooked aspects of the trade and peace debate. Although I discuss several overlooked impacts of commerce throughout the chapter, I focus extensively on trade's function as a signaling device. International politics, like the economy, has a knowledge problem. International politics' knowledge problem creates a permissive environment for war, preventing rational leaders from reaching prewar bargains, making it challenging for leaders to reach a peaceful settlement to disputes, or using diplomacy or other communication channels to avoid the costs and risks of fighting (Fearon 1995). The knowledge problem could emerge due to a misalignment between political and military leaders (Levy 1989). At other times, it could arise because information about a state's relative capabilities or resolve is private, and state leaders have an incentive to misrepresent such private information for political and security reasons (Fearon 1995). These theories of the causes of war fail to adequately resolve the central puzzle: why do rational actors continue to go to war despite the cost of war and the abundance of national security information and information-gathering tools? These failings are because the theories overlook an essential cause of the knowledge problem. To state it differently, these theories ignore the central human problem—the need for rapid adaptation to change.

Due to the symbiotic relationship between economic, diplomatic, and military power, Hayek's formulation of the economic problem as one of rapid adaptation to change extends to international politics and most human domains. Political actors need knowledge contingent on domestic and international factors to decide how much security to produce, when to produce it, and what kind to produce. Just like market players, they also need to make spontaneous adjustments to change since the changes they encounter are not always preplanned. For instance, unlike a country's topography, other factors that affect state and regime security, like technology, change constantly, making it challenging, if not impossible, for state actors to feel secure perpetually.

Unfortunately, international political actors lack effective mechanisms for acquiring the requisite information for decision-making in such a rapidly evolving world. Hayek's explanation of the knowledge problem in economics can help us understand the dilemma political decision-makers face and why decentralized mechanisms, like commerce, are vital peace-generating and enhancing mechanisms. There are two aspects to this knowledge problem.

First, decision-makers need knowledge of the circumstances of time and place in order to respond to changing conditions in their locality (Hayek 1978). Given the information needed and the pace at which the decision-makers should act, Hayek reasons that a decentralized system that encourages personal initiative is more appropriate. Markets, Hayek (1978) argues, excel at this task. They empower the individual on the spot to use their local and inarticulate knowledge to respond to emerging and evolving situations quickly, since they do not need to wait for instructions from a superior (Hayek 1945).

Second, the decision-maker must align their actions with the trends in the larger economic system to derive the maximum benefit. In this regard, local knowledge is insufficient. The problem solver needs system-wide information to align their actions with the trends in the larger system (Hayek 1978). This is the task assigned to the price system. Hayek (1945) explains that the price mechanism conveys the information decision-makers need to fit their decisions into the whole pattern of changes in the larger economic system. Western state actors, especially Western militaries, have achieved limited success at solving the local knowledge problem by delegating certain responsibilities to field officers, giving them discretionary power over some decisions. Unlike in economic domains, international political actors lack a price mechanism to perform the second function. As a result, state actors use diplomatic missions, espionage, and alliances to acquire some of the information they need for rapid decision-making. Nevertheless, these measures are less accurate than the price system.

Commerce's Solution to the Political Knowledge Problem

Commerce makes two channels available to partially solve the political knowledge problem for a smaller outlay than the other means available to political actors.[2] First, trade contributes to the knowledge discovery process. Understanding a ruling regime's orientation toward the international system, especially the global economy, offers a partial solution to the international political knowledge problem. A ruling coalition's preference for commerce indicates its foreign and security policy preferences. Put differently, a ruling coalition's orientation toward international trade communicates vital information about a regime's goals and attitudes to decision-makers in neighboring states and other regions. For example, when a state shifts from an outward-looking trade policy to an inward-looking approach, its policy change provides information of strategic value to investors and political actors in other states. Second, commerce functions as a feedback mechanism, allowing political actors to observe the effect of their policies (Gartzke 2005). In summary, commerce allows ruling coalitions to send and receive information vital for decision-making.

The chapter proceeds as follows: The next section discusses commerce's impact on communal peace and armed conflicts, covering four of commerce's impacts on peace and armed conflict. It synthesizes the existing literature and points out some of commerce's impacts that scholars have given little attention to or completely overlooked. Although commerce can promote peace and conflict, this chapter narrowly focuses on its pacifying effects. The chapter then examines commerce's impact on armed conflicts involving states, explaining why and how it promotes peace. The chapter also introduces three of commerce's impacts on state-centric wars. It concludes with a brief discussion of the policy implications.

COMMERCE'S IMPACT ON COMMUNAL CONFLICTS

International trade's impact on armed conflict depends on the nature of the conflict. Whether translocal, interethnic, intracommunal, or a mass uprising, communal wars do not require extensive planning like state-centric wars. Sometimes, they involve no planning. While an organized group can plan and start communal wars, they can also erupt without much forewarning.

For instance, the ethnically diverse state of Zanzibar had widespread communal violence in 1964 that started as a violent ethnic conflict but transformed into a religious conflict with minimal planning and intentionality (Mpangala 2006). Like a powder keg, such uprisings can explode and engulf communities. These wars often start due to human action, not human design: the main actors are individuals acting as their own sovereigns with no organizational constraints. While establishing a leviathan that can monopolize the legitimate use of force tames violent conflicts, it alone does not guarantee peace. Commerce also plays a role in offering multiple tools for fostering harmonious coexistence and preventing various forms of predation. I will focus on four of commerce's impacts: it improves societal moral standards, promotes good governance, brings about prosperity, and contributes to peace negotiations.

Commerce Improves Societal Moral Standards

Commerce and markets dampen conflicts by reducing prejudice and improving our moral standards and culture. Past and contemporary scholars have made different versions of this argument. An example of this argument includes,

> Commerce is a cure for the most destructive prejudices; for it is almost a general rule that wherever we find agreeable manners, there commerce flourishes; and that wherever there is commerce, there we meet with agreeable manners. Let us not be astonished, then, if our manners are now less savage than formerly. Commerce has everywhere diffused a knowledge of the manners of all nations: these are compared one with another, and from this comparison arise the greatest advantages. (Montesquieu 2018, 338)

Another argument notes,

> We simply do not find evidence that markets are monsters, transforming us into evil creatures; more greedy, more selfish, more materialistic, less trustworthy,

> less tolerant, and less connected than we would have been had we been able to avoid these monstrous markets. The evidence, in fact, suggests that markets are moral spaces that not only depend on virtue but also reward virtue and punish vice. (Storr and Choi 2019, 44–45)

These statements refer to the role commerce plays in transforming human moral values. The authors are not claiming that commerce improves morals at the individual level. Instead, they limit their claims to system-level effects. Trade, in this context, improves societal moral standards and contributes to the flourishing of a culture of peace and tolerance. It also helps people develop habits of peacefulness (Coyne, Romero, and Storr 2023).

There are three explanations for why commerce generates these effects. First, Storr (2008) explains that markets are social spaces that diffuse knowledge about multiple ways of being, promote extraeconomic dialogue, and create conditions for cross-class or interethnic interactions. Second, commerce promotes intercultural exchanges, creating opportunities for people worldwide to travel to other countries for work (Montesquieu 2018). Third, Coyne, Romero, and Storr (2023) credit entrepreneurs for providing a peaceful means of satisfying desires and developing mechanisms that make it possible for strangers in distant places to interact and enter into exchange relationships. Commerce, in these instances, acts as a diffusion mechanism, spreading knowledge about different ways of being and connecting people. These intercultural and/or interethnic exchanges reduce prejudice and promote better understanding, marriages, treaties and edicts, and cross-cultural friendships. As Montesquieu (2018) notes, these civil transactions produce great changes, making us less barbaric and more humane.

Commerce Promotes Good Governance

Commerce's second peace-enhancing effect, which is closely related to the idea that markets improve societal moral standards, focuses on the impact trade has on governance. Commerce requires the establishment of a just judiciary, laws, and government (Smith 1981). In addition, commerce encourages the adoption of rules and institutions. Hume argues,

> the ancient world ought to teach the modern that it was disastrous to base social life on people's personal qualities. Virtue unassisted by institutional structures was commonly no match for vice. Fortunately, the modern world, pressured by commerce and urban life, was developing a genius for institutional living, that is, for extending the artificial virtues of rule-following to more and more areas of life and making individuals more predictable and safer company for each other. (1994, xxiv)

As Hume's quote suggests, commerce affects how we design and manage public governance and governing agencies (see Aligică, Boettke, and Tarko 2019). The logic underpinning this argument is that institutions, which are laws, rules, norms, and the like, are necessary for markets and commerce to function correctly (North 1991; Khalil 1995). Commercially derived institutions serve larger societal functions since the institutions governing commerce interlink with or give rise to other societal institutions.

While most scholars agree that commerce-induced institutions serve non-commercial social ordering purposes, they disagree over the source of such institutions and enforcement mechanisms. Ferguson (2004) and Lal (2004) point to empires as the source and diffusion mechanism of good institutions, crediting them for establishing global rules that gave rise to the global economy and for bringing order and peace to people living in states with defective political institutions. Ferguson and Lal want us to think of institutions as human inventions designed by a global hegemon to serve a given function. Agent-based explanations, like those offered by Ferguson and Lal, advocate for a global liberal hegemonic lawgiver to establish and enforce liberal rules and institutions worldwide (Coyne, Hall, and Smith 2022).

Coyne, Hall, and Smith (2022) contest this narrative. They agree that a peaceful social order requires adopting and adhering to abstract rules or principles; however, they disagree that the institutions and their enforcement must emanate from outside a polity. The gist of the argument put forward by Coyne, Hall, and Smith (2022) is that people can design institutions to solve the collective action problems they encounter. The idea that everyday people can develop and enforce rules challenges the Hobbesian notion that a powerful actor is necessary for establishing, policing, and diffusing good institutions.

There are two reasons why people's capacity for self-governance is germane to this conversation. One, a global lawgiver, whether benign or exploitative, often provokes resistance. Indigenous people worldwide did not acquiesce to Western imperialism and colonialism. Almost all local opposition led to wars of independence, which undermined the growth and development of those communities. Two, attributing the origins of social order to the actions of a powerful actor distorts the source of authentic and sustainable institutions. Most institutions originate from the activities of multiple actors, not the work of one divine mind or government. Powerful political actors work like aggregators that create processes for harmonizing and standardizing emergent institutions. Institutions evolve from attempts by ordinary people to solve the problems they face in their daily lives. Governments and multilateral governmental actors only aggregate, diffuse, and normalize the emergent institutions they prefer. In some ways, the globalizers truncate the institutional evolutionary process, picking winners and losers, which could undermine their social ordering function by provoking a backlash against those institutions.

Instead of agent-based explanations, process-based explanations provide a better understanding of the mechanisms and how they contribute to the observed outcome. Process-based narratives, like those offered by Hume, Montesquieu, Hayek, and North, describe the role of commerce as a catalyst for institution-building. According to this perspective, institutions evolve through successive decisions and actions that individuals take to exploit profit opportunities or solve the challenges presented by the main economic problems.

Hayek (2014) defines the economic problem as one of rapid adaptation or adjustment to change. Because economic actors, who also double as sociopolitical actors in some instances, live in a world of constant and rapid change, they need to develop mechanisms for successfully conducting their activities. In effect, these actors adopt abstract rules and principles, which narrow their choices and impose constraints on them (Hayek 2014). These abstract rules, norms, principles, and enforcement mechanisms gain legitimacy when they emanate from the people's daily practices (North 1991). When institutions evolve or arise from people's lived experiences, they provide the certainty, predictability, and security that individuals and groups need to carry out their activities peacefully. Moreover, such institutions better reflect the social dynamics and aspirations of the different social groups in that state or system. When that happens, the institutions will provide a basis for human flourishing, peaceful coexistence, and orderliness. While addressing Smith on this point, Hayek argues,

> The crucial fact of our lives is that we are *not* omniscient, that we have from moment to moment to adjust ourselves to new facts which we have not known before, and that we can therefore not order our lives according to a preconceived detailed plan in which every particular action is beforehand rationally adjusted to every other. Since our whole life consists in facing ever new and unforeseeable circumstances, we cannot make it orderly by deciding in advance all the actions we shall take. The only manner in which we can in fact give our lives some order is to adopt certain abstract rules or principles for guidance, and then strictly adhere to the rules we have adopted in our dealing with the new situations as they arise. Our actions form a coherent and rational pattern, not because they have been decided upon as part of a single plan thought out beforehand, but because in each successive decision we limit our range of choice by the same abstract rules.
>
> His implied assumption, however, that the extensive division of labor of a complex society from which we all profited could only have been brought about by spontaneous ordering forces and not by design was largely justified. At any rate, neither Smith nor any other reputable author I know has ever maintained

> that there existed some original harmony of interests irrespective of those grown institutions. What they did maintain, and what one of Smith's contemporaries, indeed, expressed much more clearly than Smith himself ever did, was that institutions had developed by a process of the elimination of the less effective which did bring about a reconciliation of the divergent interests. (Hayek 2014, 48)

We can deduce three essential points from Hayek's statement. One, the evolutionary process offers a peaceful means for reconciling divergent interests. Instead of attempting to freeze institutions, it is in humanity's interest to unfreeze and allow them to evolve. Two, spontaneous orders do not mean anarchy; they refer to any order that develops due to human action, not human design (Hayek 2014).[3] Spontaneous orders encourage human creativity and resourcefulness; they create opportunities for everyday people to devise and design institutions and practices to facilitate their activities (Ostrom 2015).

Three, during crises, indigenous institutions prove more resilient and adept at promoting peace and harmonious coexistence. For example, Gacaca courts, an indigenous justice system, have contributed to Rwanda's effort for justice, communal healing, and restoration in the aftermath of that country's genocide (see Pillay and Scanlon 2008). Ghana's informal arbitration systems, which involve chiefs, elders, and religious leaders, prevented electoral conflicts after the closely contested 2008 election from escalating into militarized conflict. In essence, productive and effective institutions are not dictated but are a product of many individuals who may not always know each other or might even be working at cross-purposes (Hayek 1978). If we set aside the debate over the origin of institutions, it is worth emphasizing that a rule-based trading system has positive public governance spillovers, which limit the range of issues that would trigger armed conflict.

Commerce Creates Posterity

The third peace-enhancing effect of commerce is its ability to generate wealth. Trade and manufacturing create prosperity, which cures many social ills that cause war. Poverty creates a permissive condition for war: people who live in poverty are more susceptible to the influence of bad actors, like terrorists, transnational criminals, and warlords. These bad actors, with a promise of riches, power, and freedom, can easily recruit impoverished youth to commit hideous crimes on their behalf. This is the case in developing countries like Kenya, where politicians can easily recruit, train, and deploy thousands of unemployed youth (see Government of Kenya 2013).

However, when the spirit of commerce prevails in a state, the people are more likely to use their ingenuity, creativity, and resourcefulness to solve societal problems, giving individuals a sense of purpose, hope, and a means to cater to their basic needs. Trade also enables individuals and societies to become wealthy, allowing them to lift more of their citizens out of poverty, which eradicates most of the social problems associated with widespread poverty. The expanding economic prospects will also increase the cost of maintaining private militias, reducing the number of militias in that polity. All these efforts tame conflict and enhance negative peace.

Additionally, trading states can invest some of their wealth in fostering positive peace, such as improving hard and soft public infrastructure, reducing income inequality, investing in cutting-edge innovations, and providing quality education for all citizens. Alshamy et al. (2023) point out that some entrepreneurs in trading states contribute to peace by aligning their products to social causes or purposes, like racial harmony or civic engagement, as a differentiation strategy. They also sometimes fund research on obscure but vital topics that become game changers when their usefulness becomes apparent.

The point is not to claim that innovation happens only in commercial societies: commercial societies simply allow for more innovations than non-commercial societies. The reason is that there is more funding in commercial societies than in noncommercial societies. The proliferation of funding agencies, governmental and nongovernmental, boosts innovation since it increases the odds of funding good research ideas, especially those whose commercial value cannot be immediately demonstrated. The downside is that some dangerous ideas might end up receiving funding. However, the net effect of the innovative ecosystem would be positive (Graham 2023).

Furthermore, interstate trade and the various corresponding economic activities offer an alternative means for investing capital. The proliferation of investment opportunities is another important but often neglected way trade decreases the likelihood of conflict escalation and enhances peace (see Smith 1981). It is often the case that peace and political stability are elusive in countries whose political economy incentivizes owners of capital to become warlords. Raising private militias allows the wealthy to acquire de facto power, which they can use to obstruct the establishment and administration of justice or disturb the country's peace. When the wealthy have alternative uses for their resources, especially more productive alternative investment vehicles, the practice of individuals keeping a loyal cadre of people loses its lure (Smith 1981). Most rational wealthy people would invest their resources in pursuit of higher profits, which would reduce the number of people with sufficient de facto power to interfere with the administration of justice. Reducing the number of warlords and cartels will reduce homicide rates and gun violence. It will also improve people's sense of security and tame extrajudicial killings. In other words, fewer warlords and cartels mean less opportunity for communal violence and, in some instances, less cross-border raids and armed conflict potential.

Commerce Contributes to Peace Negotiations

Commerce's contribution to negotiation at the individual and communal levels is an often-overlooked impact. Suppose the maxim that most conflicts end in a negotiated settlement is true. In that case, it means that people living in market societies are more likely to find negotiated settlements to conflicts before they escalate into armed conflict. Three skills are foundational to thriving in market societies.

One is the ability to acquire, process, and retain information. For example, knowing the normal price of maize is necessary for understanding that the price has gone up or down. Individuals also need to compare and choose between competing interests; they must understand the relative value of things and decide which best meets their needs. Two, people need to be able to choose and engage in exchange relationships. People in market societies must be able to compete, exchange, compromise, and exercise their exit rights at will. Three, individuals need to have the ability to negotiate to get the best value in the marketplace. The negotiation can be in the form of a discussion between a buyer and a seller or a buyer collecting multiple pieces of information before making a purchasing decision. People living in actual market societies get opportunities to practice these three essential skills regularly, increasing the likelihood of them developing a proclivity for exchange and negotiation, which will make them more willing to compromise and pursue win-win solutions during disputes.

In addition to the three basic skills, other advanced skills that help people succeed in commercial societies include critical thinking, creativity, communication, analytical skills, collaboration, and relationship-building skills (Winthrop and McGivney 2016). These are vital to an individual's ability to notice profit opportunities, explore, and capture them. They also help people think outside the box and find novel solutions to problems (Dondi et al. 2021). These skills enable individuals to connect with others, develop shared understanding, solve problems, and deliver value to interlocutors.

All these skills are directly transferable to conflict resolution. Having difficult conversations during a conflict requires training: conflict resolution experts have long held that people can learn how to negotiate, compromise, build trust, and communicate during conflicts, empowering them to resolve most disputes before they escalate into full-blown wars (Chetkow-Yanoov 1996). The ability to solve conflict does not depend on an individual's level of academic education (Dondi et al. 2021). People can learn these skills through other avenues, like markets. In other words, the skills people learn from market participation can help them better manage low-level conflict situations.

We need not underestimate the importance of decentralized conflict resolution mechanisms. Peaceful orders depend on them since disagreement is a natural part of human existence. Unfortunately, all disputes have escalation potential: to illustrate, the Guinea Fowl War was an inter-ethnic conflict in Northern Ghana from 1994 to 2015 that led to about 2,000 deaths and 150,000 displacements. It started as a disagreement over the price of a guinea fowl. Interestingly, when conflicts escalate, they take a life on their own. In the case of the Guinea Fowl War, even though it started as a dispute over the price of a guinea fowl, it metamorphosed into a war over land ownership between three ethnic groups. Whereas it is challenging to quantify the number of wars that do not occur because conflicting partners deescalate the situation, we cannot ignore trade and market systems' role in equipping people with the skills necessary for resolving conflicts. These systems help prevent some civil wars and play constructive roles in peacebuilding, especially when it comes to creating positive peace.

COMMERCE AND CONFLICTS INVOLVING THE STATE

Unlike communal wars, wars that involve states, whether inter or intrastate, do not break out spontaneously. War and the preparation for war by the state occur within a system with a chain of command: a legitimate state actor must give a command for such wars to start and end. Most importantly, although the number of key decision-makers varies depending on the polity, they are always few in number, which sets wars involving states apart from mass uprisings or communal wars. Commerce influences conflict involving states in three ways. One, trade changes the incentives of state actors. Two, it serves as a signaling mechanism that reduces information asymmetry. Three, it influences negotiation between state actors. While there is an extensive discussion of the first impact in the existing literature, there is less focus on the last two.

Commerce's Impact on Incentives

The security-focused international political economy (IPE) literature has extensively explored how international trade alters our incentives. A dominant view asserts that states wage wars to extract resources for development. Students of political economy who subscribe to this view claim that economic gain from war makes war lucrative and attractive to states (Khalili

2020). Contrarily, scholars who embrace the trade-leads-to-peace argument disagree with this thesis, arguing that commerce weakens the economic rationale for war (see Gartzke 2005). Commerce alters our incentives for making war, positively and negatively. Positively, trade offers a humane and less costly path for achieving states' stated economic and sociopolitical goals (Pinker 2011; Lehmann and Lehmann 2010). To illustrate, Rosecrance (1986) points out that the rise of trading states makes it easier for states to gain access to lucrative markets and scarce inputs through bilateral, plurilateral, or multilateral arrangements. It is also cheaper for states to pursue resource competition through markets than military campaigns (Gartzke 2007). The post-World War II development of China, Japan, Germany, and the Asian Tigers are excellent examples of the pacifying effect of trade (Mahbubani 2010). China did not need nuclear weapons or a strong military before rising to become the second-largest economy in the world and the largest trading partner of many countries. The high levels of trade openness and production integration offer states a reason to avoid militarizing conflicts.

Negatively, commerce alters the incentive for war in two ways. First, Norman (1910) posits that the low payoffs from war combined with the high cost of governing conquered states or running an empire disincentivize state actors from waging war. Aside from natural resources, it has become challenging for conquerors to obtain the economic resources of a conquered state for their own use since most economic goods are now highly mobile (Norman 1910; Gartzke 2007). Moreover, the direct cost of administering and securing a conqueror's interest in a colony has increased substantially (Norman 1910).

In addition to the high direct cost, the opportunity cost is equally high. For example, the Overseas Contingency Operations budget consumed $1 trillion of the $2.26 trillion the United States spent on the war in Afghanistan between 2001 and 2021 (Sabga 2021). Aside from the operational and reconstruction costs, Americans must now pay for long-term medical care and disability compensation for service members, veterans, and families, military supplies replenishment, and rebuilding its credibility as a peace-loving nation (Bilmes 2013). Available estimates from Crawford (2021) and Bilmes (2013) show that these future costs will be significant budgetary outlays. These resources could have gone to other programs.

In 2021, the U.S. president, Joseph Biden Jr., alluded to these cost concerns in two separate addresses on his decision to withdraw from Afghanistan. On July 08, 2021, Biden Jr. (2021a) said,

> After 20 years—a trillion dollars spent training and equipping hundreds of thousands of Afghan National Security and Defense Forces, 2,448 Americans killed, 20,722 more wounded, and untold thousands coming home with unseen trauma

> to their mental health—I will not send another generation of Americans to war in Afghanistan with no reasonable expectation of achieving a different outcome.

On August 31, 2021, Biden Jr. (2021b) argued, "After more than $2 trillion spent in Afghanistan . . . what have we lost as a consequence in terms of opportunities? I refused to continue in a war that was no longer in the service of the vital national interest of our people." In summary, war's low economic payoff and high direct and opportunity costs make it less appealing to some political actors.

Second, the costs of rupturing economic interdependence disincentivize state actors from initiating wars. Most students of international political economy consider this causal path as the most robust means through which trade tames conflict (see Solingen 2021; Gartzke 2005). Reciprocal economic dependence serves as a disincentive for war because it disrupts economic activities in all states, increasing the economic cost of war (Tiwary and Roy 2021). Such costs could include disruptions to trade, an increase in inflation, loss of jobs, loss of investments, destruction of businesses and properties, and reduced access to critical inputs, which would degrade the productive capacity of the warring states.

In some polities, especially states where citizens have a role in choosing their leaders, the high economic cost could have political ramifications for the ruling coalition, thereby increasing the political cost. The mutual vulnerability gets both sides to commit to each other's security, but does not mean both states would endure the same suffering. The threat each state faces will differ; so too will their benefits: what is most vital is the reciprocal nature of dependence.

Simultaneously, the economic impact on third-party states incentivizes the leaders of those third-party states to intervene in a conflict. The role of third-party states in preventing conflict escalation or resolving conflicts due to war's third-order effects on them has not received much attention in the literature. In summary, economic interdependence tames armed conflict by increasing the economic and political cost of war, which dissuades some state actors from initiating war and incentivizes third-party state leaders to mediate.

However, not all scholars embrace the idea that economic interdependence leads to peace. While some scholars argue, sometimes passionately, that commerce causes war, most critics of the economic interdependence thesis (let us call them the mid-range theorists) argue that economic interdependence alone cannot guarantee peace. The mid-range theorists argue that nationalism and realpolitik (Bolton 2020; Mearsheimer 2018), the potential of trade cessation (Copeland 2015), and the allure of noneconomic goals, like the ability to dictate the terms of future engagements (McBride and Skaperdas 2014) limit economic interdependence's influence. These factors either increase the political stakes or reduce the economic cost of fighting.

The position of the mid-range theorists is not outlandish. The social world is not mechanistic and static, which implies that no system or ideology, including realpolitik, can achieve locked-in peace. In a constantly changing and dynamic world, the idea that perpetual peace and stability would emanate from establishing economic interdependence is tenuous. Despite its advantages, commerce is not the fulcrum of all political decisions; humans, as agentic beings, do not base all their decisions on economic rationality. This understanding of political decision-making is vital because the main actors in the international system are state agents, not the elusive inanimate entities called states. Thus, the interests of these agents matter, if not more than those of their principal—the state—then they matter at least as much. Put simply, state survival is a euphemism for regime survival. Whereas some agents are willing to accept a situation of mutual vulnerability, other agents are naturally opposed to that idea, preferring a situation where they, not their adversaries, have greater autonomy and a higher degree of certainty in their survivability. This tendency is why nationalism and realpolitik will remain relevant for the foreseeable future. Nonetheless, accepting the limits political factors impose on commerce's effect on peace and conflict does not negate commerce's influence.

Commerce as a Signaling Mechanism or Communication Device

Like commerce, wars are intercourse between humans with divergent interests and goals (Clausewitz 1989). However, unlike commerce, which has a price system (a vital mechanism for communicating inarticulate local knowledge and reconciling divergent interests), inter or intrastate wars unfold in the womb of politics—"a cautious, devious, even dishonest" but sometimes benevolent domain—which is often shrouded in secrecy (Clausewitz 1989, 30). To state it differently, war starts in a domain where the actors willfully obfuscate information, making it challenging for adversaries and allies to acquire and process the information they need for decision-making. The opaqueness of the political domain makes it challenging for states to know when a neighbor or a powerful state has malign intentions toward them.

Political scientists have long argued that the knowledge problem in politics causes wars because it leads to misperceptions, miscalculations, and diplomatic blunders (Van Evera 1998, 1999; Levy 1989; Ziegler 1987; Jervis 1976; Blainey 1973). The two dominant explanations for Russia's ongoing war in Ukraine, which started in 2022, involve the knowledge problem (see Kupchan 2022; Donato 2022). One explanation attributes the war to Russian miscalculation. Some commentaries focus on Russia's misreading of its support level in Ukraine and the strength of Ukrainian nationalism, while some analysts point to Russian miscalculation of its own military strength, while yet others say Putin underestimated Western nations' willingness to arm Ukraine and the duration of their commitment. Additionally, some explanations focus on the quality of information the Russian President receives, noting that Putin appeared isolated in the days leading to the war, implying that he lacked the relevant information to make a rational decision.

The second explanation blames the United States and the collective West for the war on the grounds that Western leaders subscribe to a flawed view of world politics (see Walt 2022; Mearsheimer 2014). The subtext of this argument is that the Western strategies for primacy in Eastern Europe, like NATO and EU expansions, lack a sound theoretical and empirical foundation. In summary, the knowledge problem in world politics has catastrophic consequences on human flourishing and societal well-being.

One underestimated tool that security analysts can use to overcome the knowledge problem is a ruling coalition's orientation toward the international system, especially the global economy. Although an imperfect tool, understanding a ruling coalition's posture toward the international system offers valuable insight into its military and security posture. There are two ideal-type ruling regimes—those that make "the interests of commerce yield to those of politics" and those that make "their political interests give way to those of commerce" (Montesquieu 2018, 351).

Montesquieu's classification foreshadows Etel Solingen's regime survival strategy theory. Solingen (1998) argues that ruling coalitions, driven by their desire for regime survival, embrace or shun the global economy. She calls states that pursue deeper integration into the global economy "outward looking." Put differently, outward-looking coalitions elevate commercial interests over political interests as their key strategy for gaining and keeping power. Conversely, Solingen labels the states that steer their economy away from the global economy "inward-looking." In other words, inward-looking coalitions prioritize political interests over commercial interests as their preferred strategy for guaranteeing regime survival.

In this narrative, outward-looking coalitions embrace international trade and adopt strategies for attracting Foreign Direct Investments (FDI) to their countries. Inward-looking coalitions, on the other hand, are hostile to international trade, preferring import substitution and militaristic policies. A ruling coalition's inward or outward orientation toward the global economy acts as a signal to political actors in neighboring states, serving as a proxy for that coalition's security and military posture. In other words, it communicates the coalition's policy preferences and approaches to political opponents and observers.

There are two reasons why the signaling effect of a coalition's inward or outward orientation toward the global economy is strong. One, commerce is a confidence-building mechanism because international trade and FDI thrive in stable and peaceful regions. As a result, regimes that adopt outward-looking regime survival strategies have incentives to improve regional security. They usually work with regional partners to strengthen and codify existing institutions and enforcement mechanisms. They also work to resolve regional collective action problems to provide a conducive environment for their regime survival strategy to succeed. They adopt a conciliatory approach to regional disputes, preferring to de-escalate tensions rather than hold dogmatically to their position.

For example, Vietnam moved to end its occupation in Cambodia and re-positioned itself as a regional security contributor after adopting an outward-looking development model in 1986. The change in foreign and security policy occurred because the strategic interest of the ruling coalition changed from political to economic. These efforts prevent hostilities, avert conflict escalations, reduce military tensions, and build mutual trust between countries. Therefore, a ruling regime that adopts a pro-commerce regime survival strategy boosts regional confidence and provides certainty to leaders in neighboring states.

Two, a regime survival strategy is a statement of intent and a commitment to act in a certain manner. For example, Ethiopia transitioned from being a source of regional tension to a source of regional security when its ruling coalition, under the leadership of Meles Zenawi, embraced an export-oriented developmental state regime survival model. The Meles Zenawi regime offered the following justification for its foreign and security policy:

> The failure to realize development and democracy has resulted in our security being threatened. It has meant that we have remained impoverished, dependent, and unable to hold our heads high. The prospect of disintegration cannot be totally ruled out. That is why it is imperative that we expedite development and consolidate democracy. In doing so, we can consolidate our existence as a nation, and preserve our honor. The goal of our foreign and security policy is to ensure international conditions that are conducive to achieving our development and democratic objectives. (Government of Ethiopia 2002, 9)

> When we contend that we should pursue an economy-centered strategy, we mean that our relations of friendship or otherwise should be based first of all on economic matters. We mean that we should not enter into hostilities or friendship based on matters irrelevant to our development. We also mean that our external activity should focus on promoting business and investment opportunities and identifying sources of aid and credit. It means ensuring that foreign service officers realize that they are first of all development officers and that they acquire the

> requisite competence to accomplish this mission. It also means that we should not view our economic-related tasks as just one of many in our external activities, but rather to place economic work at the center of foreign relations. When we maintain that the economy should be in the center of our security strategy, we are recognizing that it is rapid economic growth that will build our capacity to withstand internal and external security threats. Impediments to economic development are a threat to our security, and therefore, to assure security, we will have to remove obstacles in the way of rapid development. Minor impediments can be handled with greater tolerance. But even those problems that hinder development and constitute a serious threat to security, need to be dealt with in a manner that would not be economically damaging, through the use of diplomatic instruments such as negotiations and political pressure. (Government of Ethiopia 2002, 22)

Ethiopia's justification for its policy orientation shows that regime survival strategies do not produce only policy changes; they also generate cultural and attitudinal changes. For example, China's Wolf Warrior diplomats gained prominence after the Chinese Communist Party (CCP) switched from an outward-looking regime survival strategy to an inward-looking (leaning hybrid) survival strategy. Another example of such attitudinal shifts occurred in Tanzania in the late 1990s: during Tanzania's transition from an inward-looking to an outward-looking regime survival strategy at the turn of the millennium, Tanzanian president Benjamin Mkapa made the remarks below to his ambassadors:

> Some people recall, with justifiable nostalgia, the days when the opinion and voice of Tanzania in world affairs carried considerable weight and influence. Statesmen and Diplomats routinely sought the opinion of Tanzania, especially, but not only, on matters concerning Africa. Our influence was predicated upon the impassioned articulation of the moral superiority of our position on matters such as decolonization, apartheid, socio-economic development of societies, human rights and international law, peace and disarmament, a new international economic order, and so on.
>
> Today, these factors have ceased to carry the weight they did before. The question, therefore, is whether it is possible for us to return to the glory days of the past in our foreign policy. My answer is that it is not possible to reach the heights of the late 1960s and the 1970s. Neither should it be our foreign policy priority to recover this lost influence in our present state of underdevelopment.
>
> We should instead strive for that influence which will bring food, shelter, and clothing for our people, as well as education, jobs, and improved health. In today's world, and in the coming century, we will be more respected for the socio-economic development of our people than only for our fervent articulation of the moral high ground. Economic growth and development will give us a more solid basis for influence, not the fact that 95% of our development budget is financed by grants and loans.

> It is clear, therefore, that our Embassies should now focus on the promotion and protection of the developmental interests of Tanzania, and the commercial interests of its private and corporate citizens abroad.
>
> In terms of foreign policy, this calls for a re-defined role of our Diplomatic Missions abroad . . . In that respect our Missions have to strive for the maintenance of the best possible relations with all foreign countries in general, and particularly with all our neighboring countries. They should also act as barometers of bilateral relations, and of local conditions in those countries. (Ministry of Foreign Affairs 1999, 95–96)

As evident from the quote, Mkapa's speech during the ambassador's retreat in 1999 advocated for a tactical and attitudinal change to match the administration's policy priorities. His instruction meant he wanted the diplomatic corps to be less aggressive and more friendly. The government no longer expected Tanzanian diplomats to be paragons of virtue and moral police but development agents who would seek and exploit exchange opportunities. The expectation of future gains from trade and globalization explains Tanzania's change in attitude. The ruling coalition that rose to power after Julius Nyerere was not pro-market pacifists. They were Socialists who became convinced that they had to change their approach to the global economy to ensure their regime's survival (see Mkapa 2019). The Mkapa government asked the diplomats to change their approach because it realized that "it is foolhardy to . . . contemplate an arrogant or dismissive attitude towards the IMF, the World Bank, and bilateral donors and creditors" since Tanzania needs these partners (Mkapa 1999, 318). Put plainly, Mkapa told the warriors to become doves because he thought the change in attitude would allow them to realize the benefits of global economic integration. Nevertheless, this willingness to compromise, cooperate, and be tolerant contributed to regional stability by easing longstanding tensions between Tanzania and Kenya and providing the certainty traders needed to grow their businesses.

The pacifying effect of commerce emanates from outward-looking regimes' willingness to moderate their positions—they are more tolerant and subject themselves to international trading rules and norms. In game theoretical language, outward-looking regimes voluntarily choose to cooperate rather than defect. A plausible explanation put forward by Copeland (2015) for why outward-looking regimes adopt a conciliatory posture in international affairs is that they expect international trade to continue. The problem with Copeland's thesis is that it ignores what outward-looking regimes do to ensure the continuity of international trade. These regimes actively provide the institutional framework for foreign trade to bloom because international trade is a means to an end for them. In effect, international trade is a tool of choice, which is why these regimes accept the constraints it imposes on their actions. Thus, a regime's survival strategy communicates the regime's intent to allies and adversaries.

In addition to its signaling function, commerce creates opportunities for state leaders to understand the consequences of their policies: it functions as a feedback mechanism for policymaking. Gartzke (2005) posits that it is economic freedom that has the most robust connection to conflict reduction. Of Gartzke's reasons, I will focus only on one here. Gartzke (2005) notes that actions that create uncertainty and frighten markets and market players discourage investment, worsen domestic economic conditions, provoke retaliatory measures, and dampen foreign trade. Markets' ability to react to political activities allows them to act as a sounding board, providing political leaders with credible real-time feedback on their actions, utterances, and policies. For some leaders, especially isolated leaders or those who surround themselves with sycophants, market reactions or retaliatory measures would probably be the closest thing to objective feedback they would ever receive. Such feedback allows leaders to evaluate and alter their policies if they want a different outcome. While there is no guarantee that the leaders will learn the right lessons from the situation, it can also tip the balance away from war.

In sum, commerce is vital in solving the knowledge problem in politics and international security. Despite lacking a price system that conveys critical information necessary for decision-making, commerce and a regime's orientation toward the global economy can partially fulfill that role. A latent function of commerce is that it conveys relevant information for policymaking in a mutually reinforcing manner. On the one hand, it enables a state to signal its intent and communicate its resolve to other states, while on the other hand, it acts like a mirror, providing specific feedback to policymakers on the impact of their policies.

Commerce Influences International Negotiation

Trade's role in international negotiation is often overlooked. Trade is vital at every stage of the negotiation process. At the pre-negotiation stage, it nudges ruling coalitions to adjust to accommodate the interests of trading partners, because they know it is only under a specific institutional arrangement and business-friendly climate that they can derive the true benefit of commerce. Thus, they willingly compromise to create or maintain those institutional arrangements or conditions. Given their incentive to maintain and deepen trading relationships, they are more likely to consider their counterparts' needs and views.

Boca et al. (2018) find that hostility decreases significantly when parties to a conflict use their perspective-taking skills. According to Brett and Thompson (2016), actors who take the perspective of others, which entails cognitively viewing an issue from another actor's point of view, understand the outcome potential of a situation better, and take constructive actions that improve those outcomes. Prenegotiation adjustment is an example of constructive action that political actors who do not discount the value of trade take during conflicts with current or prospective partners.

In addition to decreasing hostility between the conflicting parties, prenegotiation adjustments also lower the political temperature and/or expand the Zone of Possible Agreement (ZOPA). More often than not, conflicts create tensions, suspicion, outrage, fear, and distrust (Hernández-Requejo and Graham 2008). In such instances, each actor develops tunnel vision by taking a position, proclaiming the righteousness of that position, and expecting the opponent to adopt their position or at least make concessions (Fisher, Ury, and Patton 2011). International negotiation experts call this tendency positional bargaining. Fisher, Ury, and Patton (2011) say positional bargaining makes it challenging for conflicting parties to be open to new perspectives and solutions since their ego gets attached to their initial positions. Some political actors can move away from positional bargaining because existing trading relations compel them to educate themselves on how their interests intersect with those of the other party in the conflict. Becoming aware of the interdependent interest could inspire them to take actions that lower the political temperature and expand the ZOPA, increasing the probability of reaching an agreement. Often, the adjustments are not major. It can be a microlevel adjustment like adopting a mindset of "I will do my best to listen and be open-minded," or a political leader deciding to frame a conflict in less antagonistic terms.

Furthermore, negotiators sometimes use trade and commerce to unlock agreements on sociopolitical issues. For example, this could entail promising an interlocutor enhanced market access or inserting a managed trade provision in an agreement. The 2015 Iran Nuclear Agreement between the United States, the United Kingdom, France, Germany, China, Russia, and the European Union, on the one hand, and Iran, on the other, is a good example. One benefit Iran gained from temporarily giving up its right to a nuclear weapon and allowing for comprehensive and invasive monitoring of its nuclear program was the ability to trade freely and openly. Article III, Clause 3 of the 1979 peace treaty between Israel and Egypt is another example.

Similarly, after a year of vetoing Sweden's membership in the North Atlantic Treaty Organization (NATO), Türkiye President Recep Tayyip Erdoğan dropped his opposition unceremoniously. Although other backroom deals could have swayed Erdoğan's decision, the commerce clause in paragraph six of the written agreement was key in softening his opposition. Paragraph six states that the two countries will establish a Joint Economic and Trade Committee (JETCO), boost bilateral trade and investments, and work together to "reinvigorate Türkiye's EU accession process, including modernization of the EU-Türkiye Customs Union and visa liberalization" (NATO 2023, 1). These examples shine a spotlight on commerce's contribution to dispute settlement.

Additionally, commerce is conducive to inventive negotiating strategies. Hernández-Requejo and Graham (2008) developed the inventive approach to negotiation in the late 2000s: they describe the approach as an art of using conflict as a tool for long-term relationship building (Graham 2019). Assuming Party A and Party B are fighting over an offshore natural gas-rich territory. Suppose Party A wants to control the territory because of the resources and the sea lane. Party B also wants to control the territory because its regime is territorial and feels its security will be severely compromised if Party A controls it. If the two sides adopt an inventive negotiating approach, they might set up a joint venture to drill the gas and share the revenue, build a port facility to service vessels that use the sea lane, and regulate and secure the sea lane. They might even sign a nonaggression pact and demilitarize the conflict territory.

These solutions are not transactional and short-term-oriented: inventive negotiators pursue solutions that transform conflict into a source of long-term stability and friendship. Commerce is often a tool for inventive negotiators because it can take many forms and is conducive to long-term relationship building. For a joint commercial venture to succeed, all parties must be committed and take concrete action, often together. Peace and friendship bloom because the parties have a shared goal and take action toward its realization (Graham, Lawrence, and Hernández-Requejo 2014). The promise of this approach is that it can be used to transform many intractable and frozen conflicts. However, it calls for creativity and innovation since an inventive solution might not always be obvious or easy to implement.

CONCLUSION

In this chapter, I argue that scholarly discussions of commerce's impact on peace and conflict overlook many of commerce's effects, leading to a distorted view of the relationship between the variables. A probable reason for the omission is that it is easy to conflate different causes of war. Wars have an equifinality problem, which makes it challenging to study their causes without falling into the trap of oversimplification or obfuscation. To avoid this trap, I examine commerce's impact at communal and state levels. The nature of conflict at these two levels differs, making it easier to parse the multiple effects of commerce on peace and conflict. I synthesize the existing literature for each level and introduce new perspectives where necessary.

This chapter's discussions of commerce's effect on communal conflict focus on four impacts. First, commerce and markets dampen conflicts by reducing prejudice and improving moral standards and culture. Second, commerce promotes the establishment of good governance and institutions. Third, trade and manufacturing create prosperity, which cures many social ills that cause war. Fourth, commerce influences negotiation and conflict resolution.

Regarding conflicts that involve the state, the discussions explore three of commerce's influences. One, students of Classical Liberalism agree that commerce alters our incentive for war positively or negatively. Positively, trade and economic activities free states from the need to make wars by offering peaceful means of achieving their economic goals. Negatively, the chapter presents two paths—the unprofitability of modern warfare and economic interdependence. Two, commerce serves as a communication device or signaling mechanism that conveys vital information for political decision-making. Three, commerce plays a role in international negotiation.

The discussion in this chapter shows that commerce, on the whole, is peace-enhancing, just as Montesquieu argued when he declared, "peace is the natural effect of trade" (Montesquieu 2018, 338). It works because it makes it easier for individuals and the ruling coalition to choose peace. This effect is more robust on communal-level conflict than on state-centric conflicts. At the state level, the ruling coalition promotes peace by working within the confines of emergent institutions and creating opportunities for institutional evolution. They can also choose to ignore the institutional constraints.

The main point is that the ruling coalitions that make political interest yield to economic interests are more willing to accept and strictly follow the guidance of abstract rules or principles compared to regimes that make economic interest yield to political interests. Such regimes have an incentive to provide guardrails for commerce to thrive. The ability of politicians to choose when political interests trump economic interests and vice versa gives them a veto over commerce's impact on peace and conflict.

Therefore, the task of the defenders of liberty and freedom is to create permissive conditions for ruling coalitions to feel comfortable prioritizing economic interests over political interests: conditions that encourage ruling coalitions to opt for commerce as a tool for regime survival. For instance, explicitly including nonaggression clauses in bilateral or multilateral free trade agreements could create such a permissive environment. While the nonaggression clause would not replace the problematic national security exception clause, it could force the negotiators to provide clear guidelines on what constitutes a threat to national security, when it can be triggered, and how a signatory state can return to compliance.

Even if the agreement does not specify these conditions, it could nudge signatory states to list sunset conditions under which activating the nature security exception would be permissible. To state it differently, we ought to create a process for states or regimes to ask for security guarantees when they feel threatened. We will all benefit from normalizing the act of asking for and providing security guarantees even to our adversaries under certain conditions. This is important because the pace of change in the global era means no state or regime can feel safe perpetually. Thus, ruling coalitions must continuously invest in their relations with allies and adversaries to guarantee state and regime survival. This way of approaching international relations calls for epistemic humility and fellow feeling.

NOTES

1. I do not seek to claim here that it is a panacea or perfect tool. My argument is that it is better than all other alternatives.

2. Commerce's communication function does not eliminate the need for intelligence and alliances. It complements rather than replaces them.

3. There is an element of order even in anarchy, which implies that the existence of a government is a sufficient but not a necessary condition for order to exist.

REFERENCES

Aligică, Paul Dragoş, Peter J. Boettke, and Vlad Tarko. 2019. *Public Governance and the Classical-Liberal Perspective: Political Economy Foundations*. New York, NY: Oxford University Press.

Alshamy, Yahya, Joshua Ammons, Christopher J. Coyne, and Nathan Goodman. 2023. "The Market Process as Nonviolent Action." *The Independent Review* 28 (1): 11–28.

Biden Jr., Joseph. 2021a. "Remarks by President Biden on the Drawdown of U.S. Forces in Afghanistan." July 8. https://www.whitehouse.gov/.

———. 2021b. "Remarks by President Biden on the End of the War in Afghanistan." August 31. https://www.whitehouse.gov/.

Bilmes, Linda. 2013. "The Financial Legacy of Iraq and Afghanistan: How Wartime Spending Decisions Will Constrain Future National Security Budgets." *SSRN Electronic Journal* (RWP13-006).

Blainey, Geoffrey. 1973. *The Causes of War*. New York, NY: The Free Press.

Boca, Stefano, Maria Garro, Isabella Giammusso, and Costanza Scaffidi Abbate. 2018. "The Effect of Perspective Taking on the Mediation Process." *Psychology Research and Behavior Management* 11: 411–416.

Bolton, John R. 2020. *The Room Where it Happened: A White House Memoir*. New York, NY: Simon & Schuster.

Brett, Jeanne, and Leigh Thompson. 2016. "Negotiation." *Organizational Behavior and Human Decision Processes* 136: 68–79.

Chetkow-Yanoov, Benyamin. 1996. "Conflict-Resolution Skills Can Be Taught." *Peabody Journal of Education* 71 (3): 12–28.

Clausewitz, Carl von. 1989. *On war*. Translated by Michael Eliot Howard and Peter Paret. Princeton, NJ: Princeton University Press.

Copeland, Dale C. 2015. *Economic Interdependence and War*. Princeton, NJ: Princeton University Press.

Coyne, Christopher J., Abigail Hall, and Nathaniel Smith. 2022. "International Trade as a Peace Project." *GMU Working Paper in Economics* (22–40).

Coyne, Christopher J., Michael R. Romero, and Virgil Henry Storr. 2022. "The Market as a Space for Building a Peaceful Society." *Peace Review* 34 (3): 333–342.

———. 2023. "Entrepreneurial Pathways to Peacemaking." *Peace Economics, Peace Science, and Public Policy* 29 (2): 97–127.

Crawford, Neta C. 2021. "The U.S. Budgetary Costs of the Post-9/11 Wars." *Research Series: Costs of War*. Providence, RI: Watson Institute for International and Public Affairs.

Donato, Joseph M. 2022. "Putin's Bad Math: The Root of Russian Miscalculation in Ukraine." *Modern War Institute*. May 10. https://mwi.usma.edu/.

Dondi, Marco, Julia Klier, Frédéric Panier, and Jörg Schubert. 2021. "Defining the Skills Citizens Will Need in the Future World of Work." *McKinsey Global Institute*. June 25. https://www.mckinsey.com/.

Fearon, James D. 1995. "Rationalist Explanations for War." *International Organization* 49 (3): 379–414.

Ferguson, Niall. 2004. *Colossus: The Price of America's Empire*. New York, NY: Penguin Press.

Fisher, Roger, William Ury, and Bruce Patton. 2011. *Getting Ready to Negotiate: Negotiating Agreement without Giving In*. New York, NY: Penguin Books.

Gartzke, Erik. 2005. "Economic Freedom and Peace." In *Economic Freedom of the World: Annual Report*, edited by James Gwartney and Robert Lawson. Vancouver, BC: Fraser Institute.

———. 2007. "The Capitalist Peace." *American Journal of Political Science* 51 (1): 166–191.

Gartzke, Erik, Quan Li, and Charles Boehmer. 2001. "Investing in the Peace: Economic Interdependence and International Conflict." *International Organization* 55 (2): 391–438.

Government of Ethiopia. 2002. *Foreign Affairs and National Security Policy and Strategy*. Addis Ababa, Ethiopia: Federal Democratic Republic of Ethiopia.

Government of Kenya. 2013. National Cohesion and Integration: Sessional Paper No. 9 of 2013. Edited by The Presidency and Ministry of Interior and Co-ordination of National Government. Nairobi, Kenya: Government Printer.

———. 2014. National Policy for Peacebuilding and Conflict Management: Sessional paper No, 5 of 2014. Edited by The Presidency and Ministry of Interior and Co-ordination of National Government. Nairobi, Kenya: Government Printer.

Graham, John L. 2019. "A Third Theory: Inventive Negotiation." *The Journal of Business & Industrial Marketing* 34 (4): 703–710.

Graham, John L., Lynda Lawrence, and William Hernández-Requejo. 2014. *And? How to Build Relationships through Inventive Negotiation*. 1st ed. New York, NY: Palgrave Macmillan.

Graham, Lawrence J. 2023. *Charlotte's War*. Austin, TX: Greenleaf Book Group Press.

Hayek, Friedrich A. 1945. "The Use of Knowledge in Society." *The American Economic Review* 35 (4): 519–530.

———. 1978. *Law, Legislation and Liberty, Volume 2: The Mirage of Social Justice*. 1 ed. Chicago, IL: University of Chicago Press.

———. 2014. *The Market and Other Orders*. Edited by Bruce Caldwell. Vol. XV. Collected works of F.A. Hayek. Chicago, IL: The University of Chicago Press.

Hernández-Requejo, William, and John L. Graham. 2008. *Global Negotiation: The New Rules*. 1st ed. New York, NY: Palgrave Macmillan.

Hume, David. 1994. *Hume: Political Essays*. Edited by Knud Haakonssen. Cambridge: Cambridge University Press.

Jervis, Robert. 1976. *Perception and Misperception in International Politics*. Princeton, NJ: Princeton University Press.

Khalil, Elias L. 1995. "Organizations versus Institutions." *Journal of Institutional and Theoretical Economics* 151 (3): 445–466.

Khalili, Laleh. 2020. *Sinews of War and Trade: Shipping and Capitalism in the Arabian Peninsula*. New York, NY: Verso.

Kupchan, Charles A. 2022. "Why Putin's War with Ukraine is a Miscalculation." *Council On Foreign Relations*. February 24. https://www.cfr.org/.

Lal, Deepak. 2004. *In Praise of Empires: Globalization and Order*. 1st ed. New York, NY: Palgrave Macmillan.

Lehmann, Fabrice, and Jean-Pierre Lehmann. 2010. *Peace and Prosperity Through World Trade*. Cambridge: Cambridge University Press.

Levy, Jack S. 1989. "The Causes of War: A Review of Theories and Evidence." In *Behavior, Society, and Nuclear War*, edited by Philip E. Tetlock, Jo L. Husbands, Robert Jervis, Paul C. Stern, and Charles Tilly, 209–333. New York, NY: Oxford University Press.

Mahbubani, Kishore. 2010. "Trade in the New Asian Hemisphere." In *Peace and Prosperity through World Trade*, edited by Fabrice Lehmann and Jean-Pierre Lehmann, 5–8. Cambridge: Cambridge University Press.

McBride, Michael, and Stergios Skaperdas. 2014. "Conflict, Settlement, and the Shadow of the Future." *Journal of Economic Behavior & Organization* 105: 75–89.

Mearsheimer, John Joseph. 2014. "Why the Ukraine Crisis is the West's Fault." *Foreign Affairs*. Accessed July 8, 2023.

———. 2018. *The Great Delusion: Liberal Dreams and International Realities*. New Haven, CT: Yale University Press.

Miller, Steven E. 2015. "Introduction: The Sarajevo Centenary—1914 and the Rise of China." In *The Next Great War? The Roots of World War I and the Risk of U.S.-China Conflict*, edited by Richard N. Rosecrance and Steven E. Miller. Cambridge, MA: The MIT Press.

Ministry of Foreign Affairs. 1999. "Tanzania Ambassadors' Conference." White Sands Hotel, April 19–23.

Mkapa, Benjamin William. 1999. "A New Partnership in Higher Education." In *The Mkapa Years: Collected Speeches*, edited by Ombeni Sefue. Dar es Salaam, Tanzania: Mkuki na Nyota.

———. 2019. *My Life, My Purpose: A Tanzanian President Remembers*. Dar es Salaam, Tanzania: Mkuki na Nyota Publishers.

Montesquieu, Charles Louis. 2018. *Montesquieu: The Spirit of The Laws*. Edited by Anne Cohler, Basia Miller, and Harold Stone. Cambridge: Cambridge University Press.

Mpangala, Gaudens P. 2006. "The Zanzibar Conflict: A Search for Durable Solutions." In *Civil-Security Relations in Tanzania: Investigating the Relationship between the State, Security Services and Civil Society*, edited by Martin Rupiya, Jonathan Lwehabura, and Len Le Roux, in ISS Monograph Series, 63–80. Pretoria, South Africa: Institute for Security Studies.

NATO. 2023. "Press Statement Following the Meeting between Türkiye, Sweden, and the NATO Secretary General." July 10. https://www.nato.int/cps/en/natohq/news_217147.htm.

Norman, Angell. 1910. *The Great Illusion: A Study of the Relation of Military Power to National Advantage*. New York, NY: G.P. Putnam's Sons.

North, Douglass C. 1991. "Institutions." *The Journal of Economic Perspectives* 5 (1): 97–112.

Ostrom, Elinor. 2015. *Governing the Commons: The Evolution of Institutions for Collective Action. Canto Classics*. Cambridge: Cambridge University Press.

Pillay, Suren, and Helen Scanlon. 2008. *Indigenous Justice? The Cases of Rwanda and Mozambique*. Cape Town, South Africa: Centre for Conflict Resolution.

Pinker, Steven. 2011. *The Better Angels of Our Nature: Why Violence has Declined*. New York, NY: Viking.

Putin, Vladimir. 2022. "Putin's Declaration of War on Ukraine." Edited by Russia The Presidential Executive Office. London: The Spectator.

Rosecrance, Richard N. 1986. *The Rise of the Trading State: Commerce and Conquest in the Modern World*. New York, NY: Basic Books.

Sabga, Patricia. 2021. "The US Spent $2 Trillion in Afghanistan—and for What?" *Al Jazeera*, August 16. https://www.aljazeera.com/economy/2021/8/16/the-us-spent-2-trillion-in-afghanistan-and-for-what

Smith, Adam. 1981. *An Inquiry into the Nature and Causes of the Wealth of Nations*. Indianapolis, IN: Liberty Fund.

Solingen, Etel. 1998. *Regional Orders at Century's Dawn: Global and Domestic Influences on Grand Strategy*. Princeton, NJ: Princeton University Press.

———, ed. 2021. *Geopolitics, Supply Chains, and The International Relations of East Asia*. Cambridge University Press.

Storr, Virgil Henry. 2008. "The Market as a Social Space: On the Meaningful Extra-economic Conversations that Can Occur in Markets." *The Review of Austrian economics* 21 (2–3): 135–150.

Storr, Virgil Henry, and Ginny Seung Choi. 2019. *Do Markets Corrupt Our Morals?* 1st ed. Cham, Switzerland: Springer International Publishing.

Tiwary, Bipin K., and Anubhav Roy. 2021. "Partnering a Rival: The Sustenance of India's Complex Interdependence with China, 2010–20." *Strategic Analysis* 45 (5): 375–394.

Van Evera, Stephen. 1998. "Offense, Defense, and the Causes of War." *International Security* 22 (4): 5–43.

———. 1999. *Causes of War: Power and the Roots of Conflict. Cornell Studies in Security Affairs*. Ithaca, NY: Cornell University Press.

Walt, Stephen M. 2022. "Liberal Illusions Caused the Ukraine Crisis." *Foreign Policy*. Accessed July 8, 2023.

Winthrop, Rebecca, and Eileen McGivney. 2016. *Skills for a Changing World: Advancing Quality Learning for Vibrant Societies*. Washington, DC: The Brookings Institution.

Ziegler, David W. 1987. *War, Peace, and International Politics*. 5th ed. ed. Boston, MA: Little, Brown.

Chapter 10

Transaction Costs and Authoritarian Institutions

Early Coalition Size and Regime Party-Building

Curtis Bram

In this chapter, I argue that authoritarian governments establish political organizations when the costs of political action between the leader and political elites are high. Regime parties serve a purpose beyond merely distributing private goods to cronies or securing loyalty by containing potential challengers. Instead, they function as cooperative mechanisms for both the dictator and elites to ensure distribution, transparency, and loyalty. The factor that accounts for the variation in the costliness of political coordination, linked to the variation in regime party emergence, is the size of the political and economic elite, which consequently determines the transaction costs of political action.

The first section of this chapter reviews the existing literature on regime parties, while the second section examines the conditions that facilitate the emergence of such organizations. The third section presents a comparative analysis of North and South Korea between 1945 and 1960, highlighting the distinctive challenges faced by each country's political elite. In North Korea, the large elite faced particularly high costs of collective action, whereas the small and incidentally cohesive elite in South Korea led to the Rhee regime's dismantling of the institutions that underpin an enduring authoritarian rule.

When the Rhee regime eventually formed a party several years later, it signified an expansion of the regime's coalition. Specifically, the emergence of newly independent centers of wealth and power outside politics spurred party formation. I argue that this organization effectively amassed substantial kickbacks and redistributed those gains back to the political elite through non-competitive auctions. To substantiate these claims, I draw upon a combination of primary and secondary sources. These findings imply that the size of the elite coalition plays a crucial role in explaining the empirical variation in the presence of political organizations.

LITERATURE REVIEW

Extensive research on authoritarianism delves into the existence of and variation in political institutions. In dictatorial systems, political parties and organizations may seemingly serve as a facade, given that dictators are unaccountable to the people. One might think that "overt dictatorships should have little use for ostensibly democratic institutions such as legal opposition parties, popularly elected parliaments, and partially free presidential elections" (Guriev and Treisman 2019, 110). If these institutions, including regime parties, were only a form of marketing, one would expect them to be prevalent primarily in weaker regimes that need to invest in public relations, both internationally and domestically. Nevertheless, institutionalized autocracies exhibit long tenures and are remarkably resilient to economic crises (Gasiorowski 1995, 883). What accounts for the variation in the emergence of parties within regimes, and how does this relate to regime durability?

Geddes (2005) posits that authoritarian leaders establish parties to address conflicts within the regime. As Gandhi (2010) puts it, leaders may employ organizations to facilitate, compromise, and moderate policy. Conversely, some scholars argue that parties as institutions are created by the coalition after the elite have resolved internal conflicts (Brownlee 2007, 36). These frameworks for examining political organizations might overlook the reciprocal nature of institution-building (Wagner 2016): given that both the leader and the coalition reap benefits, it is likely that both groups come together to form a regime party.

In other words, authoritarian party formation may be a dual, bottom-up and top-down phenomenon, requiring the cooperation of both the leader and the supporting coalition. If organizations are established solely to serve the dictator by coercing elites, the coalition may not endorse their formation and could undermine their strengthening. Likewise, if organizations cater only to the coalition by redistributing benefits to political elites, the leader may oppose their creation. This reciprocal relationship in party-building is vital, as all dictators need resources (Slater 2010) that they can allocate to their essential backers (Bueno de Mesquita et al. 2005, 416). These distributions could be to those who are especially loyal, or even those in the opposition, as Gordon Tullock writes: "Rewards for loyalty and bribes for people who you suspect of potential disloyalty are the main motivating factor in both cases" (Tullock 1986, 12).

I contend that a structural feature accounting for variation in the costs of aggregating and redistributing resources is the size of the elite, which must act collectively to provide resources to the regime and individually to receive patronage such as kickbacks. The mechanism connecting these structural considerations to regime party-building is transaction costs—the costs incurred when using the market or other institutions to exchange goods and services (Pejovich 2006, 2). In practice, I assume that transaction costs rise with the size of the elite coalition. Consequently, instead of concentrating on resource distribution between the leader and the elite, I emphasize the size of the elite.

THEORETICAL FRAMEWORK

There are at least two paths by which the elite can support an authoritarian regime. On one extreme, a small elite coalition implies low transaction costs of political action. On the other extreme, a large coalition may require the establishment of organizations to overcome higher costs of facilitating political action. While both systems could result in long-lasting authoritarian regimes, studies of authoritarianism have predominantly focused on small, homogenous elite coalitions and paid less attention to large ones. Large coalitions differ in that they are effectively tied to the dictatorship through the organizations they create. As transaction costs increase with the growth of the elite, organizations become increasingly beneficial. The cases chosen for analysis in the following section are close to the two extremes: a notably large North Korean elite and a smaller predemocratic South Korean elite.

Elite Size and Organizational Strength

Political coalitions of different sizes necessitate distinct organizational structures to ensure transparency and reciprocity between the regime and elites. One reason for this is that regime parties are resource-intensive organizations with benefits that can vary depending on the context. These benefits often revolve around providing and distributing information about resource transfers between the dictator and the coalition. Given the disparity between the immediate costs of establishing a regime party and the potential long-term benefits, focusing solely on the institutions' outcomes might not reveal their initial purposes. For instance, researchers might observe cohesive and well-funded party organizations in enduring authoritarian regimes; however, this doesn't mean that cohesion was required to form the organizations. The incentives of authoritarian regimes might initially lead to the creation of organizations, which then promote collective action and durability. Party formation becomes more likely when a large group of elites cannot act collectively without an organization.

Even though small, cooperative coalitions may be able to build parties at lower costs, it doesn't guarantee that they will establish regime parties. Additionally, it might appear that only small coalitions capable of collective action would invest resources in organizations. However, focusing exclusively on expenditure reveals just one aspect of the situation. Organizational strengthening always involves costs, and the benefits fluctuate according to the coalition's size. Small coalitions may not benefit from the reduced transaction costs of governance that organizations offer, so forming a party may not be worthwhile.

Transaction Costs and Regime Parties

This framework's emphasis on reciprocity between the coalition and the leader encourages viewing regime parties as analogous to firms. Firms serve as mechanisms for facilitating exchange between entrepreneurs, who cannot implement their ideas alone, and employees, who are willing to work for others in exchange for compensation (Leeson and Boettke 2009, 253). Likewise, regime parties can facilitate exchanges between dictators who cannot rule independently and coalition members willing to support the dictator in return for some form of compensation. For instance, postwar South Korea saw newly wealthy individuals join the regime's party and receive substantial state transfers in exchange for donations to the Rhee regime. In this case, elites were defined by their wealth and effectively "hired" by the autocrat. Corporations are thought to emerge to overcome transaction costs (Coase 1937); this concept might extend to the political realm, explaining divergent party-building patterns.

In both democracies and authoritarian systems, transaction costs of political action can be high. In democracies, coalitions tend to be large and loosely connected, making it inefficient for democratic policy and electoral entrepreneurs to form new political coalitions for each legislative or electoral endeavor. However, in authoritarian regimes, dictators rely on a smaller group of key supporters for maintaining power (Bueno de Mesquita et al. 2005, 68). As long as they secure minimal support from this core coalition, dictators might have more freedom in daily policy decisions.

This implies that transaction costs of coalition building in autocracies are particularly high during leader selection. However, authoritarian leaders often hold office longer than their democratic counterparts (Bueno de Mesquita et al. 2005, 941). Under the selectorate theory, authoritarian leaders might avoid actions that reduce their coalition's flexibility, and consequently, they might not establish a party, as doing so could hinder their ability to coerce or co-opt existing members and make it more difficult to alter the coalition's composition. These costs are not directly related to party-building expenses but rather to the benefits of creating organizations, which may increase with coalition size.

Distinguishing between the benefits and costs of party-building is crucial, as the expense of building and strengthening parties only partially explains the relationship between varying coalition sizes and the need for a party. Autocrats face a constant challenge in resource extraction, with lasting regimes being those that extract rather than contract (Slater 2010; Brownlee 2007; Smith 1999). As extraction is always necessary for coalition payoff, there must be some factor explaining when extraction becomes particularly difficult. For large coalitions, sustaining high levels of extraction is challenging due to numerous individuals with diverse interests and opaque information. As a result, regimes benefit from building and strengthening organizations, which aggregate rents from a defined, relatively transparent group, and reallocate extractions to benefit the core constituency.

This notion that parties redirect, rather than merely absorb, rents could challenge Svolik's (2012) view on party formation variation. He argues that dictatorships supported by traditional elites, such as landed aristocracy or capital owners, may not build party organizations due to the costs of channeling resources through them. However, the question remains as to why such dictatorships, backed by a presumably small group of elites, would need party organizations in the first place, as these elites may have no reason to relinquish their rents.

Svolik contends that parties serve three unique functions that prolong regime lifespans: hierarchical assignment of service and benefits, political control over appointments, and selective recruitment and repression (Svolik 2012, 194). These features are costly, requiring resources to build a party, formalize governance, vet appointments, and balance benefits with repression. Svolik's argument is that small coalitions do not build parties, not because they are unwilling, but because they will not benefit from investing resources in such organizations.

Transaction costs become particularly significant when the elite coalition is large. Building authoritarian organizations can help address this issue by ensuring credibility and fostering information flow over time (Pepinsky 2014, 663). Coalition members seek a continuous flow of patronage, while leaders aim for sustained support. Regime parties facilitate this reciprocal relationship by making resource transfers in both directions explicit and overt, enabling coalition members to easily track donations and receipts. This, in turn, reduces transaction costs when dealing with regime officials and vice versa. Empirical case studies demonstrate the value of this knowledge for both the regime and the coalition. When the benefits of formalization outweigh the costs, coalition members and the leader collaborate to form political organizations that provide information about each other's involvement in the reciprocal transfer of rents.

If a leader relies on a small coalition, organizations should not emerge, as the leader can micromanage transfers within the coalition. Additionally, coalition members can trust the leader since they can easily monitor rent flows between other elites and the regime. These information problems drive the transaction cost mechanism: when information is inexpensive, there may be little need for a regime party; although the party provides information, it does so at a high cost. When the regime relies on a large group of key backers, negotiating and concluding separate patronage agreements may become too costly and even unsustainable, as transaction costs rise with the number of backers. Consequently, the varying benefits are determined by the transaction costs associated with coalition size; as Coase (1937, 390) states, the costs of negotiating and concluding a separate contract for each exchange transaction on a market must be considered.

The assumption that a leader's coalition size is highly and negatively correlated with collective action is strong. There may be instances where large coalitions can act collectively (and thus not require a regime party) or small coalitions cannot cooperate (and thus require a party). What this means is that value heterogeneity between elites may be more important than the sheer number of elites for determining the costs of collective action. At the same time, those preferences may themselves result from exogenous factors like urbanization or early settlement (Nathan 2022; Bram and Munger 2022), or even the natural world (Nathan 2023). But even if this key assumption does not hold, what matters most are the incentives implied by the coalition size. As one factor among many, larger coalitions tend to indicate fractionalization, all else being equal. Other factors may dominate the mechanisms in this analysis, but unless they challenge the incentives' direction as coalition size varies, they remain less relevant to these arguments. Moreover, evolving patterns of elite politics in North and South Korea suggest that coalition size is a reasonable predictor of elite collective action, at least in these cases.

CASE STUDIES

This section presents a comparative analysis of party formation under Kim Il Sung in North Korea and Syngman Rhee in South Korea. Numerous factors contributed to the construction of the Korean Workers' Party in North Korea, factionalization and the ensuing divisions within the elite being among them. Conversely, Syngman Rhee in South Korea disbanded the initially supportive Korean Democratic Party (KDP) and only established the Liberal Party six years later. While countless factors influenced these decisions, many of which are unobservable, Rhee faced a united coalition before the Korean War, making it unnecessary to maintain the costly KDP. Later, after the war, when rapidly growing business interests started developing independent power centers, establishing an organization became cost-effective.

The theoretical sections of this chapter link variations in the presence of authoritarian institutions to differences in elite coalition sizes. Transaction costs account for a significant portion of the puzzle surrounding authoritarian institution-building. A historical analysis of North and South Korea between 1945 and 1955 offers empirical support for this hypothesis. The end of World War II marks the historical moment that solidified the enduring division of the peninsula, representing a critical juncture that produced a stable equilibrium outcome (Mahoney and Thelen 2015, 159). Although international factors played a role, domestic politics on each side and the subsequent variation in institutionalization highlight the importance of scale in consolidating regime parties. Both North and South Korea faced similar political situations immediately after the war, grappling with power vacuums, legitimacy deficits, and the need to mobilize resources for reconstruction and defense. However, their elite coalitions differed in size and composition.

When the Soviet Army arrived in Pyongyang and the Americans reached Seoul, local People's Committees were present throughout the entire peninsula. These organizations were not dominated by Communists; in fact, leftists tended to be a minority, and there was often friction between People's Committees (PCs) and the local communist parties (Armstrong 2004). These groups operated across the peninsula, but the Americans pursued a policy that "rejected any preexisting Korean political authority and dismantled each PC in the South" (Armstrong 2004).

In contrast, the Soviet occupiers in the North acknowledged the authority of the PCs and sought to use them to promote communism (Armstrong 2004). However, no organized communist parties existed in Korea in the early 1940s, and none had been present since the 1920s (Cumings 2002, 79). Overall, the conditions at the beginning of the occupation were similar; variations largely stemmed from political decisions made after the occupation of the peninsula and not from a preexisting communist movement in North Korea. Furthermore, North Korea (the Democratic People's Republic of Korea, or DPRK) did not start with a vanguard party. When Kim Il Sung became the head of the Korean Workers' Party (KWP) in 1945, its membership comprised 30 percent workers, 34 percent peasants, and 56 percent intellectuals or entrepreneurs (Armstrong 2004).

While international factors influenced many political developments on the Korean Peninsula after World War II, my hypothesis focuses on explaining one crucial aspect: the effect of variation in coalition size on the incentives driving institutionalization. Unfortunately, direct measures of elite coalition size are unattainable, along with much historical data on the early years of the Kim Dynasty. Rather than providing a definitive measure, I infer the direction of incentives from relative levels of factionalization, secondary sources, and primary statements from Korean and foreign policymakers.

North Korea

There were significant divisions among a large group of elites from the very beginning of North Korea's existence. The leadership consisted of four competing centers of power, each with distinct interests, experiences, and aspirations: the Domestic, Yanan, Soviet, and Guerrilla factions (Lankov 2002, 78). Each group held its own ideas on governing the country, leading to disputes over ideology and policy (Armstrong 2004). The numerous factions likely made it difficult to disseminate information on transfers between groups and the regime. With different interests and goals, the Kim regime probably faced initial challenges in extracting and redistributing resources, given the sheer number of individuals seeking to contribute to the regime in exchange for transfers.

Politics was largely conducted through the People's Committees (PCs), which aimed for centralization during the Joint Conference of People's Committees in the Five Provinces of North Korea. PCs had been responsible for managing local affairs, providing essential services, and maintaining social order: the meeting's objective was to integrate the previously autonomous PCs and incorporate the grassroots politics that followed liberation (Armstrong 2004) under the central authorities in Pyongyang. PCs were subsequently transformed and integrated into the emerging political system of the Democratic People's Republic of Korea (DPRK) under the leadership of Kim Il Sung and the Korean Workers' Party (KWP).

The North Korean regime relied on a variety of diffuse groups, all of which sought political authority in an uncertain, competitive environment. People's Committees consisted of diverse social groups, including workers, peasants, and intellectuals. Intense internal competition and disagreement led to the consolidation of power within the Korean Workers Party. The party functioned to reduce transaction costs inherent in garnering support from numerous individuals for political action. The differences between North and South Korea were significant:

> Unlike the Americans with their military government in the South, the Soviets in the North allowed Koreans to take charge early on while exerting a powerful influence behind the scenes. And at the local level, as we have seen, Koreans were indeed in control, with the bottom-up structure of the PCs ensuring that

> Korean input would move from the periphery to the center. (Armstrong 2009, 68)

This quote speaks to the theoretical framework outlined earlier. The emergence and strengthening of the Korean Workers Party was not just the inevitable progression of a Soviet satellite or the result of Kim Il Sung's maneuvers: the interplay between the incentives facing each of the PCs likely played a crucial role. A government report from 1946 supports this assertion and states that power was relatively diffuse in the North (Jarman 2005, 116). In contrast, the South Korean regime was cohesive from the start and controlled by a select few. Only when economic growth led to the development of a newly independent political power center did Syngman Rhee establish a regime party.

South Korea

The U.S. approach to governing the South differed from the Soviet approach to the North. The United States relied on a small Korean Advisory Council that worked with various South Koreans to secure elite and popular support for President Rhee (Jarman 2005, 155). The U.S. allies in Korea were mostly Japanese collaborators and other elites who opposed any social change or leftist influence (Cumings 2002, 179). A 1944 British report confirms this, stating that

> [B]ourgeois nationalist groups want no important changes in the Korean social order after the achievement of independence, the Communists and other Left-Wing groups do advocate a large measure of social change, particularly in land redistribution, much as do the Chinese Communists. In foreign affairs the Right-Wing groups look to the United States for support in the struggle for Korean independence. (Jarman 2005, 674)

When Rhee became president, he protected these elites from being dispossessed by any communist or nationalist regime (Cumings 2002, 208). He did not need to build organizations to maintain their loyalty as they already had strong incentives to back his rule. A 1946 telegram from Rhee's secretary of the interior Yoon Chiyoung shows that the regime recognized only the "Interim Legislative Assembly" and wanted to dissolve the "Representative Democratic Council" (Rhee et al. 2000, 628). The regime dismantled existing organizations and did not invest in new ones.

Rhee secured the support of the elite by protecting their interests and privileges. This contrasted with the land reform policies in North Korea, where about 70 percent of farmlands were redistributed (Armstrong 2004). Rhee delayed land redistribution until after the Korean War, when he faced more political pressure from a larger number of actors. An American officer who understood the nature of Rhee's regime said that the U.S. mission in Korea was to prevent the landlords from being abandoned (Cumings 2002, 209). The landlords, who were few in number, also had the implicit backing of the United States, unlike in the North. The elite in the South rallied behind Rhee because they saw his dictatorship as the best way to preserve their status.

They did not need a costly party to coordinate their actions; they had similar interests and shared information. This was different from the North, where there was more political competition and diversity among the elite. Kim Il Sung built and strengthened the KWP, while Syngman Rhee shut down the KDP. The implication is that political parties and organizations must be worth their costs: if they are not useful to the elite, they will not be maintained or developed. The pattern here is the opposite of what happened in North Korea. A government report on the political situation in South Korea aptly describes the Rhee regime's unique position:

> [Rhee's] group was not a combination of political parties, for Rhee had exalted himself above the party level to the position of national leader. It was an organization of societies united in the desire for immediate sovereign independence and in the belief that Rhee was the man to lead them to their goal. (Jarman 2005, 325)

To account for Syngman Rhee's establishment of the Liberal Party (LP) in 1951, I argue that the elite coalition supporting his rule expanded and diversified between the end of World War II and the middle of the Korean War. The LP was not very effective or deep as a regime party, but it still represented an attempt to organize support (Pyung-guk and Vogel 2011, 204). My framework predicts that a larger and more divided elite coalition would require more organizational investment. This is supported by archival evidence that shows high levels of internal conflict during the LP's founding (Jarman 2005, 105). It is also consistent with existing studies of South Korea's political and economic development after the end of World War II, which attribute some of its success to increasing state capacity in response to external threats (Doner and Slater 2005, 3). My framework complements these studies by emphasizing internal rather than external vulnerabilities as drivers of institutionalized autocracy. Other authors also note that Rhee faced more political competition from a new group of businessmen who emerged after the War and sought government support for their manufacturing activities (Haggard et al. 1991, 857). This suggeststhat Rhee's coalition became larger and more diverse over time.

As resources became less concentrated in a small group of political elites, Rhee had to aggregate support from a larger and more difficult to manage coalition (Jarman 2005, 158). A 1952 UN Report provides further evidence of these divisions: the document describes the increasing number of opposition figures that Rhee initially attempted to include in his cabinet. These people were from the opposition Democratic Nationalist Party (DNP), which the United Nations describes as the only initially organized political entity (Reports of the United Nations Commission for the Unification and Rehabilitation of Korea, Seventh Session, 1960). When inclusion failed, Rhee made a number of attacks on the DNP while simultaneously working toward the establishment of a new party. Statements from the president speak to this conclusion:

> Synghman Rhee, in his speech at a ceremony to commemorate the anniversary of the establishment of the Republic of Korea, said that he thought the time had come for the formation of a new political party of "laborers and farmers." He followed this, on 25 August 1951, with a further statement that the new party would be based on his 'one people' principle. (Reports of the United Nations Commission for the Unification and Rehabilitation of Korea, Seventh Session, 1960, 4)

The U N Report describes Rhee's participation in the formation of the Liberal Party as a reversal of the nonparty position that he had consistently taken since Korean independence. This reversal suggests the need to aggregate support from a newer and larger group of individuals. Further evidence comes from conflicts between the legislature and the President (Jarman 2005, 161), along with reports of growing splits between new factions just as those same factions were intentionally entering into the Liberal Party (Jarman 2005, 410).

Rhee had to create distribution mechanisms to redirect resources to his cronies, as well as gather resources from increasingly independent elites, so he sold land confiscated from Japanese industrialists at a low price (Wonhyuk et al. 2003, 42). The buyers made huge profits and gave kickbacks to the Liberal Party. Wonhyuk Lim gives an example of this system: "Using political connections, top industrial capitalists borrowed money from the banks in order to make bids for the ownership of the same banks" (Wonhyuk et al. 2003, 42). This shows the mutual transfers between the regime and the entrepreneurial elite: these were symbiotic relationships; the implication is that the exchange between the party and its key backers was never one-sided and increased as independent sources of political and economic power emerged. Recall that this chapter's theoretical framework argues that regime parties are costly organizations that will only form when the benefits to both the regime and elites outweigh the costs.

Exchange between the coalition and the regime is mutual, as the case of South Korea's banking sector and government illustrates. The Liberal Party enabled the holders of wealth to channel resources into an organization and not just a person. The party also facilitated the noncompetitive auctions that resulted in large transfers of wealth back to the same elites who had been funding the party. Without a party, it may have been harder for government officials to use noncompetitive auctions, because they needed kickbacks to redistribute these transfers. While the Liberal Party was not necessarily a strong or effective organization, it still served as a mechanism for resource exchange between the regime and the elite. The party also helped Rhee to secure his political survival by mobilizing support for his constitutional amendments and suppressing opposition. The party's formation and function reflect the changes in the size and composition of Rhee's coalition over time.

Discussion

One objection to this account of the variation in authoritarian organization-building in North and South Korea is repression. Kim Il Sung may have been able to dominate the political system in the North with his personality-driven party because he was more brutal than Syngman Rhee, but Rhee also used widespread repression and committed several massacres with his security apparatus. Another possible objection is that the Soviet Union's policy was to institutionalize a Leninist Party in the North, but this may not be enough to explain the historical record. Communism in North Korea did not start with a single party, but with three competing parties: the Communist, Korean Democratic (Christian), and Young Friends parties. These parties represented the three main ideologies that shaped the internal political divisions of North Korea after the liberation from Japan (Wonhyuk et al. 2003, 42). They competed in local elections, where the Communists often lost to the others. Moreover, the NKWP (Communists) were not proletarian: half of their delegates at the first party congress were from wealthy and educated backgrounds, while workers only made up about twenty percent (Wonhyuk et al. 2003, 42).

Party-building in North Korea "was not a simple process of imposing a vanguard party on society, but rather one of building a mass party from the bottom as well as from the top, accompanied by difficulties and conflicts" (Wonhyuk et al. 2003, 42). Kim Il Sung also tried to reduce Soviet influence (Lankov 2002, 62). Therefore, Soviet involvement likely does not fully explain the consolidation of the KWP as a regime party. Rather, the party emerged as a result of the complex interactions among various political actors, both domestic and foreign, who had different interests and ideologies. The party also served as a mechanism for Kim Il Sung to manage his diverse and divided coalition, which included workers, peasants, intellectuals, nationalists, and communists. The party enabled him to aggregate and redistribute resources among his supporters, as well as to mobilize and suppress opposition. The party's formation and function reflect the changes in the size and composition of Kim Il Sung's coalition over time.

The consolidation of the KWP may not be fully attributed to Soviet influence, as it also depended on the complex interactions among various political actors in North Korea. Similarly, the dismantling of the KDP and the creation of the LP in South Korea cannot be fully attributed to U.S. influence, as they also depended on the changing dynamics among the political elites in South Korea. Both Kim Il Sung and Syngman Rhee were repressive, received financial support from a superpower and aimed to retain political power, but they used different strategies to do so. Kim Il Sung built a robust party to aggregate diverse supporters, while Syngman Rhee relied on the internal security force. When he faced more independent and divided elites, Rhee and his followers built the LP to aggregate and distribute resources. The relative sizes of their political coalitions constrained their choices and explained a significant part of the variation in institution building. This variation at the onset of authoritarian rule does not capture all the factors that shaped the long-run divergence on the Korean Peninsula, but it supports the theoretical framework for analyzing authoritarian party formation.

CONCLUSION

This chapter focused on how the size of authoritarian coalitions affects regime party-building. Either the dictator can rely on a small coalition, which has little need for institutions because the elite can easily share information about transfers, or the dictator can rely on a large coalition, which is more likely to institutionalize because information about transfers is scarce. The framework that I have outlined predicts that the probability of formalized party arrangements increases as the coalition expands and the transaction costs of mutual transfers between the regime and elites increase.

The main variable in the analysis is the number of relevant social groups. Autocrats with small coalitions prefer weak organizations. They only face constraints that require the creation of organizations and institutions when their elite rule is challenged: this conflict can have different sources, but I focused on the divisions within the elite that are likely to emerge in large coalitions. In this case, the transaction costs of sending and receiving patronage are high, so both the coalition and the leader have incentives to build a regime party to facilitate the transfers. In contrast, when the coalition is small, transaction costs are low and there is little need for the organizations and institutions that support the most durable regimes.

This framework opens several possibilities for future research. One is to examine how South Korea's democratic transition was influenced by the early elite unity that led to the collapse of the dictatorship. There are many accounts of South Korea's transition, and a future project may incorporate this variable into that literature. Another potential avenue for future research is to explore how the Kim Dynasty in North Korea has survived despite many challenges to its legitimacy. The North Korean regime cannot claim successful economic development, as few gains have occurred even during periods of increased liberalization. The elite are not well compensated for giving up the rights that they would have in a democracy. These points suggest that repression is the main source of regime stability. A future project may investigate the potential links between repression, elite coalition size, and long-run regime durability.

REFERENCES

Armstrong, Charles K. 2004. *The North Korean Revolution, 1945–1950*. Ithaca, NY: Cornell University Press.

Bram, Curtis, and Michael Munger. 2022. "Where You Stand Depends on Where You Live: County Voting on the Texas Secession Referendum." *Constitutional Political Economy* 33 (1): 67–79.

Brownlee, Jason. 2007. *Authoritarianism in an Age of Democratization*. Cambridge: Cambridge University Press.

Bueno de Mesquita, Bruce, Alastair Smith, Randolph M. Siverson, and James D. Morrow. 2005. *The Logic of Political Survival*. Cambridge, MA: MIT Press.

Coase, Ronald H. 1937. "The Nature of the Firm." *Economica* 4 (16): 386–405.

Cumings, B. 2002. *The Origins of the Korean War. Liberation and the Emergence of Separate Regimes 1945–1947*. Vol. I. Princeton, NJ: Princeton University Press.

Doner, Richard F., Bryan K. Ritchie, and Dan Slater. 2005. "Systemic Vulnerability and the Origins of Developmental States: Northeast and Southeast Asia in Comparative Perspective." *International Organization* 59 (2): 327–361.

Gandhi, Jennifer. 2010. *Political Institutions under Dictatorship*. Cambridge: Cambridge University Press.

Gasiorowski, Mark J. 1995. "Economic Crisis and Political Regime Change: An Event History Analysis." *American Political Science Review* 89 (4): 882–897.

Geddes, Barbara. 2005. "Why Parties and Elections in Authoritarian Regimes?" Presented at Annual Meeting of American Political Science Assoc., Washington, DC.

Guriev, Sergei, and Daniel Treisman. 2019. "Informational Autocrats." *Journal of Economic Perspectives* 33 (4): 100–127.

Haggard, Stephan. 2004. "Institutions and Growth in East Asia." *Studies in Comparative International Development* 38 (4): 53–81.

Haggard, Stephan, Byung-kook Kim, and Chung-in Moon. 1991. "The Transition to Export-Led Growth in South Korea: 1954–1966." *The Journal of Asian Studies* 50 (4): 850–873.

Jarman, R. L. 2005. Korea Political & Economic Reports 1882–1970. Archive Editions.

Lankov, Andrei N. 2002. *From Stalin to Kim Il Sung. The Formation of North Korea, 1945–1960. New* Brunswick, NJ: Rutgers University Press.

Leeson, Peter T., and Peter J. Boettke. 2009. "Two-Tiered Entrepreneurship and Economic Development." *International Review of Law and Economics* 29 (3): 252–259.

Haggard, Stephan, Wonhyuk Lim, and Euysung Kim, eds. 2003. *Economic Crisis and Corporate Restructuring in Korea.* Cambridge: Cambridge University Press.

Mahoney, James, and Kathleen Thelen. 2015. *Advances in Comparative-Historical Analysis.* Cambridge: Cambridge University Press.

Reports of the United Nations Commission for the Unification and Rehabilitation of Korea. The United Nations Official Records: Seventh Session, The United Nations, Vol. 14.

Nathan, Charles. 2022. "The Urban/Rural Divide in Athenian Political Thought." *American Political Science Review* 116 (4): 1490–1502.

Nathan, Charles. 2023. "Anthropoligarchy: Politics and the Nonhuman in the Anthropocene." *Theory & Event* 26 (2): 232–257.

Pejovich, Svetozar. 2003. "Understanding the Transaction Costs of Transition: It's the Culture, Stupid." *The Review of Austrian Economics* 16: 347–361.

Pepinsky, Thomas. 2014. "The Institutional Turn in Comparative Authoritarianism." *British Journal of Political Science* 44 (3): 631–653.

Rhee, Syngman, Yonse Taehakkyo, and Hyondae Hangukhak Yonguso. 2000. *The Syngman Rhee Telegrams.* Seoul: Institute for Modern Korean Studies, Yonsei University.

Slater, Dan. 2010. *Ordering Power: Contentious Politics and Authoritarian Leviathans in Southeast Asia.* Cambridge: Cambridge University Press.

Smith, Benjamin. 1999. *Hard Times in the Lands of Plenty. Oil Politics in Iran and Indonesia.* Cambridge: Cambridge University Press.

Svolik, Milan W. 2012. *The Politics of Authoritarian Rule.* Cambridge: Cambridge University Press.

Tullock, Gordon. 1986. "Industrial Organization and Rent Seeking in Dictatorships." *Journal of Institutional and Theoretical Economics (JITE)/Zeitschrift Für Die Gesamte Staatswissenschaft* 142 (1): 4–15.

Wagner, Richard E. 2016. *Politics as a Peculiar Business: Insights from a Theory of Entangled Political Economy.* Cheltenham: Edward Elgar Publishing.

Chapter 11

Disaster Recovery, Entrepreneurship, and the American Revolution

Women in the Foundations of American Political Economy

Kirstin Anderson Birkhaug

The instinct to separate the public and the private pervades social science, dating to the ancient Greeks. Hannah Arendt, the great twentieth-century political theorist, wrote in *The Human Condition* that "the distinction between a private and public sphere of life corresponds to the household and the political realms, which have existed as distinct, separate entities at least since the rise of the ancient city-state" (Arendt 1956, 28). The public sphere of politics, by definition, suffers a crisis of identity when forced to confront issues of the private. It is for this reason that the term *political economy* is troublesome for many who follow in the tradition of the ancients. The word *economy* derives from the Greek *oikos*, meaning house or home. For the ancients, Arendt writes that "the very term 'political economy' would have been a contradiction in terms: whatever was 'economic' related to the life of the individual and the survival of the species, was a non-political, household affair by definition" (Arendt 1956, 29).

Without proposing to reject the whole of ancient philosophy, it may suffice to say that the relationship between the public and the private, the nexus of political economy, is more complicated than the ancients deduced. This bears out in a wealth of scholarship in economics, political science, and other social scientific disciplines that offer evidence for a symbiotic relationship between the public and the private. As Elinor Ostrom put it:

> A competitive market—the epitome of private institutions—is itself a public good. Once a competitive market is provided, individuals can enter and exit freely whether or not they contribute to the cost of providing and maintaining

> the market. No market can exist for long without underlying public institutions to support it. In field settings, public and private institutions frequently are intermeshed and depend on one another, rather than existing in isolated worlds. (Ostrom 2015, 15)

But even the great scholars of this tradition have been met with skepticism. Ostrom herself saw her ideas critiqued as "radical" and "potentially offending to 'everyone's sense of propriety'" (Ostrom 2015). However controversial, it was Ostrom's refusal to draw bright lines between the public and the private that gave way to her Nobel-prize-winning research on the governance of the commons.[1] The public and the private often walk together, a truth revealed through the study of economics, and more specifically, of political economy.

There are few instances in which the interdependence between the public and the private is more obvious than in times of disaster and crisis. When superstructures of politics, society, and economics collapse in the face of life-or-death situations, it often falls not to public institutions, but to private citizens, to preserve what remains of their way of life and recover from the damage. Beyond simply exposing the reliance of public goods on private individuals, these times of crisis are often moments that define the identity of a people or a place. The United States is no exception to this, born as it was from the ashes of the American Revolution, which was a complete upheaval of the colonial way of life. When the North American colonists overthrew British rule, the people of the American colonies were plunged into chaos. Caught between an adversarial, attacking British government and a weak, burgeoning, wartime American government, most existing structures of political and economic life in the colonies began to break down. Those who did not fight in the Revolution (primarily women) thus had to make do to ensure their survival during a time of political and economic upheaval. Examining historical evidence from this time—in particular the life and letters of Abigail Adams—reveals that American civilians, especially women, developed modes of informal entrepreneurship in the wake of disaster to protect and provide for their households. In turn, these modes of behavior laid the groundwork for the future of American political economy.

The contributions of this project are twofold. First, this case study offers additional historical evidence for contemporary theories of entrepreneurship and disaster recovery and indicates that these are original elements of American politics—part of the Founding. Second, this project adds to the historical texture of these theories by offering an understanding of the political and economic contributions of women—who were not, at the time of the Founding, formally allowed autonomy in either sphere. This case study examines the informal, nonlegal ways in which an unrecognized class of Americans helped shape the nation's political and economic frontier. Given that the history of political economy tends to focus on economic and political events from which women were generally excluded, this is an exciting new avenue for future study. Who, in history, has better understood the tenuous, complicated connection between the public and the private known as "political economy" than those relegated to the *oikos* itself? Indeed, it seems there can be little study of the history of political economy without attempting to parse out the complicated and often obscure role of women.

This chapter will proceed by first outlining contemporary research on entrepreneurship and disaster recovery. It then details the case study of Abigail Adams as evidence for these theories. It concludes with a brief discussion of the implications of this case study.

DISASTER RECOVERY: A THEORETICAL FRAMEWORK

When disaster strikes, recovery is never assured, especially given that the locations hardest hit by disaster are often those with fewer economic resources to mitigate the damage (Peacock 2003; Norris et al. 1999; Blanchard-Boehm 1998; Fothergill and Peek 2004). Given the tenuous conditions of disaster recovery and the assumption of risk by those who stay and attempt to recover their communities, Chamlee-Wright and her coauthors have identified community disaster recovery as a collective action problem (Chamlee-Wright 2010; Chamlee-Wright and Storr 2009, 2010). While, as Storr and his coauthors point out, those who experience disaster tend to turn to their governments in order to recover, there is evidence that nongovernmental entrepreneurs are also an effective catalyst for community recovery after disaster (Storr, Haeffele-Balch, and Grube 2016). Storr et al. define entrepreneurs as "agents of social change," and thus encompass within the term a variety of types of people. In their terms:

> When we describe someone as an entrepreneur, we do not mean to suggest that the person is necessarily the decision agent in a commercial enterprise who notices and seeks to exploit profit opportunities . . . We also think of the individual who organizes a food drive in their neighborhood and the community leader who organizes community members to protest some societal injustice as entrepreneur. We also think of the religious leader who cares for his flock as an entrepreneur. (Storr, Haeffele-Balch, and Grube 2016, 4)

What bounds this term for Storr et al. is an attention to opportunity and vision that the entrepreneur must possess. Entrepreneurs are those who identify and chart paths forward, and may direct others to follow in their footsteps. Grube and Storr (2018) also find that postdisaster entrepreneurs tend to be those with high levels of social capital, strong place attachment, and dedication to both commercial and social goals. These entrepreneurs are "embedded," or as Grube and Storr put it, "motivated by connection to their communities, possess the requisite local knowledge to assess how they might contribute to community rebound, and want to promote community rebound in addition to and maybe instead of making a profit" (ibid., 803).

Storr et al. identify three core ways in which entrepreneurs assist in disaster recovery efforts at the community level: "1) they provide needed good and services; 2) they help to restore or replace disrupted social networks; and 3) they signal that community rebound is likely and, in fact, underway" (Storr, Haeffele-Balch, and Grube 2016, 46). This last task is especially important for Storr and his coauthors because they identify a community's capacity to rebound with its capacity to self-govern. Rebounding from disaster, then, reflects the restoration of community self-governance, a conclusion also borne out in Grube and Storr (2014). A number of case studies support these theories, including Chamlee-Wright and Storr (2009), which examines club goods provision by the Mary Queen of Vietnam Catholic Church in the wake of Hurricane Katrina as essential to (1) rebuilding the New Orleans East Vietnamese-American community, (2) overcoming social coordination challenges, and (3) a successful organization of political action on behalf of that community. Storr and Haeffele-Balch (2012) found that the effects of entrepreneurial efforts post-Katrina were not reserved to homogenous, tight-knight communities but might also be observed in heterogenous, loosely knit communities as well.

In essence, this literature maintains the importance and significance of entrepreneurs in disaster recovery. When a place returns from the brink of destruction to restored self-governance, it happens largely on the backs of embedded entrepreneurs (found in both tight-knit and loosely knit communities) who seize opportunities to provide needed goods and services to their disaster-stricken communities. Not only do these entrepreneurs preserve economic ways of life by providing goods and services, but they are also essential in rebuilding political and social ways of life. While Hurricane Katrina is often the case study for examinations of disaster recovery and entrepreneurship, American history offers us no shortage of examples of disaster, and people of entrepreneurial spirit who triumph over it. In fact, one could argue that the United States emerged out of a disaster—the American Revolution—which upended social, political, and economic life for those who lived in the former British colonies. With the American Revolution, as in the case of Hurricane Katrina, what emerged from the rubble resulted not from the dictates of a centralized government, but from the disparate efforts of embedded entrepreneurs (many, if not most, of whom were women) who sought to hold together the bonds of their social, economic, and political lives in the wake of disaster. Entrepreneurship is at the heart of the American political project, and this bears out in examinations of primary sources from that time.

DISASTER RECOVERY AND ENTREPRENEURSHIP IN THE CORRESPONDENCE OF ABIGAIL ADAMS, 1775–1783

The Political Economy and the American Revolution

When scholars discuss political economy in juxtaposition to the American Revolution, it is usually an effort to understand what role, if any, economics played in forming the ideology of the revolutionaries. This debate, well summarized by Ernst (1976), has historically been between scholars such as Bernard Bailyn (1967, 1973) who view economic matters as fundamentally unimportant to the formation of revolutionary ideology in America, and scholars such as Wood (1966), Pocock (1975), Lockridge (1973), Appleby (1976), and Greene (1970, 1973), who understand this view to be myopic, with some maintaining that economics constitute an essential element of revolutionary ideology. Ernst himself articulated a third way of considering political economy during the Revolution: as an ideology in and of itself (Ernst 2014). The debate over the role of political economy in motivating the Revolution continues to this day and counts among its intellectual successors a number of culturally important projects, including the 1619 Project. This chapter sets that debate aside in order to examine the political economy of the Revolution from a different angle. Instead of examining economics as a potential spark of the Revolution itself, this project examines the economic realities of Americans during the Revolution and seeks to understand how everyday nonideological actions during wartime—actions taken to remain alive, to provide for families, to rebuild ways of life—formed a basis upon which the American political project was then built. For this, a historical account of the wartime economic landscape of the American Revolution is necessary. Given that Abigail Adams is the centerpiece of this case study, and her observations are limited to New England, this chapter specifically examines the political economy of that region.

The British Navigation Acts of 1651 and 1660 ensured that Britain remained an intermediary for trade to and from the British colonies (Pollio 2022, 113). These acts served as the bedrock for the commercial operations of the American colonial project. While these policies did not necessarily hinder the economic growth of the American colonies, the intercession of the British in American trade was troubling for many—the British insistence upon levying taxes against the unrepresented American colonists, for example, led to the famous Boston Tea Party. Furthermore, in the lead-up to the American Revolution, as colonists expressed increased desire for control over trade conducted in their harbors, many decried these British policies as monopolistic. Britain undercut trade competition in the American colonies, and as colonists reacted increasingly negatively to British attempts to rein them in with the Stamp and Townshend Acts, many colonists suspected that Britain might use price controls to extort the American colonies should tensions continue to mount (Dorfman 1966, 206; Pollio 2022, 127–156). Indeed, after the outbreak of the war, British-backed merchants with monopolies on trade goods quickly inflated prices for the American colonists. As Dorfman records it: "Imports . . . were 500 to 600 per cent of the prime cost, and they retailed at the 'unreasonable profit' of 40 or 50 per cent more in addition" (Dorfman 1966, 214). A number of prominent politicians brought economic issues to the floor of the Continental Congress during the Revolution, explicitly lamenting this very thing:

> Prices are higher than they ought to be in proportion to the quantity of money . . . Every new cargo instead of lowering prices, raises them. The prices of rum, tea, sugar, flour, coffee have risen without any real cause. The lax laid on us by forestallers and monopolists the last six months has been sufficient to prosecute the war for a year . . . By stepping in between importers and retailers, monopolizers can introduce a scarcity when they choose and, by transporting goods from one state to another, create a scarcity in one or all. (Dorfman 1966, 219)

Even Washington "complained bitterly of the high prices and their effect on the Army" (Dorfman 1966, 216). Not only the Army felt the sting of the economic upheaval; American civilians were met with serious economic challenges. Some essential goods (many of which Abigail Adams mentioned explicitly to her husband within their correspondence) became difficult to purchase, which put even further burden on the shoulders of those tasked with family and household management during the wartime years—many of them women.

American politicians worked throughout the war to alleviate these economic concerns. Several individual colonies attempted to pass price-fixing legislation during the war, though none were individually successful. Price-fixing itself became a point of contention among serious political thinkers of the day, including John Witherspoon, who could not justify the infringement upon liberty inherent in mandated price-fixing. Other important politicians, including Gouverneur Morris and Benjamin Franklin, attempted to leverage the printing of paper money against war expenses, all the while acknowledging that to do so might undermine the financial stability of American citizens, as the money would quickly devalue. So too, the Continental Congress began the arduous discussions regarding the funding of the war effort, considering how taxes might be levied and even exploring such extreme options as confiscation and foreign loans (Pollio 2022, 177–194, 203–212). While politicians debated and attempted to institute correctional policy amid an ongoing war by way of a weak, decentralized governing body, American civilians did not sit idly by. Instead of waiting for formal fixes from the federal government (which took months and years to implement), those affected by the war and its economic consequences at home had to make do with what they had. In a time of disaster, it fell to those who remained in their communities to find a way out. Leading the way in these efforts, seizing opportunities to provide necessary goods and services to their neighbors, were quintessential entrepreneurs of the variety described by Chamlee-Wright and her coauthors. These were, in large part, the "war widows," left behind to tend to farms and children while their husbands served in some capacity in the Revolution. Perhaps the example *par excellence* of the war widow entrepreneur was the future First Lady Abigail Adams, in whose correspondence we find evidence that these entrepreneurial efforts laid the groundwork for establishing a self-governing United States in the wake of the Revolution.

Abigail Adams: The Political Economy of a Forgotten Founder

That Abigail Adams as a "forgotten Founder" is a recurring idea in the history of American political thought (Dreisbach et al. 2009; Holton 2009; Roberts 2004). Her husband, John Adams, was the second president of the United States, as well as a prominent lawyer, statesman, and patriot. Although most of the Founders were married, Abigail Adams stands out among the wives of these great men as a clever and sophisticated thinker herself. Perhaps no other Founder took to heart his wife's ideas and advice as much as John Adams. However, Abigail, unlike most of the Founders, used her pen to discuss politics sparingly; when she did, it was usually in response to her husband's prompting. A famous exception is her letter urging her husband to "consider the ladies" in structuring American governance, a somewhat veiled plea to rescind the coverture laws that prevented women from owning property. Adams's precise thoughts on political economy, as many of her opinions, are rarely explicit, but it is clear from reading her letters during the American Revolution that economic issues were important to her. John was frequently gone from their family homestead in Braintree, Massachusetts (and their city lodgings in Boston) to convene with fellow Founders in Philadelphia. Throughout the course of the war, John trusted Abigail to handle their Massachusetts assets on her own. Though John never served in the military, Abigail certainly sacrificed marital comforts for the sake of the new nation. In 1777 she wrote to her husband, "Tis almost 14 years since we were united, but not more than half that time have we had the happiness of living together"

(Adams 1777b). It would be many more years until they would consistently cohabitate once more.

Given the remarkable degree of control John gave Abigail over their family's finances in his absence–especially given that most American women did not have explicit economic or political rights at this point due to coverture laws (Dabling 2022)–it should come as no surprise that many of her letters to her husband recount their financial situation, and the economic tumultuousness that marked the years of the Revolution. Particularly insidious for the families left to manage in the wake of the war was inflation: as Britain attempted to box its unruly colonies back into submission, the prices for everyday goods skyrocketed. Abigail Adams makes note of this to John repeatedly throughout their wartime correspondence. As early as 1775, Abigail writes to John:

> Formerly we used to purchase cotton wool at 1 Shilling Lawfull money pr. Bag, now tis 3, and the scarcity of that article distresses us, as it was wrought up with less trouble than any other article of cloathing. Flax is now from a Shilling to one and Sixpence pr. pound, Sheeps wool Eighteen pence and linnens not to be had at any price. I cannot mention the article in the English goods way which is not double, and in the West India Molasses by retail I used formerly to purchase at one and Eight pence now tis 2 and Eight pence, rum 3 Shillings, coffee one and 3 pence. (Adams 1775)

Later, in 1776, Abigail detailed that the inflated price of goods had snowballed into inflated prices for hired labor:

> There is such a demand of Men from the publick and such a price given that the farmer who Hires must be greatly out of pocket. A man will not talk with you who is worth hireing under 24 pounds per year. Col. Quincy and Thayer give that price, and some give more. Isaac insisted upon my giving him 20 pounds or he would leave me. (Adams 1776)

By the following year, the inflation crisis reached its fever pitch, despite the efforts of the Continental Congress to curtail the ever-rising prices. Again, Abigail wrote to John:

> The extravagance of Board is greater there than here tho here every thing is at such prices as was not ever before known. Many articles are not to be had tho at ever so great a price. Sugar, Molasses, Rum, cotton wool, Coffe, chocolate, cannot all be consumed. Yet there are none, or next to none to be sold, perhaps you may procure a pound at a time, but no more. I have sometimes stoped 15 or 20 Butchers in a day with plenty of meat but not a mouthfull to be had unless

I would give 4 pence per pound and a pence per pound for bringing. (Adams 1777e)

These are far from the only times Abigail mentioned inflated prices to her husband.[2] For those who wished to provide food, shelter, and clothing to their loved ones, it was a time not only of political and social upheaval, but of uncertain survival—a disaster in any sense of the word. As prices rose, the weak American dollar devalued and became as worthless as paper, and access to necessary goods became more limited. In response, Abigail recorded the efforts of her community and those nearby to produce and provide some of these goods for themselves. Entrepreneurs, including Abigail herself, began to emerge, seizing the equipment and resources at their disposal in order to provide for themselves and their communities. Abigail understood the importance of these events, as evidenced by her communication of them to her husband. The entrepreneurial work of Abigail and others that she observed during this time of crisis led the United States out of the disaster of the Revolutionary War and into a new era of self-governance. Without any assistance from a top-down governmental authority, Abigail Adams observed entrepreneurs seizing opportunities in such a way that these New England communities survived in the midst of political and economic upheaval, and emerged from the war primed for self-governance.

REVOLUTIONARY WAR ENTREPRENEURSHIP AS OBSERVED BY ABIGAIL ADAMS

When considering Abigail Adams's correspondence during the war, what she left unsaid is nearly as important as what she said. Abigail chose her words carefully. There is a marked difference between her communications with her husband, her sisters, and her friends (and even variations across different friendships). Her concerns about the distance between her and John, and her occasional venting about his dismissal of her ideas, for example, are reserved for Mercy Otis Warren, a friend sixteen years her senior and also a fellow wife to a powerful man. Her letters to her husband during the Revolution, though perhaps the most numerous in her collected correspondence, are never individually longer than a few pages. She doesn't detail every tiny aspect of her life, but clearly privileges certain themes over others. Repeatedly, she laments the separation between her and John, wishing to be reunited with the person she calls her "dearest friend." There are several letters from Abigail to John that might well be considered letters of business, as they recount her handling of the Adams farm and assets. She usually mentions their children and relatives, and frequently gives accounts of the war as she observes it. She makes note of community disasters such as sickness and drought, and generally provides an overview of the goings-on of the community. Day-to-day minutiae are lost in these letters, and with them, some of her own actions on behalf of her community. For example, in September 1777, she wrote to John that "My children have never cried for Bread, nor been destitute of cloathing—nor have the poor or the needy gone empty from my Door whenever it was in my power to assist them" (Adams 1777f). While she offers her husband some details on the provision for her family in this letter and others, she never indulges him with any description of her charity. Her correspondence with John highlighted what she determined to be his priorities in hearing from her. Thus, it is safe to assume that the events Abigail *did* include as a matter of correspondence with her husband were, in her mind, significant events of which her husband should remain aware.

This project identifies three situations involving three different goods in Abigail's correspondence that indicate entrepreneurship throughout small Massachusetts communities during the war. Two receive extensive details in letters from Abigail to John, while the third is briefly mentioned between Abigail and John and further discussed in Abigail's correspondence with Mercy Otis Warren. They are as follows: the development of local molasses mills throughout rural Massachusetts towns, the women-led Boston coffee riots, and fabric-sharing between Abigail and Mercy Otis Warren.

Molasses

"Necessity is the mother of invention," Abigail wrote to John in early September 1777 (Adams 1777c). The "necessity" she referred to was that of foodstuffs. Though these goods were not themselves limited, their high prices (charged by monopolistic merchants using British channels of commerce) had set them beyond the reach of average Massachusettsans. In the same letter, Abigail treated her husband to yet another roll call of inflated goods, although this message came with a new note of urgency. Inflation had increased steadily since 1775, but by 1777, Abigail had begun to despair. She wrote:

> What can be done? Our money will soon be as useless as blank paper. Tis True I have not much to be anxious about, but it will soon take all I have to pay my day labourers, mowing 12 shillings a day, and much obliged to them to come at that. Butter is 3 shillings, cheeses 2, Mutton 18 pence,Beaf 18 pence, Lamb 1 & 4 pence. Corn at no price, none to be had. Barly 8 shillings a Bushel, Rye none, sold only by way of Barter. Sugar 15 pounds per hundred, Coffe 10 shillings per pound, Molasses 24 per Gallon, Rum 28 ditto. What is to become of sallery people? With Hard money not one article of the produce of this Country but

> what I could purchase cheeper than ever it was sold, nor do they value offering 8 dollors for one. (Adams 1777c)

But even as Abigail despaired, she also made note of the ingenious ways rural Massachusettsans had begun to circumvent their lack of resources. "Necessity is the mother of invention," she wrote to John: the inability to procure certain goods prompted entrepreneurs to seek out ways to produce these goods themselves for the sake of their communities. Specifically, they had begun producing their own molasses. Abigail wrote to John, "There is a Manufactory of Molasses set up in several Towns. Green corn Storks ground and boild down to Molasses, tis said an acer [*sic*] will produce a Barrel. I have seen some of it, it both tastes and looks like Sugar Bakers molasses" (Adams 1777c). Presumably, local farmers contributed parts of their own crops to these manufactories, which were manned by community members and produced molasses at a price affordable for those within these communities. For Adams, this signaled the resolve and independence of American communities—in an additional letter, she elaborated on the molasses mills in Massachusetts, writing:

> Necessity of the times will . . . put us upon seeking Resources among ourselves. An instance of that may be seen in the progress which is made of grinding corn storks and boiling the Liquor into Molasses. Scarcly a Town or parish within 40 miles of us but what have several mills at work, and had the experiment been made a month sooner many thousand Barrels would have been made, no less than 80 have already been made in the small Town of Manchester. It answers very well to distill, and may be boild down to Sugar. There are two mills sitting up in this parish. They have 3 Rollers one with cogs and two smooth, the storks are striped of the leaves and tops so that tis no Robbery upon the cattle, and the juce groundout. but Tis said 4 Barrels of juice will make one of Molasses, but in this people differ widely. They have a method of refining it so that it looks as well as the best imported molasses. Thus you see we go from Step to Step in our improvements. We can live much better than we deserve within ourselves. (Adams 1777g)

Faced with the inability to procure sugar and molasses, entrepreneurs emerged within these communities, equipping the production of needed goods at prices their communities could afford. With this, not only were they able to craft a comparable product to what they might have received by way of British-regulated trade, but even a better product: from town to town, Abigail notes that there were different strategies and recipes for the sugar and molasses in accordance with the tastes of the community members. This proved to Abigail that the Americans would be able to survive off their own products and that they could provide for themselves the essential necessities of life. Outside of the distribution of goods by government-backed merchants, these entrepreneurs produced and provided necessities for their own communities. This molasses production was an entrepreneurial effort within these communities, and as such shows these towns moving toward self-governance despite the economic upheaval of the war.

Coffee

Among Abigail's most frequently mentioned inflated goods was coffee. Though not, per se, a *necessity* in the same way as molasses and sugar, coffee was a staple of the New England diet. It was also one of the few goods that were genuinely difficult to obtain during the Revolution— but this was manufactured scarcity. As Edith Gelles puts it: "many consumers began to suspect . . . middlemen were deliberately holding commodities back from the market in order to drive the price still higher" (Gelles 1995, 127). As the war raged on and the relationship between America and Britain continued to sour, Bostonians plundered the city's British-backed merchants. This looting was not merely for the sake of theft, however. The purpose of these riots was "not exactly to steal the merchandise but to put it up for sale at a reasonable price, with the revenue going to the shopkeeper" (Gelles 1995, 127). In July 1777, Abigail wrote to John about the situation, with particular attention to one detail: the women of Boston had joined the fray.

> You must know that there is a great Scarcity of Sugar and Coffe, articles which the Female part of the State are very loth to give up, expecially whilst they consider the Scarcity occasiond by the merchants having secreted a large Quantity. There has been much rout and Noise in the Town for several weeks. Some Stores had been opend by a number of people and the Coffe and Sugar carried into the Market and dealt out by pounds. It was rumourd that an eminent, wealthy, stingy Merchant (who is a Batchelor) had a Hogshead of Coffe in his Store which he refused to sell to the committee under 6 shillings per pound. A Number of Females some say a hundred, some say more assembled with a cart and trucks, marchd down to the Ware House and demanded the keys, which he refused to deliver, upon which one of them seazd him by his Neck and tossd him into the cart. Upon his finding no Quarter he deliverd the keys, when they tipd up the cart and dischargd him, then opend the Warehouse, Hoisted out the Coffe themselves, put it into the trucks and drove off. (Adams 1777d)

Gelles adds one detail that Abigail neglects: the women who led this riot were largely shopkeepers whose clientele included the poorest within their community. When the monopolized wartime market refused to provide for the needs of Bostonians, the Bostonians (including the women) commandeered the provision of these goods. These individuals might be considered entrepreneurs of a kind. While this is perhaps not an *ideal* form of entrepreneurial engagement (it is certainly not legally above-board, even during wartime chaos), this vignette does show a group of individuals identifying an opportunity to provide a necessary good to their community for which the efficient allocation was stymied by intrusive governmental forces. Local shopkeepers—in this instance acting as embedded entrepreneurs with an eye more toward community survival than toward profit margins—sold the reclaimed coffee back to Bostonians without price-gouging. This slightly shocking story, at its base, is simply one more signal that individuals throughout towns in Massachusetts were entrepreneurial in their efforts to produce and provide goods for their communities during the crisis of the American Revolution.

Fabric

These first two examples of entrepreneurship happened within communities: entrepreneurs organized to establish their own sugar and molasses mills within their towns, and the lady shopkeepers of Boston commandeered their own supply of essentials. The third example, however, happened on a smaller scale and was very personal to Abigail herself. At the root of all community-centric governance are personal relationships. Entrepreneurs organize community members to fulfill community needs and often personally know and care for those they organize. In this sense, postdisaster entrepreneurship at a community level can happen in small instances of sharing and exchange. These networks, which throughout history have often belonged to women, constitute an essential part of any political economy, but especially a postdisaster one. Such was the context for the supply of fabric in New England during the Revolution. Most rural Massachusettsans at this time retained some remnants of Puritan stock; they were not particularly refined or wealthy people. The materials they needed were not fineries, but the everyday wools and linens needed to make sturdy clothing, patch old clothing, and otherwise keep them warm and dry in the sometimes-cruel northeastern climate.

Abigail worried about clothing her children during the Revolution as fabric prices spiked. She often recorded the price of linen and wool in her letters to John regarding inflated prices. Perhaps the personal nature of this good's provision prevented her from explaining to her husband just how she procured it, but in any sense, her only mention of fabric to John noting her entrepreneurial efforts in obtaining it is as follows:

> As to cloathing I have heithertoo procured materials sufficent to cloath my children and servants which I have done wholy in Home Spun. I have contracted

> no debts that I have not discharg'd, and one of our Labourers Prince I have paid seven months wages to since you left me. (Adams 1777h)

When one looks to Abigail's other correspondence at this time, it is clear that she leaned on her personal relationships to furnish these necessary goods. Mercy Otis Warren (otherwise known as "The Muse of the Revolution" for the fame she accrued by way of her pen) was her supplier and trading partner. Abigail explicitly addresses this partnership with Warren in a letter from August 1777, wherein she writes:

> You mention some French cotton. I am much obliged to you but I have since I saw you been accommodated in that way. The Russel I should be very glad of either one or two yards just as you can spair it, and Shooe binding, if it is to be had. Garlick thread I am in great want of, if you should know of any be so good as to let me know. I am really asshamed to tell my Friend that I have not yet been able to get Home the cloth. All that was in my power to do to it, has been done 3 months ago and I have been sending and going almost every week since. I saw the Man yesterday and he has promissed me that I shall have it next week, but if his word prove no better than it has done I cannot say you may depend upon it. (Adams 1777a)

Adams and Warren took advantage of their personal connections in order to produce and provide a good that they could not obtain on the market. They coordinated these entrepreneurial efforts between their families to ensure that neither the Adams nor the Warren children went without. There is no reason to believe that Mercy and Abigail were the only women in rural Massachusetts who, by way of their entrepreneurial spirit, created these pools of resources. However, given the relative anonymity in which most women of this generation lived their lives, there is little way to know for sure the extent of their entrepreneurial activities. The historical record provided by Mercy Otis Warren and Abigail Adams by way of their correspondence shows a clear example of two women engaging in entrepreneurship in the face of disaster so as to provide necessities for themselves and their families. Even at this small scale, these efforts were essential building blocks of community self-governance that allowed the United States to recuperate from the effects of the Revolution and become, in itself, a self-governing nation.

AMERICAN ORIGINS: THE CONTINUING INFLUENCE OF THE FOUNDING GENERATION

This case study offers several key takeaways for the future study of postdisaster entrepreneurship, political science, and history. First, and perhaps most importantly, this case study shows that entrepreneurship is at the heart of the American project. To know how a nation functions, and what it values, one must look closely at its origins. This examination of Abigail Adams's correspondence does just that. When observing the actions of American civilians in Massachusetts during the Revolutionary War, it is clear that they were involved in entrepreneurship for the provision of necessary goods. Entrepreneurship, performed by community leaders without the interference of any centralized power, is baked into the foundations of the United States.

Moreover, this case suggests that further study is necessary to parse the contributions of women to early American entrepreneurship. Some of the neglect of women is due to the comparative lack of information we have of their contributions. While the men of the Founding era signed great documents and cherished a legal status that ensured their names were recorded in ledgers and logbooks, women were often explicitly and legally subsumed into the identities of their husbands. They had no ability to contribute in a formal capacity to their political and economic systems, and yet, as half of the population, played a significant role in determining the direction of these institutions. These contributions are difficult to observe historically and even more difficult to measure; as a result, few women-centric historical or political theory studies appear in the bibliographies of projects on entrepreneurship and disaster recovery. This case study is a step toward closing this gap in knowledge.

Abigail Adams and her letters provide a rare glimpse into the everyday life of American citizens during the Revolution. Further, her perspective as a woman offers unique insight into the complex relationship between the public and the private—the *polis* and *oikos*—that is essential for the study of political economy. Her letters reveal a world that sets the stage for ours: one in which communities engaged in entrepreneurship to solve the resource shortages that emerged from a crisis situation, and efficiently solved their own problems without assistance from a Leviathan.

NOTES

1. What Ostrom referred to as "political economy" is today considered "institutional analysis." Nonetheless, Ostrom's terminology holds for capturing the perceived tensions between public and private with regard to economic policy research (McGinnis 1999, 10).

2. See also Adams, Abigail. 1777f. "Letter from Abigail Adams to John Adams, 20–21 April 1777 [electronic edition]." Adams Family Papers: An Electronic Archive. Massachusetts Historical Society; Adams, Abigail. 1777d. "Letter from Abigail Adams to John Adams, 10–11 July 1777 [electronic edition]." Adams Family Papers: An Electronic Archive. Massachusetts Historical Society.

REFERENCES

Adams, Abigail. 1775. "Letter from Abigail Adams to John Adams, 10 December 1775 [electronic edition]." Adams Family Papers: An Electronic Archive. Massachusetts Historical Society.

———. 1776. "Letter from Abigail Adams to John Adams, 14 May 1776 [electronic edition]." Adams Family Papers: An Electronic Archive. Massachusetts Historical Society.

———. 1777a. "Abigail Adams to Mercy Otis Warren, 14 August 1777" Founders Online, National Archives, https://founders.archives.gov/documents/Adams/04-02-02–0252. [Original source: The Adams Papers, Adams Family Correspondence, vol. 2, June 1776–March 1778, ed. L. H. Butterfield. Cambridge, MA: Harvard University Press, 1963, pp. 313–315.].

———. 1777b. "Letter from Abigail Adams to John Adams, 5 August 1777 [electronic edition]." Adams Family Papers: An Electronic Archive. Massachusetts Historical Society.

———. 1777c. "Letter from Abigail Adams to John Adams, 10 September 1777 [electronic edition]." Adams Family Papers: An Electronic Archive. Massachusetts Historical Society.

———. 1777d. "Letter from Abigail Adams to John Adams, 10–11 July 1777 [electronic edition]." Adams Family Papers: An Electronic Archive. Massachusetts Historical Society.

———. 1777e. "Letter from Abigail Adams to John Adams, 17 April 1777 [electronic edition]." Adams Family Papers: An Electronic Archive. Massachusetts Historical Society.

———. 1777f. "Letter from Abigail Adams to John Adams, 21 September 1777 [electronic edition]." Adams Family Papers: An Electronic Archive. Massachusetts Historical Society.

———. 1777g. "Letter from Abigail Adams to John Adams, 21–24 September 1777 [electronic edition]." Adams Family Papers: An Electronic Archive. Massachusetts Historical Society.

———. 1777h. "Letter from Abigail Adams to John Adams, 22 August 1777 [electronic edition]." Adams Family Papers: An Electronic Archive. Massachusetts Historical Society.

Arendt, Hannah. 1956. *The Human Condition*: Chicago: University of Chicago Press.

Bailyn, Bernard. 1967. *The Origins of American Politics*. Vol. 604. New York: Vintage.

———. 1973. "The Central Themes of the American Revolution: An Interpretation." In *Essays on the American Revolution*, edited by Stephen G. Kurtz and James H. Hutson, 3–31. Chapel Hill, NC: University of North Carolina Press.

Blanchard-Boehm, R. Denise. 1998. "Understanding Public Response to Increased Risk from Natural Hazards: Application of the Hazards Risk Communication Framework." *International Journal of Mass Emergencies & Disasters* 16 (3): 247–278.

Chamlee-Wright, Emily. 2010. *The Cultural and Political Economy of Recovery: Social Learning in a Post-Disaster Environment*. Vol. 12. New York: Routledge.

Chamlee-Wright, Emily, and Virgil Henry Storr. 2009. "Club Goods and Post-Disaster Community Return." *Rationality and Society* 21 (4): 429–458.

———. 2010. "The Role of Social Entrepreneurship in Post-Katrina Community Recovery." *International Journal of Innovation and Regional Development* 2 (1–2): 149–164.

Dabling, Brandon. 2022. *A New Birth of Marriage*. Notre Dame, IN: University of Notre Dame Press.

Dorfman, Joseph. 1966. *The Economic Mind in American Civilization*. Vol. 1. New York: Augustus M. Kelley.

Dreisbach, Daniel L., Mark David Hall, Jeffry H. Morrison, and Mark A. Noll, eds. 2009. *The Forgotten Founders on Religion and Public Life*. Notre Dame, IN: University of Notre Dame Press.

Ernst, Joseph. 1976. "Political Economy and Reality: Problems in the Interpretation of the American Revolution." *Canadian Review of American Studies* 7 (2): 109–118.

———. 2014. *Money and Politics in America, 1755–1775: A Study in the Currency Act of 1764 and the Political Economy of Revolution*. Chapel Hill: UNC Press Books.

Fothergill, Alice, and Lori A Peek. 2004. "Poverty and Disasters in the United States: A Review of Recent Sociological Findings." *Natural Hazards* 32: 89–110.

Gelles, Edith B. 1995. *Portia: The World of Abigail Adams*. Bloomington, IN: Indiana University Press.

Grube, Laura, and Virgil Henry Storr. 2014. "The Capacity for Self-Governance and Post-Disaster Resiliency." *The Review of Austrian Economics* 27: 301–324.

———. 2018. "Embedded Entrepreneurs and Post-Disaster Community Recovery." *Entrepreneurship & Regional Development* 30 (7–8): 800–821.

Holton, Woody. 2009. *Abigail Adams*. New York: Simon and Schuster.

Lockridge, Kenneth A. 1973. "Social Change and the Meaning of the American Revolution." *Journal of Social History* 6 (4): 403–439.

McGinnis, Michael Dean. 1999. "Introduction." In *Polycentricity and Local Public Economies: Readings from the Workshop in Political Theory and Policy Analysis*, edited by Michael Dean McGinnis, 1–30. Ann Arbor, MI: University of Michigan Press.

Norris, Fran H., Julia L. Perilla, Jasmin K. Riad, Krzysztof Kaniasty, and Evelyn A. Lavizzo. 1999. "Stability and Change in Stress, Resources, and Psychological Distress following Natural Disaster: Findings from Hurricane Andrew." *Anxiety, Stress & Coping* 12 (4): 363–396.

Ostrom, Elinor. 2015. *Governing the Commons*. Cambridge: Cambridge University Press.

Peacock, Walter Gillis. 2003. "Hurricane Mitigation Status and Factors Influencing Mitigation Status Among Florida's Single-Family Homeowners." *Natural Hazards Review* 4 (3): 149–158.

Pocock, John Greville Agard. 1975. *The Machiavellian Moment: Florentine Political Thought and the Atlantic Republican Tradition*. Vol. 93. Princeton, NJ: Princeton University Press.

Pollio, Gerald. 2022. *The Rise and Fall of Britain's North American Empire: The Political Economy of Colonial America*. Cham: Springer Nature.
Roberts, Cokie. 2004. *Founding Mothers*. New York: HarperCollins.
Storr, Virgil Henry, and Stefanie Haeffele-Balch. 2012. "Post-Disaster Community Recovery in Heterogeneous, Loosely Connected Communities." *Review of Social Economy* 70 (3): 295–314.
Storr, Virgil Henry, Stefanie Haeffele-Balch, and Laura E. Grube. 2016. *Community Revival in the Wake of Disaster: Lessons in Local Entrepreneurship*. Cham: Springer.
Wood, Gordon S. 1966. "Rhetoric and Reality in the American Revolution." *The William and Mary Quarterly: A Magazine of Early American History* 23 (1): 3–32.

Index

About the Contributors

Kirstin Anderson Birkhaug, assistant professor of political science, Hope College, Holland, Michigan.

Andrew Berryhill, PhD student in economics, Indiana University Bloomington.

Donald J. Boudreaux, professor of economics, George Mason University; senior fellow, F. A. Hayek Program for Advanced Study in Philosophy, Politics, and Economics, Mercatus Center at George Mason University.

Curtis Bram, assistant professor of political science, University of Texas, Dallas.

Jason Lee Byas, PhD student in philosophy, University of Michigan, Ann Arbor.

Christopher J. Coyne, professor of economics, George Mason University; associate director, F. A. Hayek Program for Advanced Study in Philosophy, Politics, and Economics, Mercatus Center at George Mason University.

Paa-Kwesi Heto, visiting professor of Soka University of America, Aliso Viejo, California.

Jordan J. Hunter, PhD student in public affairs, Indiana University Bloomington.

Sargis Karavardanyan, PhD candidate in political economy, University of California, Irvine.

Brian Kogelmann, associate professor of philosophy and political science at Purdue University, West Lafayette, Indiana.

Todd Maslyk, PhD student in Germanic languages and literatures, University of Michigan, Ann Arbor.

Alexander W. Morales, Mellon assistant professor in communication of science and technology, Vanderbilt University, Nashville, Tennessee.

Eryn Rozonoyer, PhD student in political science, Boston College, Chestnut Hill, Massachusetts.

Mariam Sedighi, PhD student in educational policy studies, University of Wisconsin, Madison.

www.ingramcontent.com/pod-product-compliance
Ingram Content Group UK Ltd.
Pitfield, Milton Keynes, MK11 3LW, UK
UKHW041834031026
15587UKWH00002B/758

9 781666 945416